Knowledge-Intensive Entrepreneurship in Low-Tech Industries

Knowledge-Intensive Entrepreneurship in Low-Tech Industries

Edited by

Hartmut Hirsch-Kreinsen

Professor of Economic and Industrial Sociology,
TU Dortmund University, Germany

Isabel Schwinge

Research associate and lecturer at the Chair of Economic and
Industrial Sociology, TU Dortmund University, Germany

Edward Elgar
Cheltenham, UK • Northampton, MA, USA

© Hartmut Hirsch-Kreinsen and Isabel Schwinge 2014

Published by
Edward Elgar Publishing Limited
The Lypiatts
15 Lansdown Road
Cheltenham
Glos GL50 2JA
UK

Edward Elgar Publishing, Inc.
William Pratt House
9 Dewey Court
Northampton
Massachusetts 01060
USA

A catalogue record for this book
is available from the British Library

Library of Congress Control Number: 2013958029

This book is available electronically in the ElgarOnline.com
Economics Subject Collection, E-ISBN 978 1 78347 204 8

MIX
Paper from
responsible sources
FSC
www.fsc.org   FSC® C013056

ISBN 978 1 78347 203 1

Typeset by Servis Filmsetting Ltd, Stockport, Cheshire
Printed and bound in Great Britain by T.J. International Ltd, Padstow

Contents

Contributors

Yannis D. Caloghirou is Professor of Economics of Technology and Industrial Strategy and head of the Innovation and Entrepreneurship Unit at the National Technical University of Athens (NTUA), Greece. He is leading two research groups at the Laboratory of Industrial and Energy Economics, one on 'Innovation and Entrepreneurship Studies' and the second on 'Information Society and the Knowledge-based Economy'. In this capacity he has acted as a scientific coordinator in a number of European research projects in the broader area of socioeconomic research. He has served in top policy-making positions in Greece, among them as Secretary General for Industry and as Secretary for the Information Society. He has also sat in a number of EU high-level expert and policy groups.

Teresa Farinha Fernandes is an assistant researcher at the Research Unit on Complexity and Economics (UECE) of the School of Economics and Management (ISEG), University of Lisbon, Portugal. She has a Master's degree in Monetary and Financial Economics and a four-year degree in Economics. Her academic interests are in economics of innovation, employment and monetary policy and monitoring and evaluation.

Manuel Mira Godinho is a Full Professor of Economics at the School of Economics and Management (ISEG), University of Lisbon, Portugal, and a member of the Research Unit on Complexity and Economics (UECE). His main research focuses are on intellectual property rights, innovation and economic development and knowledge-based entrepreneurship.

Attila Havas is a Senior Research Fellow at the Institute of Economics, Research Centre for Economic and Regional Studies, Hungarian Academy of Sciences and regional editor of the *International Journal of Foresight and Innovation Policy*. His academic interests are in economics of innovation, theory and practice of innovation policy, and technology foresight. He has been a member of EU expert groups and advised national governments and international organizations on innovation, science, technology and innovation policies, as well as on foresight and prospective analyses.

Hartmut Hirsch-Kreinsen is Professor of Economic and Industrial Sociology at TU Dortmund University, Germany. He holds academic degrees in Sociology and in Business Administration and Engineering. He is a member of high-ranking national and international advisory councils in the field of innovation policy. His main research focuses are on company strategies and company networks, development of work, and innovation studies.

Glykeria Karagouni is a lecturer at the Technological Educational Institute of Thessaly, Greece, and a PhD candidate at the Laboratory of Industrial and Energy Economics, National Technical University of Athens, Greece. She holds a BSc and an MSc in Mechanical Engineering and an MSc in Modern Industrial Management. Her main research interests focus on entrepreneurship, knowledge-intensive entrepreneurship, strategic management, innovation studies and industrial management, especially in low-tech industries.

Ioanna Kastelli holds a PhD in Economics of Technology, a DEA from Paris X-Nanterre in Industrial Economics and a BSc in Economics from the National and Kapodistrian University of Athens. She is a researcher at the Laboratory of Industrial and Energy Economics and coordinator of the Innovation and Entrepreneurship Unit at the National Technical University of Athens, Greece. She is teaching as adjunct professor at the Hellenic Open University and at the National and Kapodistrian University of Athens. Her research interests include the fields of economics of technology and industrial economics, with emphasis on the dynamics of knowledge creation and diffusion, entrepreneurship and industrial and technology policy.

Ricardo Paes Mamede is Assistant Professor of Political Economy at ISCTE, the Higher Institute of Business and Labour Sciences, Lisbon University Institute, Portugal, and a researcher at Dinâmia'CET. Since 2008 he has also coordinated the Research and Evaluation Department at the NSRF Observatory, the government agency responsible for monitoring the use of EU structural funds in Portugal. He has a PhD in Economics from Bocconi University, Italy and a Master's in Economics and Management of Science and Technology from ISEG, the School of Economics and Management, Technical University of Lisbon. His research interests are in the fields of innovation and industry dynamics, structural change, European integration, and public policies.

Aimilia Protogerou holds a PhD in Business Strategy and Industrial Policy and is research fellow at the Laboratory of Industrial and Energy Economics, National Technical University of Athens, Greece. Her research interests revolve around strategic management of technology and innovation, technology policy and cooperative research and development, innovation networks and knowledge-intensive entrepreneurship.

Isabel Schwinge, MA, is a research associate, lecturer and PhD candidate at the Chair of Economic and Industrial Sociology of TU Dortmund University, Germany. She studied Sociology, Political Sciences and Ergonomics at Technische Universität Braunschweig. Her main research interests are entrepreneurship and innovation in low-tech industries, as well as inter-organizational processes of innovation along supply chains.

Aggelos Tsakanikas holds a diploma in Chemical Engineering and a PhD in Technology, Economics and Business Strategy from the National Technical University of Athens (NTUA), Greece. He is currently Research Director at the Foundation for Economic and Industrial Research (IOBE) and Assistant Professor at the Laboratory of Industrial and Energy Economics at NTUA in the field of economic analysis of technological systems. His main research interests are in the areas of business and technology strategy, economics of innovation, entrepreneurship and relevant public policies.

Andrei Yudanov is Professor of Economics and Doctor of Economic Science (DSc) at the Department of Microeconomics of the Financial University under the Government of the Russian Federation, Moscow. He is a member of the editorial boards of the *Russian Management Journal* and 'The Modern Competition' journal, Moscow. His current fields of scientific interest are high-growth firms ('gazelles'), low-tech and medium-low-tech (LMT) innovations, entrepreneurship and theory of competition.

Foreword

This book is about knowledge-intensive entrepreneurship (KIE) in low-tech industries. It originates from a large-scale collaborative project concerning knowledge-intensive entrepreneurship – AEGIS (Advancing Knowledge-Intensive Entrepreneurship and Innovation for Economic Growth and Social Well-being in Europe, 2009–12) – which was funded by the European 7th Framework Programme in the Social Sciences and Humanities and which involved several European research centers and universities, each trying to understand knowledge-intensive entrepreneurship in specific ways, either with a sectoral, country, company or an individual focus.

Low-tech industries occupy a relevant share of employment and production both in advanced and in developing countries: therefore they deserve detailed analytical scrutiny for a deep understanding of their characteristics and dynamics. In the last years these industries have been undergoing change and transformation, and KIE is one of the main driving forces at the base of these processes. Therefore a full understanding of the relevance, origin and impact of entrepreneurship in this sector represents something of vital importance for several reasons: a comprehension of the evolution of these industries, an identification of the factors of change, an analysis of the drivers of innovation in low-tech industries and a base for the setting up of policies that may revitalize and rejuvenate this sector.

However, while lots of analyses have been done regarding knowledge-intensive entrepreneurship in high- and medium-tech industries and services, much less work has concentrated on the low-tech sector. This gap needs to be filled by studies that address this type of entrepreneurship in these industries: it is necessary to identify the characteristics, specificities and differences of knowledge-intensive entrepreneurship in this sector compared to other sectors. This is what the book very timely aims to do.

One of the strengths of this book is that it focuses on KIE at various levels and dimensions and that it uses various methodologies, from case studies, to surveys, to country analyses. In particular, the book utilizes an extensive survey of KIE (AEGIS Survey) done at the firm level in various European countries and focused on several aspects of knowledge-intensive entrepreneurship: origin, characteristics, strategy, organization, innovativeness, performance and growth. In sum, the book combines a multilevel analysis of this phenomenon, complementing in-depth qualitative case studies with quantitative studies.

What emerges from this book is a rich and articulated picture of knowledge-intensive entrepreneurship in low-tech industries which is indeed diffused across countries and regions but it presents several differences compared to knowledge-intensive entrepreneurship in medium- or high-tech industries. These specificities have to be well kept in mind if policies aim to target KIE in order to foster innovation and transformation in these industries.

Franco Malerba
Professor of Applied Economics
President of CRIOS
Bocconi University
Milan

Preface

This book presents for the first time research findings dealing with opportunities for knowledge-intensive entrepreneurial activities in so-called low-tech or mature industries. This topic covers an issue of high novelty and great scientific and public interest. It links two issues which at first glance have little in common: on the one hand there is an ongoing scientific discussion over knowledge-intensive entrepreneurship (KIE) which mainly focuses on start-ups in the new technology-based, high-tech sector. On the other hand little or no attention so far has been paid to sectors that conduct only a few or no formal research and development (R&D) activities and can be characterized as non-research-intensive or low- and medium-low-tech (LMT). The underlying assumption of that perspective is that LMT sectors, with their mature character, offer only very limited opportunities for KIE activities. However, there is strong evidence from LMT industries that there, too, successful KIE activities take place.

The main objective of the volume is thus to contribute to a scientific discussion of the relevance of KIE activities in LMT industries for industrial innovativeness in the emerging knowledge economy. Additionally, the book aims to contribute to the ongoing political debate on the policy measures needed to promote future industrial innovativeness. It is argued among other things that policy first has to raise its awareness of the relevance of LMT industries for future economic and societal development. The issues covered in the volume center on the identification and analysis of KIE processes in LMT firms and sectors. The focus is mainly on typical KIE patterns, their prerequisites and consequences, the distribution of KIE in LMT sectors in Europe and policy recommendations to promote these activities.

The volume is mainly based on the research findings of the recently completed large-scale EU-funded project 'Advancing Knowledge-Intensive Entrepreneurship and Innovation for Economic Growth and Social Wellbeing in Europe' (AEGIS, 2009–12) coordinated by Franco Malerba (Bocconi University, Milan). One of the premises of this project was that KIE is highly industry-specific. Its features and impact depend on the knowledge base of an industry, the main public and private actors embedded in the industry, and the associated institutions. Therefore it was assumed at the outset that KIE was as relevant to low-tech and mature industries as to high-tech and new industries. This was the reason a specific work package within this large project dealt with the evolution and the characteristics of KIE in LMT manufacturing sectors, the relevance of interrelationships between low-tech and high-tech activities for KIE, and the impact of this phenomenon on the growth and competitiveness of European traditional industries. The main findings of this work package and the results of a related discussion are presented in this volume. Methodologically the empirical findings are based on case-study research and the analysis of statistical data, especially data from a large-scale survey conducted in the context of the AEGIS project.

The editors of this volume heartily thank the work-package partners from the AEGIS project for their collaboration and their research on this stimulating issue. Bram Timmermans, Christian Østergaard, Eun Kyung Park and Kenney V. Christiansen from Aalborg University (AAU), Guido Bünstorf, Christina Guenther and Matthias Geissler from Max Planck Institute of Economics (MPI), Glykeria Karagouni, Ioanna Kastelli and Yannis Caloghirou from National Technical University of Athens (LIEE-NTUA) and Alexandra Rosa, Manuel Mira Godinho and Ricardo Mamede from Technical University of Lisbon (UECE) participated in this work package. We furthermore especially thank all contributors for their commitment to the book. They all generously provided original work for which there were already many alternative publication opportunities.

1. Introduction: knowledge-intensive entrepreneurship in low-tech industries

Hartmut Hirsch-Kreinsen and Isabel Schwinge

1.1 THE DEBATE ON KNOWLEDGE-INTENSIVE ENTREPRENEURSHIP

The ongoing discussion over knowledge-intensive entrepreneurship (KIE) underscores its relevance to future economic growth and societal well-being (Audretsch et al., 2002; Malerba, 2010; Malerba and McKelvey, 2010). Moreover, this term is narrowly linked to the discourse on the emerging 'knowledge economy' and the debate on entrepreneurial activities. Heretofore research on KIE has mainly focused on firms or start-ups in the new technology-based high-tech sector. Altogether KIE is a vital mechanism for economic renewal, giving rise to new industries but also driving renewal within existing industries. The latter function of industrial revitalization, in particular, makes KIE an important phenomenon for the mature low-tech sector.

The overall objective of this volume is to introduce the discussion over KIE into the context of low-tech industries. The authors contributing to this book address diverse aspects – from *characteristics* and *impacts* (Part I), to specific *strategies* (Part II), all the way to *political and policy preconditions* (Part III) for KIE in this specific industrial context. Thereby different foci and approaches are applied to the KIE phenomenon that can be subsumed best by Malerba's (2010: 5) broad perspective on KIE as 'new innovators in a technology or sector that can be either de novo entrants or established firms active in a process of technological diversification'.

Initially a more detailed definition of KIE is outlined by its main features (Section 2). To start from a common ground, the relevance of and differences in the low-tech dimension at the sectoral and firm level are re-elaborated (Section 3). Following this an introduction of, first, constraints and opportunities for KIE in low-tech industries build the starting point for distinguishing this phenomenon from other sectoral contexts (Sections 4 and 5) before the structure of the volume is presented (Section 6).

1.2   THE MAIN FEATURES OF KNOWLEDGE-INTENSIVE ENTREPRENEURSHIP

The volume follows a broad concept of KIE, especially that based on Malerba (2010) and Malerba and McKelvey (2010), the following characteristic features of which are briefly outlined here.

The first feature of KIE refers to the *organizational form* of innovation activities (Malerba and McKelvey, 2010: 7). This relates to entrepreneurship as undertaking new activities and innovation as creating new economic value. This follows a Schumpeterian approach arguing that a fundamental change in existing activities as well as the introduction of entirely novel activities should keep providing the 'fuel' to the capitalist engine. Thus, KIE is considered an activity dealing with the uncertainties of discovering and exploiting new opportunities, often driven by individuals but also by established organizations in terms of 'corporate entrepreneurship'. The latter organizational form is thought to be particularly relevant with respect to the institutional context and constraints of low-tech industries.

The second feature of KIE is *knowledge*, which is primarily defined in relation to scientific, engineering and design knowledge. As Malerba explains (2010: 6 et seq.), this special notion of knowledge refers to systematic problem-solving knowledge, which is very different from that having a primary emphasis on experience and skills. Therefore entrepreneurs are considered to be 'knowledge operators' dedicated to the innovative utilization of existing knowledge, the new integration and coordination of different knowledge assets, and the creation of new knowledge aimed at the implementation of new products and technologies. Thus, KIE means the launch of new activities and organizations that intensively use existing scientific and technological knowledge, or that intensively create new scientific and technological knowledge for commercial purposes or for bringing new products or services to markets. In consequence, the 'absorptive capability' of entrepreneurs or – in the case of KIE as corporate entrepreneurship – of firms is a necessary condition. And, an increasing share of the workforce that is scientifically educated is thought to be one of the main preconditions for successful KIE activities.

The third feature is that KIE is shaped by *systems of innovation* that differ among sectors (Malerba, 2010: 8 et seq.). Networks, as relations to commercial and non-commercial actors, are regarded as a key prerequisite for entrepreneurship. They offer essential sources of knowledge, new capital, new potential employees, strategic alliance partners, and service providers (lawyers, accountants, consultants). Also networks allow entrepreneurs to share information and their assessments of markets and technologies. In addition to looking at business organizations, this network perspective analyses the contribution of universities, research organizations and other types of organizations to the emergence of KIE; particularly in academic organizations where knowledge from scientific research is assumed to generate new technologies for commercial exploitation. Also, users and suppliers may be a source of entrepreneurship and innovation in various ways, generally through knowledge related to market opportunities and customer demands. In addition, this view of innovation systems reconsiders the role of institutions as a key factor shaping entrepreneurship (ibid.: 12). Institutions include norms, routines, common habits, established practices, rules, laws, standards and so on, which shape the entrepreneurs' cognition and action and affect their interactions with other agents. Institutions and related organizations differ greatly in terms of their types of effect on the behavior of entrepreneurs. These effects can range from those that bind or impose constraints on KIE, to those that are created by interactions among agents (such as contracts) – from formal to informal (such as patent laws or specific regulations vs. traditions and conventions). Many institutions are national (such as the patent system), while others are specific to sectoral innovation systems related to industries, such as industry-specific labor markets or financial institutions. In general, these industry-specific institutions and knowledge-intensive entrepreneurs that are active in different contexts affect KIE as well.

The fourth feature of KIE refers to *opportunities for innovation* (Malerba and McKelvey, 2010: 8 et seq.). An innovation opportunity is here defined as the possibility to realize the economic value inherent in a new combination of resources and market needs. Opportunities can emerge from changes in the scientific or technological knowledge base, customer preferences, or the interrelationships between economic actors. The concept of innovative opportunities comprises both aspects related to the demand as well as to the scientific and technological knowledge needed to serve this specific market. The individual entrepreneurs or entrepreneurial firm must be able to identify the value to a customer, mobilize the resources and capture the economic benefits from innovating. This feature of KIE thus focuses the attention on organizational processes.

As aforementioned, entrepreneurship research still concentrates distinctly on the high-tech sector. However, in more recent debate on KIE, scholars underscore that KIE cannot be exclusively limited to high-tech industries. Rather, the KIE phenomenon is seen to emerge in different sectoral contexts (Malerba and McKelvey, 2010: 9). That means sectoral conditions greatly affect the opportunities of KIE through divergent stocks of knowledge, specific technological domains, different agents and networks, specific market conditions and institutional regulations. As a consequence, the patterns, opportunities and determining factors of KIE are highly sector-specific and the possibilities for growth are affected in very different ways. It seems that the exploration of low-tech specific characteristics of KIE has just begun.

1.3   THE 'LOW-TECH' DIMENSION

1.3.1   The Relevance of Low-Tech Industries

The term 'low-technology' (low-tech) sector denotes those industries that have low-level or no research and development capacities and do not spend large amounts of money on R&D activities. The basis of this categorization is the 'R&D intensity' indicator, which measures the ratio of the R&D expenditure to the turnover of a company or to the output value of an industry. By means of this indicator, industries with an R&D intensity of more than 5 per cent on average are characterized as 'high-tech', and those with an R&D intensity between 3 and 5 per cent as 'medium-high-tech', or 'complex technologies'.[1] Sectors with an R&D intensity between 3 and 0.9 per cent are classified as 'medium-low-tech' and those with an R&D intensity below 0.9 per cent as 'low-tech'. All these classed industries are further aggregated in the high-tech sector or the low-tech sector and the medium sectors respectively (cf. Table 1.1). In the following, the term 'low-tech industries' refers to both 'low- and medium-low-technology' (LMT) sectors. Regarding the industry level, industries such as household appliance manufacture, the food industry, the paper, publishing and print industry, the wood and furniture industry and the manufacture of metal products – such as the foundry industry – as well as plastic products manufacturing are grouped in LMT sectors. In contrast, pharmaceuticals, the electronics industry, medical engineering and vehicle construction, the aerospace construction industry as well as large parts of the mechanical engineering and the electrical industries are aggregated in high-tech and medium-high-tech (HMT) sectors (OECD, 2005).

Recent years have seen a growing body of innovation literature devoted to the innovativeness of low-tech industries. This research interest is mainly motivated by criticism of the mainstream of innovation research and innovation policy which regards a high investment in R&D and advanced technologies as the key to growth and prosperity. This has led to the almost exclusive focus of many scholars and policy-makers on the economic

Table 1.1   Classification of manufacturing industries into categories based on R&D intensity

High-tech industries	Medium-high-tech industries
Aircraft and spacecraft	Electrical machinery and apparatus, n.e.c.
Pharmaceuticals	Motor vehicles, trailers and semi-trailers
Office, accounting and computing machinery	Chemicals excluding pharmaceuticals
Radio, television and communications equipment	Railroad equipment and transport equipment
Medical, precision and optical instruments	Machinery and equipment
Medium-low-tech industries	**Low-tech industries**
Building and repairing of ships and boats	Manufacturing, n.e.c.; Recycling
Rubber and plastics products	Wood, pulp, paper, paper products, printing and publishing
Coke, refined petroleum products and nuclear fuel	Food products, beverages and tobacco
Other non-metallic mineral products	Textiles, textile products, leather and footwear
Basic metals and fabricated metal products	

Note: n.e.c.: not elsewhere covered.

Source: OECD (2011).

sectors of high R&D intensity, while the economic importance and specific innovative ability of LMT sectors is overlooked. Contrastingly, low-tech research as a whole has clearly shown that LMT firms and industries are by no means technologically and economically stagnant. LMT industries play a decisive role in shaping current economic structures and are essential to the future economic and technological development of advanced countries (Robertson et al., 2009). In other words, the surprising viability of the non-research-intensive industrial sectors in the developed economies of Western countries up to the present day cannot be ignored.

The large share that LMT industries contribute to the value added of the whole of manufacturing industry is a convincing indicator of this. In 2010 this share accounted for about 53 per cent in EU–27, while the respective share of HMT sectors was around 47 per cent; the high-tech sector stood at 12 per cent.[2] The share of employment is another important indicator. In relation to the manufacturing industry as a whole, the LMT sectors in the EU-27 had an employment share of approximately 65 per cent in 2010.

The respective share of the HMT sectors accounted for about 35 per cent; the high-tech sector, only 7 per cent.[3] The development of the different sectors in the EU–27 has been characterized by different trajectories in recent years. Annual average growth rates between 2005 and 2011 were negative for the LMT sectors – between -0.4 and -0.7 per cent – whereas the respective figures for HMT sectors were between 1.0 and 3.3 per cent.[4] However, these data also underscore the relative high stability of the LMT sectors in the EU.

1.3.2   Differentiations between Sectoral and Firm Level

As low-tech research shows, the term 'LMT' does not sufficiently define the sectoral system. At least three aspects should be taken into consideration in dealing with LMT companies and sectors in further research activities. First, while this concept may be useful with regard to a first statistical definition, the term 'traditional industries' probably more appropriately specifies the industrial structure in question. To describe it one has to add further specifications. For example, the industries of these sectors are characterized by well-established technologies and production regimes. They have undergone a shorter or longer evolution, resulting in the emergence of established standards, methods and knowledge related to both products and processes. In other words, these industries are mostly well advanced along their industrial life cycles. This is perhaps one of the most important reasons for the difficult competitive position of many of these industries in Europe: the basic technologies and procedures relevant in the industries are well known and can often be easily copied by foreign competitors with a lower cost base. Another consequence of the established character of the technologies is that the technological change is predominantly incremental. Radical innovations based on fundamentally new scientific findings or erratic shifts in buyers' preferences can happen but are an unusual event in traditional industries. This applies to both products and processes. Consequently, growth rates in these industries are relatively low (EuroStat, 2013a; Jaegers et al., 2013).

Second, when speaking about LMT we should differentiate between the sectoral and the company level. At the sectoral level there are typical low-tech industries characterized by a low level of R&D intensity. However, at the company level the situation is not so clear. Empirical data show that there are LMT companies (with low levels of R&D intensity) in typical HMT sectors such as the pharmaceutical industry or mechanical engineering and – vice versa – high-tech companies in typical LMT sectors. These findings show that there are industries with fewer and industries with more low-tech companies, the latter being the above-mentioned low-tech industries (Kirner et al., 2009). Therefore the area of research on entrepreneurship in the context of LMT should discriminate between 'entrepreneurial activities in industries dominated by LMT companies' and 'research on LMT companies'.

1.4   CONSTRAINTS ON KIE IN LMT SECTORS

Because of the structural conditions of LMT firms and sectors, the constraints on KIE activities in this field seem to be significant. The main features of KIE are considered to be the focus on unexploited opportunities, having to deal with uncertainties, the creation of new knowledge and the necessity of overcoming established routines on the company and sectoral level (Cohendet and Llerena, 2010). However, the context of LMT sectors and firms would seem to offer only very limited opportunities for these activities. The reason for this is that innovations in LMT sectors are known to be path-dependent and based on a relatively slow accumulation of capabilities surrounding previously known technological specializations. This path-dependency is continuously stabilized by incremental innovation activities, by increasing returns as the result of the continuously optimized processes in the existing technologies, and the therefore slowly emerging momentum of these developmental paths.[5] As available research findings show, this holds true in particular for entrepreneurial activities in the context of established companies (Parhankangas and Arenius, 2003). Unlike the high-tech sector with its prevailing technological contingency, the technologies of the LMT sectors are well known and established, and the processes and products are not only highly standardized and routinized but also often rather advanced in complexity. The same holds for the knowledge base, which includes mostly codified, transferable and well-known elements such as design methods, engineering routines or the know-how of markets and customer preferences. Therefore technological norms, methods and leitmotifs as well as occupations and skills are well developed and have existed for many generations in these mature industries.

Furthermore, sales market conditions do not trigger KIE activities. The reason is that these conditions are mainly characterized by strong international competition based on prices and costs, forcing companies to optimize continuously their processes and technologies rather than pursuing risky innovation activities. In other words, the economic success of LMT companies is normally linked to professionalized managers whose job it is to optimize, rationalize in economies of scale and streamline the processes of their companies along the given trajectories in order to meet the needs of the intensive price competition on the internationalized sales markets.

Thus, the chances for carrying out knowledge-intensive entrepreneurial experimentation in the aforementioned sense are limited by the fixed technological trajectories of LMT sectors and the cost uncertainties they may entail.[6] To sum up, it cannot be denied that unlike the field of high-technology, the socio-technical field of LMT industries offers relatively few opportunities to step up economic success. Aggregated economic data on growth rates and the development of employment in LMT industries convincingly prove this (Jaegers et al., 2013). From this perspective one has to admit that 'valuable opportunities' (Radosevic, 2010) for KIE in LMT are greatly limited.

1.5   OPPORTUNITIES FOR KIE IN LMT SECTORS

However, the constructive tendencies that accompany opportunities for KIE in low-tech should not be overlooked either. Theoretically it can be argued that – paradoxically – the situation of a fixed path-dependency can stimulate new ideas and, by attempts to overcome the obstacles they present, new paths can be created. The majority of actors involved may look upon new ideas and inventions as a cul-de-sac, but for a minority of economic actors this situation offers opportunities with a high potential for economic success (Deutschmann, 2008). It may also be argued that competitive pressure forces managers to change their role by adopting an increasingly reflective approach towards established practices and to look for breakthrough innovations (Beckert, 1991). This reflective approach may be triggered by a situation in which formerly increasing returns may cease to increase or even decrease (Deeg, 2005: 173). That may be caused in turn by continuously intensifying market competition and growing pressure from low-cost competitors. Generally it can be assumed that the intensive competitive pressure on low-tech industries forces actors not only to adopt managerial strategies of cost cutting and optimizing existing routines, but may also compel them to adopt a reflective stance towards the established practices in order to overcome this situation. Especially because of the great persistence and stability of LMT industries, entrepreneurial activities and a successful deviation from established practices and technological paths promise competitive advantage and high profitability.[7]

Recent research findings show that opportunities for KIE in LMT industries do in fact exist. Among these are, first, some long-term empirical studies which show that knowledge diversification tends to prevail over a mere deepening of the existing technological paths (Mendonça, 2009), and also draw attention to the overall surprising stability of LMT industries in many OECD countries (Kaloudis et al., 2005). From this it may be concluded that, usually, research findings have tended to underestimate the true extent and depth of entrepreneurial change in traditional businesses (Mendonça, 2009: 479).

Second, recent findings of case-study research emphasize the specific innovation ability of the low-tech sector and its companies (von Tunzelmann and Acha, 2005; Hirsch-Kreinsen, 2008). According to these findings, LMT companies very often not only pursue incremental innovation strategies but also try to overcome the routine paths of their knowledge and technology use through more far-reaching innovation activities such as architectural or modular innovation strategies. In part, such companies explicitly pursue strategies aiming at a leading position in niche markets beyond the main fields of standardized mature products or even try to create new market segments.

Third, research findings show the impressive success of so-called 'gazelles', e.g. fast-growing companies, often from the low-tech sector, which induce sectoral growth and create new jobs and new markets. Such companies can be found both in Western countries and in particular in the countries of Middle and Eastern Europe (Yudanov, 2007).[8]

These first findings can be interpreted as indicators for existing KIE processes in LMT sectors. However, even so the prerequisites, the mechanisms and, generally, the distinctive features of KIE in the low-tech context are still rather unclear.

1.6 THE STRUCTURE OF THIS VOLUME

These still open issues will be discussed in the following chapters from various methodological angles. Whereas Malerba (2010) and his contributors mainly applied quantitative analysis, the important contribution of case studies to this complex field of research is illustrated by McKelvey and Lassen's (2013) recent collection of case studies on KIE. A particular feature of our volume on the other hand is the broad mix of quantitative and qualitative methods that is necessary to deepen the understanding of the interplay between the emergence of KIE and the context of LMT sectors and/or firms (in the case of corporate entrepreneurship).

In Part I the question of the characteristics and patterns of, and the impact of KIE activities on LMT industries is broached. First, Yannis Caloghirou, Aimilia Protogerou and Aggelos Tsakanikas show in their contribution that KIE can also exist in the traditional industries of LMT sectors (Chapter 2). On the basis of a quantitative analysis of data from the large-scale AEGIS Survey they examine specific KIE characteristics in LMT sectors and posit similarities and differences to those of high- and medium-technology sectors. In this way they try to shed some light on the features of KIE in LMT firms and at the same time reveal some characteristics in common with high-tech companies which may help managers, policy-makers and scholars to better understand this 'high-potential' type of entrepreneurship.

Then, Hartmut Hirsch-Kreinsen specifies these findings on the empirical basis of case-study research on KIE processes in LMT sectors in different European countries (Chapter 3). He first presents a conceptual framework on KIE processes in LMT sectors as a guideline for the interpretation of empirical findings. Then he outlines four patterns of KIE in LMT sectors. These patterns represent distinguishable types of the opportunities and determining factors of KIE which describe and explain similarities and differences amongst KIE activities in LMT industries. This typology leads to an understanding of the determining factors, firm behavior and directions of KIE processes in LMT industries in this still mainly uninvestigated field of innovation research.

In Chapter 4 Ioanna Kastelli and Yannis Caloghirou present their findings on how KIE impacts the competitiveness and growth of European traditional industries. The authors argue that KIE in LMT sectors can contribute to overcoming competitive pressures from low-wage economies because it builds on knowledge-intensive assets, promotes innovation and continuous technological upgrading, and can also create new economic value by exploiting knowledge bases 'belonging' to other industries or scientific fields that use widely applicable knowledge. This topic has also important policy implications. Fostering the application of key enabling technologies in interactions between developers and users of these technologies can boost competitiveness. In addition, development of absorptive and technology management capabilities in these industries can transform them into knowledge-intensive users.

In Part II the contributions reveal prospects of knowledge-intensive activity in LMT industries by addressing different (country-) specific perspectives on business strategies and relations. Ricardo Mamede, Teresa Fernandes and Manuel Godinho illustrate in Chapter 5 how trademarks are used by various types of firms to differentiate their products. Their chapter provides the first results drawn from an integrated database that crosses information on national trademark applications with micro-data on all the firms with employees in Portugal. The main patterns of trademark use are identified and the characteristics of firms that are typically associated with trademark use are examined. The results indicate that trademark use is not primarily dependent on the knowledge intensity of the industries the firms belong to but rather on certain individual characteristics of the firms. An implication for the more innovative firms operating in the low-tech and less knowledge-intensive industries is that the use of trademarks may be an option to reinforce their innovative strategies.

In Chapter 6 Andrei Yudanov deals with the widespread phenomenon of firms termed 'gazelle', i.e. those showing rapid growth over a long period of time. Surprisingly, gazelle-type firms can be found not only in high-tech but also in LMT sectors, especially in countries undergoing rapid economic change processes. The author presents the findings of an empirical study of gazelle firms in Russia. He outlines how in the first decades of the post-socialist development the existing R&D-oriented way of developing KIE almost disappeared for Russian firms because of the catastrophic decrease in state demand for high-tech production and the destruction of the former vertically integrated national innovation system. Internal structural changes began to develop in Russia mainly as LMT-type – or gazelle-type – businesses. These operations were to a lesser degree connected with inventive activity than with adaptation to, recombination and/or system integration of the world experience in Russia.

The authors Aimilia Protogerou, Yannis Caloghirou and Glykeria Karagouni then discuss the 'dynamic capabilities' perspective in low-tech industries in Chapter 7. Using extensive quantitative and qualitative data, the authors explore the relationship between dynamic capabilities (DCs) and firm performance measures in the novel context of young entrepreneurial ventures in LMT industries. In this way more light is shed on the still open issue of whether DCs have a role to play in an environment which by definition is characterized as stable but lacking in any significant amount of innovation. Rich survey data reveal how dynamic capabilities have a positive impact on diverse performance measures, indicating that they can indeed play a significant role in low-tech industries. The authors show convincingly that DCs are present in knowledge-intensive low-tech firms; however, their development appears to be sector-dependent and deeply impacted by the individual firms' evolutionary paths and choices.

In the concluding chapter of this part Isabel Schwinge aims to readjust the prevalent perspective on LMT firms in product supply chains in the debate on low-tech innovations and knowledge intensity (Chapter 8). In addition to the established perspective of 'supplier-dominated LMT firms', the supplying LMT firms and their interactions with customers are also considered as well as their internal knowledge activity. For this reason the analysis of empirical findings draws on the interaction model of the Industrial Marketing and Purchasing Group (IMP) and extends it to include the dimension of distributed knowledge bases. Different positions of LMT firms in product supply chains are presented, whereby recourse to qualitative case studies from the AEGIS project sheds light on knowledge-intensive activity of LMT companies with regard to sources of knowledge and the conditions for extending knowledge bases.

In Part III of the volume, policy implications of the findings on KIE activities in LMT industries are summarized and some necessary requirements of policy measures are discussed. Attila Havas examines policy strategies in a conceptual manner (Chapter 9). He juxtaposes the analyses of innovation in mainstream economics vis-à-vis evolutionary economics of innovation, as well as their concomitant policy rationales. By discussing the indicators selected for the Innovation Union Scoreboard and another major EU report, he argues that the 'science-push' model of innovation is still highly influential in policy circles, despite a rich set of research insights stressing the importance of non-R&D types of knowledge in innovation processes. In conclusion, the chapter highlights the potential drawbacks of the persistent high-tech myth, considers possible reasons for its perseverance and discusses policy implications of the systemic view of innovation. One of them is that STI policies should promote knowledge-intensive activities in all sectors, including LMT industries and services.

The concluding chapter to this volume, offered by Hartmut Hirsch-Kreinsen and Isabel Schwinge, outlines policy recommendations for the promotion of KIE in low-tech industries (Chapter 10). The authors reveal that KIE activities in LMT sectors have received only limited support from public measures and policy so far. This situation is consistent with the limited awareness of the importance of policy for traditional industries in general. Despite this, promising fields of action are emerging for policies to promote KIE in low-tech industries. These include improving access to distributed, trans-sectoral knowledge, promoting activities that improve the specific capabilities of LMT firms, policy measures that better target the needs of KIE in LMT sectors, particularly the funding of start-up activities, and a generally increased awareness and better understanding of innovation processes in low-tech industries. The authors argue that there are considerable opportunities for pushing forward KIE activity and improving the severe competitive situation of many LMT firms despite the strong path-dependency of traditional industries and their technologies.

NOTES

1. This indicator covers in-house R&D expenditures on R&D staff, further R&D costs and investments as well as out-of-house expenditures, e.g. on R&D tasks assigned to other companies and organizations (OECD, 2002: 108).
2. EuroStat, http://epp.eurostat.ec.europa.eu/statistics_explained/index.php/High-technology_versus_low-technology_manufacturing (accessed 19 September 2013).
3. Our own approximation based on: EuroStat, Structural Business Statistics 'sbs_na_sca_

r2', http://epp.eurostat.ec.europa.eu/portal/page/portal/european_business/data/database (accessed June 2013).
4. EuroStat, http://epp.eurostat.ec.europa.eu/statistics_explained/index.php/High-technology_ versus_low-technology_manufacturing (accessed 19 September 2013).
5. See the concept of path-dependency in social sciences and innovation theory (Garud and Karnøe, 2003). In this perspective incremental innovations can be regarded as 'small events' not changing but only stabilizing existing paths.
6. Whereas a manager orients his decisions on routines, adaptation and imitation, entrepreneurs are characterized by a reflective stance towards taken-for-granted scripts and existing institutional regulations – following Schumpeter's distinction between the manager and the entrepreneur (Schumpeter, 1997: 110).
7. This argument refers to the debate in organizational sociology on 'institutional entrepreneurship' which reintroduces agency, interests and power into an institutional analysis of organizational change (Beckert, 1991; Garud and Karnøe, 2003; Garud et al., 2002).
8. See also Yudanov in this volume (Chapter 6).

REFERENCES

Audretsch, D., B. Bozeman, K. Combs, M. Feldman, A. Link, D. Siegel, P. Stephan, G. Tassey and C. Wessner (2002), 'Economics of Science and Technology', *Journal of Technology Transfer*, **27** (2), 155–203.

Beckert, J. (1991), 'Agency, Entrepreneurs and Institutional Change: The Role of Strategic Choice and Institutionalized Practices in Organizations', *Organizational Studies*, **20** (5), 777–99.

Cohendet, Patrick and Patrick Llerena (2010), 'The Knowledge-Based Entrepreneur: The Need for a Relevant Theory of the Firm', in Franco Malerba (ed.), *Knowledge-Intensive Entrepreneurship and Innovation Systems: Evidence from Europe*, London, UK and New York, USA: Routledge, pp. 31–51.

Deeg, Richard (2005), 'Change from Within: German and Italian Finance in the 1990s', in Wolfgang Streeck and Kathleen Thelen (eds), *Beyond Continuity: Institutional Change in Advanced Political Economies*, Oxford, UK: Oxford University Press, pp. 169–204.

Deutschmann, Christoph (2008), *Kapitalistische Dynamik: Eine gesellschaftstheoretische Perspektive*, Wiesbaden: VS-Verlag.

EuroStat (2013a), 'High-Technology versus Low-Technology Manufacturing', available at http://epp.eurostat.ec.europa.eu/statistics_explained/index.php/High-technology_versus_low-technology_manufacturing (accessed 19 September 2013).

EuroStat (2013b), 'Structural Business Statistics: sbs_na_sca_r2', Luxembourg: European Commission, available at http://epp.eurostat.ec.europa.eu/portal/page/portal/european_business/data/database (accessed June 2013).

Garud, R. and P. Karnøe (2003), 'Bricolage versus Breakthrough: Distributed and Embedded Agency in Technology Entrepreneurship', *Research Policy*, **32** (2), 277–300.

Garud, R., S. Jain and A. Kumaraswamy (2002), 'Institutional Entrepreneurship in the Sponsorship of Common Technological Standards: The Case of Sun Microsystems and Java', *Academy of Management Journal*, **45** (1), 196–214.

Hirsch-Kreinsen, H. (2008), '"Low-Tech" Innovation', *Industry and Innovation*, **15** (1), 19–43.

Jaegers, T., C. Lipp-Lingua and D. Amil (2013), 'High-Technology and Medium-High Technology Industries Main Drivers of EU–27's Industrial Growth', Eurostat Statistics in focus, 1 (2013), available at http://epp.eurostat.ec.europa.eu/cache/ITY_OFFPUB/KS-SF-13-001/EN/KS-SF-13-001-EN.PDF (accessed 15 August 2013).

Kaloudis, Aris, Tore Sandven and Keith Smith (2005), 'Structural Change, Growth and Innovation: The Roles of Medium and Low Tech Industries, 1980–2000', in Gerd Bender, David Jacobson and Paul L. Robertson (eds), *Non-Research-Intensive Industries in the Knowledge Economy*, published in *Perspectives on Economic, Political and Social Integration*, **XI** (1–2), special issue, 49–74.

Kirner, E., S. Kinkel and A. Jaeger (2009), 'Innovation Paths and the Innovation Performance of Low-Technology Firms – An Empirical Analysis of German Industry', *Research Policy*, **38** (3), 447–58.

Malerba, Franco (2010), *Knowledge-Intensive Entrepreneurship and Innovation Systems: Evidence from Europe*, London, UK and New York, USA: Routledge.

Malerba, F. and M. McKelvey (2010), 'Conceptualizing Knowledge Intensive Entrepreneurship: Concepts and Models', paper presented at the DIME – AEGIS – LIEE/NTUA Athens 2010 Conference, 29–30 April 2010.

McKelvey, Maureen and Astrid Heidemann Lassen (eds) (2013), *How Entrepreneurs Do what They Do: Cases Studies in Knowledge Intensive Entrepreneurship*, Cheltenham, UK and Northampton, MA, USA: Edward Elgar.

Mendonça, S. (2009), 'Brave Old World: Accounting for "High-Tech" Knowledge in "Low-Tech" Industries', *Research Policy*, **38** (3), 470–82.

OECD (2002), *OECD Frascati Manual: Proposed Standard for Surveys on Research and Experimental Development*, 6th edition, Paris: OECD.

OECD (2005), *Oslo-Manual, Proposed Guidelines for Collecting and Interpreting Technological Innovation Data*, 3rd edition, Paris: OECD.

OECD (2011), 'ISIC REV. 3 Technology Intensity Definition – Classification of Manufacturing Industries into Categories Based on R&D Intensities', available at www.oecd.org/sti/ind/48350231.pdf (accessed 21 May 2012).

Parhankangas, A. and P. Arenius (2003), 'From a Corporate Venture to an Independent Company: A Base for a Taxonomy for Corporate Spin-off Firms', *Research Policy*, **32** (3), 463–81.

Radosevic, Slavo (2010), 'What Makes Entrepreneurship Systemic?', in Franco Malerba (ed.), *Knowledge-Intensive Entrepreneurship and Innovation Systems: Evidence from Europe*, London, UK and New York, USA: Routledge, pp. 52–76.

Robertson, P.L., K. Smith and N. von Tunzelmann (2009), 'Innovation in Low- and Medium-Technology Industries', *Research Policy*, **38** (3), 441–6.

Schumpeter, Joseph (1997/1934), *Theorie der wirtschaftlichen Entwicklung*, Berlin: Duncker & Humblot.

Von Tunzelmann, Nick and Virginia Acha (2005), 'Innovation in "Low-Tech" Industries', in Jan Fagerberg, David C. Mowery and Richard R. Nelson (eds), *The Oxford Handbook of Innovation*, New York, USA: Oxford University Press, pp. 407–32.

Yudanov, A. (2007), 'Fast-Growing Firms and the Evolution of the Russian Economy', *Problems of Economic Transition*, **50** (8), 7–28.

PART I

Characteristics, patterns and impact

2. Exploring knowledge-intensive entrepreneurship in high-tech and low-tech manufacturing sectors: differences and similarities

Yannis D. Caloghirou, Aimilia Protogerou and Aggelos Tsakanikas

2.1 INTRODUCTION

In recent years, learning and knowledge in industry have gained increasing attention among scholars and policy-makers in view of the fact that knowledge-intensive industries are now considered to be at the core of growth in emerging knowledge-driven economies (Smith, 2002; Robertson and Smith, 2008). The concept of 'knowledge economy' emerges when knowledge is recognized to be useful in producing economic benefits (Garavaglia and Grieco, 2005). In fact, as Mokyr suggests, 'all economies in human history are knowledge economies' (2002). However, the difference in the use of the term today is related to the change in the relative weight of knowledge compared to other factors (such as physical assets, natural resources and unskilled labor); it has assumed greater importance both in quantitative and qualitative terms (Caloghirou et al., 2006).

'Knowledge is becoming the main raw material in many manufacturing industries' (Rodrigues, 2002: 5), while the knowledge-intensity of products and services is increasing in almost all industries. Unique knowledge, be it internal or external, is the most valuable asset of a firm for achieving competitive advantage (Liebeskind, 1996; Ihrig et al., 2006), as it provides a platform for decisions on what resources and capabilities to deploy, develop or discard as the environment changes (Ndofor and Levitas, 2004). In this context, knowledge-intensive entrepreneurship (KIE) can be understood as a necessary mechanism mediating between the creation of knowledge and innovation and its transformation into economic activity, i.e., KIE represents a core interface between two interdependent systems: the knowledge generation and knowledge diffusion system on the one hand, and the productive system on the other. (Audretsch et al., 2002; Malerba, 2010; Malerba and McKelvey, 2010; Hirsch-Kreinsen and Schwinge, 2011).

It can be argued that, by definition, the notion of KIE is closely related to knowledge-intensive contexts or industries. But what does a 'knowledge-intensive' industry actually stand for? Policy analysis and discussion of innovation has taken a rather narrow view of this question, equating these industries with a very limited group of economic activities that tend to be closely associated with high levels of direct R&D and patenting (Robertson and Patel, 2007; Kirner et al., 2009).

Moreover, 'it is common to use the terms "high technology" or "knowledge-intensive industries" in a somewhat loose way, as though in fact they were both meaningful and interchangeable terms' (Robertson and Smith, 2008: 98). The standard classification in this area remains that of the OECD which was developed in the mid-1980s, distinguishing between industries on the basis of R&D intensity[1] and proposing three sectoral categories: high-tech, medium-tech and low-tech. This classification was later modified to divide the medium-tech category into high-tech and medium-high-tech (HMT) and low-tech and medium-low-tech (LMT) industries (Hatzichronoglou, 1997).

The OECD's discussion of the proposed industry classification was rather careful, pointing out that technology intensity is not only traced by R&D expenditures. However, in policy circles and in the press it was used as a basis for defining and discussing knowledge-intensive in contrast to traditional or non-knowledge-intensive industries. This approach has three fundamental limitations. First, it focuses on knowledge that is formally created through investments in R&D, ignoring at the same time other forms of knowledge that may have economically important characteristics. Second, the focus on the direct creation of knowledge puts significant limitations on our understanding of the complexity of economic processes which essentially involves the interdependence and diffusion of knowledge between different fields and sectors of economic activity (Smith, 2002; Robertson and Smith, 2008). That is, knowledge that is relevant to a specific industry may be distributed across many independent actors or sectors, and thus a low-R&D industry may be a heavy user of knowledge produced elsewhere. Third, such an aggregate sectoral perspective might be criticized because it does not consider differences at the firm level. It is worth noting that within an industry there tends to be a wide variation across firms in terms of their R&D intensities, so that it is common to find low-tech firms in high-tech industries and vice versa (Kirner et al., 2009).

Knowledge-intensive entrepreneurship is also strongly connected to innovation (Malerba and McKelvey, 2010), while according to Schumpeter the term entrepreneurship implies the introduction of new innovative activities which may be new to the firm-specific knowledge base but also new to the sectoral knowledge base or technology field (Hirsch-Kreinsen and Schwinge, 2011).

The notion of innovation and technological change has been primarily applied to high-tech industries (von Tunzelmann and Acha, 2005). Yet, the low- and medium-tech (LMT) sector, although quite old and even mature in some cases, is reasonably innovative. They implement regular changes in both product and process technologies which, although less impressive than some of the innovations in high-tech industries, still make a considerable contribution to their own productivity and competitiveness and to better macroeconomic performance (Robertson and Smith, 2008). Furthermore, LMT industries not only innovate for their own benefit but, by being active users of products and ideas of newer industries, they contribute to the growth of high-tech industries as well.

Thus LMT firms when they follow innovative paths may not engage extensively in formal intramural R&D activities, but essentially exploit information and knowledge obtained from diverse sources (mostly external) which they in turn combine and use in internal adaptations. In consequence, the discussion on the phenomenon of knowledge generation and innovation at the level of firms and their transformation into economic activity, i.e. knowledge-intensive entrepreneurship, should not be limited solely to the science-based high-tech sector but should be extended to the low-tech sector as well.

At present the debate on KIE is mainly focused on firms or start-ups in the high-tech sector. Only limited attention has been paid to low-tech or mature industries. In this chapter acknowledging the ability of low-tech firms to engage in knowledge-seeking activities and frequent technological upgrading, we suggest that KIE can also exist in established industries. In addition, taking into consideration that established industries constitute by far the greatest part of economic activity in manufacturing and services in the developed economies, we will attempt to examine specific KIE characteristics in low- and medium-to-low-tech manufacturing sectors and examine similarities and differences to high- and medium-to-high-tech sectors. In this way we try to shed light on the features of KIE in LMT firms and at the same time reveal some common characteristics they may have with high-tech firms, in order to increase understanding of this 'high-potential' type of entrepreneurship on the part of managers, policy-makers and scholars.

2.2   THEORETICAL BACKGROUND

2.2.1   Knowledge-Intensive Entrepreneurship

Contemporary entrepreneurship research appears to be moving from the view that 'all forms of entrepreneurship are good' towards a more nuanced view that 'high-potential entrepreneurship' is an important driver of economic development (Autio and Acs, 2007; Henrekson and Johansson, 2010).

Knowledge-intensive entrepreneurship can be considered a type of high-potential entrepreneurship. It indicates ventures whose initiation or expansion is based on the dynamic application of new knowledge. Also, new knowledge-intensive firms in particular can play an important role in sectoral, local and national innovation systems by operating as problem-solvers, knowledge brokers, knowledge-intensive service providers, or specialized suppliers.

Following Malerba and McKelvey (2010), we rely on a formal definition of knowledge-intensive entrepreneurship developed during a large-scale, integrated, EU-funded research project.[2] Here, KIE is associated with four basic characteristics; it concerns: (a) new firms (new ventures); (b) new ventures that are innovative; (c) new ventures engaging in activities that are knowledge-intensive; and finally (d) new ventures that are not to be found solely in high-tech industries, but may well be active in low-tech industries.

Perhaps the best way to understand the notion of KIE is to compare it with related but distinct concepts. First, a KIE venture is not simply a new venture or start-up firm; it is a new venture that pursues innovative opportunities by purposefully and systematically utilizing knowledge in its operational activities. Second, KIE ventures transform not only scientific and technological knowledge into new products and services, since technological assets are but one class of resource or capability needed for the successful commercialization of innovation. Thus the ultimate objective in KIE is market success – not 'simply' the development of a radical innovation. Third, 'knowledge intensive' does not equate with high-tech manufacturing (Delmar and Wennberg, 2010), as knowledge matters in a variety of settings, in high- and low-tech environments alike (McKelvey and Lassen, 2013).

Knowledge-intensive firms are considered to be of strategic importance because they are often at the leading edge of innovation practices and have an important role in the creation and dissemination of knowledge (Delmar and Wennberg, 2010). However, until recently KIE has been primarily associated with high-tech industries emphasizing the role of technology, risk capital, and technical institutions in the founding processes of firms

(Brännback et al., 2003; Rosenkopf and Nerkar, 2001). In such industries KIE has been essentially related to knowledge generated by investments in R&D and embodied in high-level human capital and skills, while the transformation of knowledge into innovative outputs has been often measured by the number of patents (KEINS project[3]).

Although it might be easier to define KIE as only occurring in certain industries such as biotechnology and information and communication technologies, or in certain special types of firms (university spin-offs), we argue that KIE is a phenomenon that can be found equally in different sectors, and especially we suggest that it can be identified in low- and medium-tech (LMT) industries as well.

2.2.2 Why is KIE also Relevant to LMT Firms?

Up to now the debate on KIE has been mainly focused on firms or start-ups in high-tech manufacturing sectors. The concept of KIE has also been recently applied to knowledge-intensive service firms (Delmar and Wennberg, 2010). This is because the vibrant 'knowledge-intensive business services' (KIBS) evolution is considered part of larger economic changes emanating from an increasingly dynamic 'market for knowledge' with decreasing transaction costs due to the introduction of sophisticated information and communication technologies (Langlois, 2003).

On the other hand, limited attention has been paid to the relevance of KIE in low-tech or mature industries. This is because KIE is primarily related to the exploitation of innovative opportunities (Malerba and McKelvey, 2010), the creation of new knowledge and the transformation of established practices both at the sectoral and firm level (Hirsch-Kreinsen and Schwinge, 2011). However, it can be assumed that the significant constraints on KIE in the mature LMT sector may be due to the very basic features of these industries.

That is because, first, the LMT sector and firms appear to offer only very limited opportunities for KIE activities, since innovations in these contexts are more or less path-dependent, i.e. based on technological knowledge and capabilities that slowly evolve around established technological trajectories (ibid.). It is also suggested that this path-dependency has been further stabilized by incremental innovation activities that tend to optimize or further upgrade existing technologies. Unlike the high-tech sector, where technological risks and uncertainties prevail, the technologies of the LMT sector are considered well-known and mature. Furthermore, low-tech products are considered to be not only highly-standardized but also at an advanced stage of their life cycle. The same applies to the LMT sector's knowledge base which largely embraces codified and transferable components such as design methods, engineering routines and knowledge about the market and customer needs.

Second, the nature of competition in LMT industries – mainly characterized by intensive price or cost antagonism – forces firms to continuously improve their existing technologies and processes rather than to involve themselves in exploring innovative and risky prospects.

However, opportunities for KIE in the LMT sector should not be ignored (Hirsch-Kreinsen and Schwinge, 2011). The frequently used assumption that technology and market conditions change slowly in the low-tech sector has been increasingly challenged in recent years, thus the path-dependency argument can always be questioned. New ideas can overcome fixed trajectories and create new, maybe more promising, development paths that may change the way these industries organize their inputs/outputs. It may also be that fierce market competition and intensive pressure imposed by low-cost competitors may force LMT firms to change established practices and look for breakthrough innovations in order to gain competitive advantage (von Tunzelmann and Acha, 2005).

Knowledge and innovation in LMT sectors
Knowledge-intensive entrepreneurship can be considered as the launching of new activities and organizations that intensively use existing scientific and technological knowledge or that intensively create new scientific and technological knowledge for commercial purposes or for bringing products to markets (Malerba and McKelvey, 2010).

The concept of KIE refers to knowledge as the very basis of all entrepreneurial activities (Hirsch-Kreinsen and Schwinge, 2011; Garavaglia and Grieco, 2005). In high-tech ventures it can be either technological knowledge about new innovations and developments in a specific field, or market knowledge (Agarwal et al., 2004) mainly oriented to a more general understanding of the application areas in which technologies are used (Adams et al., 2012). Market and technology knowledge availability and sharing are considered significant elements of firm-level entrepreneurship in mature industries (Kogut and Zander, 1992; Sciascia and Mazzola, 2008). A major feature in this case is the fact that knowledge often stems from various sources outside the firm's sectoral boundaries (Hirsch-Kreinsen and Schwinge, 2011; Robertson and Smith, 2008).

It is widely accepted that LMT firms have, in general, limited in-house R&D activity. Formalized processes of knowledge creation and use play only a marginal role, and instead, innovation activities are primarily based on 'practical and pragmatic ways by doing and using' (von Tunzelmann and Acha, 2005: 417). In this respect it appears that the knowledge most relevant for these firms is application-oriented, practical knowledge.

Unlike theoretical and scientific knowledge which can be mainly attributed to research and development activities, practical knowledge is generated and accumulated in the context of ongoing operating processes through 'learning-by-using' and 'learning-by-doing' in everyday practice (Hirsch-Kreinsen, 2008).

The acquisition and generation of knowledge in LMT sectors does not take place only within firms' boundaries. External knowledge sources such as other firms, organizations and other actors play a decisive role in the innovation strategies of LMT firms. This applies to both practical and scientifically generated knowledge. Examples of external sources are the 'customer-oriented strategy' – the experience of long-time customers in new market and demand trends – the expertise of specialized consultants or information about changing market requirements acquired at trade fairs and exhibitions. Further important external sources are machinery manufacturers and suppliers who actually provide theoretical and scientific knowledge embodied in new components, production equipment and materials (Heidenreich, 2009; Grimpe and Sofka, 2009; Santamaria et al., 2009), and the diffusion of new knowledge that takes place through learning-by-doing and -using. An analogous example is the specification of material parameters by suppliers that may be systematically used by LMT firms to further improve their products' characteristics. Thus, knowledge generation in non-research-intensive firms can be linked to the concept of 'distributed knowledge bases' (Smith, 2002; Hirsch-Kreinsen, 2008). As levels of R&D are typically very low, the use of distributed knowledge is, in fact, the main source of new ideas and techniques in LMT firms. Knowledge bases are developed, maintained and disseminated by various independent institutions and often originate in different industries and technology fields, and are claimed to be 'deep, complex and systemic' (Hirsch-Kreinsen et al., 2003). Studying the phenomenon of KIE in low-tech industries in detail, Hirsch-Kreinsen and Schwinge (2011) focus on the importance of trans-sectoral factors such as new knowledge, technologies, market knowledge and recombinations of practical knowledge in order to create new knowledge.

It is rather rare for those traditional industries to generate radical innovations, which are typically captured by the usual metrics of firm innovativeness. This means that such industries seem less innovative, because of the incremental character of their innovative performance. However, it is also argued that cumulative incremental innovations can expand, extend and leverage technological trajectories and cause major economic impacts (Dosi, 1982). In some traditional industries, incremental innovations are just as important as radical innovations – or even more so. For example, in scale-intensive industries such as mining and oil extracting, the fact that innovations are primarily incremental and process-related does not necessarily mean that they play a secondary role or that those industries are less dynamic from an innovative point of view. This is because in such industries incremental innovation can result in important productivity and profitability gains having the same positive effect as a radical innovation may have in other, less scale-intensive industries. Finally, several incremental innovations taken together can result in overcoming technological barriers and expand the production boundaries of the firms in these industries (von Tunzelmann and Acha, 2005). In addition, and very often, LMT companies not only pursue incremental innovation strategies but also architectural or modular innovation strategies (Henderson and Clark, 1990) in trying to overcome their existing paths of knowledge and technology and achieve a leading position in niche markets or create new market segments (Hirsch-Kreinsen and Schwinge, 2011; Hirsch-Kreinsen, 2008).

LMT manufacturing industries are more active in process innovations (Segarra-Blasco and Arauzo-Carod, 2008; Kirner et al., 2009; Heidenreich, 2009) that are customer- or market-driven (Bender, 2004; Santamaria et al., 2009; Grimpe and Sofka, 2009) or even derive from relevant regulatory incentives or requirements. On the other hand, R&D-based product innovations are more usual in the high-tech sector (Breschi et al., 2000; Delmar and Wennberg, 2010) that rely mainly on scientific contributions and target novel technological knowledge (Grimpe and Sofka, 2009). Although it is often difficult to discriminate between product- and process-related innovation, many LMT enterprises focus their innovation efforts on their technical and/or organizational process structures. These firms typically belong to industries for products manufactured at a relatively high degree of automation and capital-intensive process technologies such as firms in furniture or paper manufacturing (Hirsch-Kreinsen, 2008).

The knowledge base of traditional industries can be greatly expanded as products become increasingly systemic and embody knowledge emerging from scientific or technological breakthroughs in the high-tech sector. More specifically, there is a merging of knowledge and industry boundaries which can be described as 'technology fusion' that gives firms the opportunity to introduce new technologies into products and systems for improved performance and new functionalities. For example, in functional or nutraceutical foods the boundaries of food and pharmaceutical industries are blurred to create hybrid products that in addition to addressing basic nutritional requirements also provide health benefits (Robertson and Patel, 2007; Bröring et al., 2006). Furthermore, in the case of complex product and production processes the technological diversification/expansion of existing knowledge bases arises when there are strong interdependencies between what firms create themselves and what they require from suppliers of machinery, components or materials. In this case the effective use and improvement of outside components and machinery requires in-house integration, learning and coordination capabilities in order to effectuate systemic change (absorptive capacity).

In many cases LMT firms do not just adjust or adapt to existing technology paradigms already developed in other more high-tech industries. They are also key users of high-tech ideas (Santamaria et al., 2009; Garibaldo and Jacobson, 2005), and can contribute significantly to the development of technologies and knowledge diversification towards new technological fields (Mendonça, 2009). These firms, by being 'lead users', place special demands on new technologies and call for novel performance attributes that exceed the normal requirements of the average user. In addition, they often find ways to expand the performance characteristics of the new technologies themselves and then allow their improvements to be fed back to high-tech firms so that they can be applied to other uses (von Hippel, 2005). It is also suggested that lead users are particularly effective in the introduction and diffusion of innovations when they search for solutions to problems analogous to their own in other industries. Thus, LMT firms can both generate demand for high-tech innovations and also speed up productivity increases in LMT industries across the economy (Robertson and Patel, 2007).

In sum, a literature review reveals the importance of knowledge and innovation in LMT sectors and suggests that opportunities for KIE do exist in these environments. Our argument is that any sensible analysis of KIE in developed economies must examine all sectors because knowledge-intensive activities can take place across all industries. It is therefore important to enrich our empirical understanding of KIE in both LMT and HMT firms by examining their similarities and possible differences in significant elements of KIE, such as knowledge-seeking activities and innovation performance.

2.3   DATA AND DEFINITIONS

The data used for empirical analyses were collected during the first half of 2011 as part of the large-scale AEGIS survey by means of computer-assisted telephone interviewing using a structured questionnaire. All respondents were either the founder/entrepreneur or members of the founding team. A total of 1902 young firms operating in different manufacturing sectors responded to the survey. They were founded between 2001 and 2007 (and thus all had passed the critical three-year survival threshold)

Table 2.1   Firm distribution per country and sectoral group

Country	LMT firms	HMT firms	Total
Croatia	114	29	143
Czech Republic	78	26	104
Denmark	69	35	104
France	189	59	248
Germany	161	67	228
Greece	177	22	199
Italy	287	63	350
Portugal	154	29	183
Sweden	90	37	127
UK	160	56	216
Total	1479	423	1902

Source: AEGIS Survey, data processing by LIEE/NTUA.

in ten European countries: Croatia, Czech Republic, Denmark, France, Germany, Greece, Italy, Portugal, Sweden and the UK (see Table 2.1).

To operationalize the concepts of high- and low-tech manufacturing industries, we followed the currently used OECD four-tier model in which the basic criterion for classifying sectors is the business expenditures on research and development (BERD) over production. In particular, the OECD distinguishes between industries spending over 5 per cent of their turnover (high-tech), those spending 3–5 per cent of turnover (medium-high-tech), those spending 1–3 per cent (medium-low-tech), and those spending less than 1 per cent (low-tech). A high R&D intensity is often considered to indicate commitment to knowledge creation in new technologies, while lower-tech is related to more or less traditional activities. The R&D intensity criterion, as already mentioned, has many drawbacks as a technological indicator in terms of countries, industries and firms (Smith, 2002).

In this chapter we adopt this conventional classification of sectors because it is generally known among scholars, popular among policymakers and because the ultimate goal of this research is to identify similarities and differences in terms of KIE characteristics across higher- and lower-tech industries. Table 2.2 shows that the sample includes firms from high- and medium-to-high-tech manufacturing sectors, and low- and medium-to-low-tech manufacturing sectors. However, for simplicity the empirical analysis is mainly performed for two sectoral groups: the 'high- and medium-tech' group (HMT) and the 'low- and medium-tech' group.

Table 2.2   Sample sectoral distribution

Selected Sectors	NACE rev. 1.1 code	Number of firms
High-tech manufacturing sector		
Aerospace	35.3	1
Computers and office machinery	30	6
Radio-television and communication equipment	32	51
Manufacture of medical, precision and optical instruments (scientific instruments)	33	68
Pharmaceuticals	24.4	19
Medium-high-tech manufacturing sector		
Manufacture of electrical machinery and apparatus	31	50
Manufacture of machinery and equipment	29	191
Chemical industry (excluding pharmaceuticals)	24 (excl. 24.4)	37
Low-tech manufacturing sector		
Paper and printing	21, 22	472
Textile and clothing	17, 18, 19	203
Wood and furniture	36, 20	237
Food, beverages and tobacco	15, 16	294
Medium-low-tech manufacturing sector		
Basic metals	27	35
Fabricated metal products	28	238

Source: AEGIS Survey, data processing by LIEE/NTUA.

2.4   EMPIRICAL RESULTS AND DISCUSSION

2.4.1   Some Basic Demographic Characteristics

Descriptive analysis indicates that firms do not differ significantly in terms of age as the average company age is seven years for both sectoral groups. However, this finding is also a consequence of the sampling design which considers young independent entities as eligible candidates for the survey. The firms appear to be rather small both in terms of full-time employees and annual turnover, a finding which can be primarily associated with their newness. In particular, the HMT firms are slightly larger than the LMT firms, but with marginal statistical significance (14 vs. 11.5 full-time employees respectively). Three out of four firms in the survey had an average turnover below €1 million during the period examined (2007–09). In fact, 32 per cent of the LMT firms and 25 per cent of their

HMT counterparts had a turnover only up to €250 000, suggestive of small firm size. As to profits, however, the HMT firms slightly outperform the LMT firms. Although more than half of the ventures of both groups reported annual profits of up to €50 000 (2007–09), only 11 per cent of the HMT firms had losses, compared to a 16 per cent share in the LMT group. Furthermore, 19 per cent of the HMT firms reported profits above €150 000, vs. 11.5 per cent in LMT sectors.

In addition, our findings suggest that firms belonging to LMT sectors may have been affected to a slightly greater extent by the global financial crisis that began in 2008: some 25 per cent of them have witnessed a decrease in sales in 2010, compared to 20 per cent in HMT sectors. However, the declining sales have not resulted in significant job losses, as only 10 to 12 per cent of firms from both groups appear to have reduced their personnel during the same period.

2.4.2 The Formation Phase

Professional experience, market knowledge and personal networks built up during the founders' career paths are reported as key drivers of firm formation for both groups. However, technical and engineering knowledge, and identification of opportunities deriving from technological change are perceived as more significant by HMT firms, a finding which can be attributed to the nature of knowledge and innovation related to high-tech products/artifacts. The same holds for opportunities arising from change in technology or market needs. On the other hand, the availability of finance appears to be more important for LMT firms. This can be attributed to the fact that the finance available over the last 15 years has been more favorable to high-tech ventures than low-tech ventures, which represents more traditional activities not usually considered attractive enough for risk-taking.

However, this finding is not further supported by the founders' information on the actual funding they received during the formation phase. Table 2.3 indicates that the different funding sources are used more or less to the same extent by the two sectoral groups. Founders' own savings are by far the most popular source, followed by bank loans. It is important to note that half of the firms in both groups were funded entirely by their own financial resources, whereas almost 60 per cent of ventures in both groups covered more than 75 per cent of their initial investment from the same source. Moreover, despite the fact that venture capital is used by less than 8 per cent of the HMT and 5 per cent in LMT ventures, 27 per cent of the former were able to obtain more than 75 per cent of their initial funding from venture capital. Family members and former employers seem to have

Table 2.3   Sources of funding for new firm creation

	% of HMT firms that received funding			% of LMT firms that received funding		
	at least 1%*	100%*	more than 75%*	at least 1%*	100%*	more than 75%*
Own financial resources	92	50	59	91	52	58
Family members	11	5	7	13	16	23
Former employer	3	9	9	2	23	30
Venture capital	8	15	27	5	0	6
Banks	38	8	29	39	7	23
Government	11	0	2	9	3	8
EU funds	3	0	0	5	3	6

Note: * Percentage of the investment funded by the particular source. The values are mean average on a 1 (not important) to 5 (extremely important) Likert scale.
Source: AEGIS Survey, data processing by LIEE/NTUA.

supported LMT firms more extensively, while government and EU funds have a rather peripheral role in new firm creation for both groups, with fractionally higher support for LMT firms.

2.4.3   Knowledge Sources

Our research findings suggest that there are multiple knowledge sources used by both young LMT and HMT firms to explore new technological and market opportunities. The sources of knowledge measured are: (a) internal sources (in-house R&D); (b) external sources related to industry that reflect the importance of knowledge coming from clients, suppliers and competitors; (c) external sources associated with science such as public research institutes, universities and commercial labs or R&D firms; (d) external open sources such as trade fairs, conferences and exhibitions, scientific journals and other trade or technical publications; and (e) nationally funded or EU-funded research programs.

Table 2.4 presents the founders' evaluations[4] of the significance of specific linkages that can act as sources of knowledge and technology for the firm and therefore support its knowledge-intensive entrepreneurial activity. It also shows t-test analysis results.

In-house generated knowledge appears to be quite important for both LMT and HMT firms, but internal R&D appears more significant for

Table 2.4 Sources of knowledge for exploring new business opportunities

Sources of knowledge	HMT	LMT	t-value
Clients or customers	4.43	4.41	−1.24
Suppliers	3.63	3.73	1.36
Competitors	3.34	3.41	0.85
In-house R&D	3.44	3.25	−2.89***
Trade fairs, conferences and exhibitions	3.14	3.09	−1.49
Scientific journals and other trade or technical publications	2.85	2.77	−3.12***
Universities	2.21	2.07	−2.72***
Public research institutes	2.16	2.10	−1.64
External commercial labs/R&D firms/technical institutes	2.18	2.11	−1.10
Participation in nationally funded research programs	2.08	1.89	−2.99***
Participation in EU-funded research programs (Framework Programmes)	2.05	1.91	−2.53**

Note: ***, **, denote statistical significance at $p < 1\%$ and $p < 5\%$ respectively. The values are mean average on a 1 (not important) to 5 (extremely important) Likert scale.
Source: AEGIS Survey, data processing by LIEE/NTUA.

HMT firms. This is an expected result since, in general, these firms have greater R&D capacities at their disposal and R&D activities are at the core of new knowledge creation in high-tech industries (Del Monte and Papagni, 2003; Stam and Wennberg, 2009; Breschi et al., 2000), while LMT firms lack formal R&D capabilities.

Research has shown that external knowledge bases play a more significant role for LMT innovation than internal knowledge sources. This is mainly because LMT firms try to balance their lack of internally generated knowledge with activities seeking knowledge from independent actors who may be in different industries and fields (Hirsch-Kreinsen and Schwinge, 2011; Robertson and Smith, 2008). Our results also suggest that among the low-tech firms external industry and market knowledge sources are held to be more important than internally produced knowledge.

Our findings also suggest that there are no significant statistical differences in the importance of external market and industry knowledge sources across the two groups. Although all firms ranked clients/customers and suppliers as their most important sources of knowledge, we notice that LMT firms evaluate knowledge from suppliers as higher than HMT firms. This can be attributed to the relevance of process innovation to LMT firms, which can be considered knowledge usually with reference to machines and other technological components, i.e.

embodied knowledge (Heidenreich, 2009; Grimpe and Sofka, 2009; Santamaria et al., 2009).

Regarding the external scientific knowledge sources, both groups use knowledge sources related to public research institutes and external commercial labs; however, HMT firms evaluate universities as an important knowledge source more highly than do LMT firms.

Furthermore, although HMT firms consider scientific journals and participation in research programs (nationally or EU funded) to be more significant sources of knowledge than do the LMT companies, these are ranked at the bottom of the list for both groups. These results are in line with Protogerou et al. (2013), who find that, in general, young firms have a relatively limited presence in EU-funded research projects because new entrepreneurial ventures need some time to develop essential administrative and project management competences as well as the necessary research resources and technical knowledge to become attractive partners in such research networks.

2.4.4 Networking Activities in Day-to-Day Firm Operations

Firms were also asked to evaluate the extent to which the networks that they have gradually created contribute to improving various operations. The purpose of this question was to determine the importance of interpersonal and interorganizational relationships or linkages to specific operations of the company. It is assumed that these linkages can be viewed as the media through which entrepreneurs gain access to a variety of market, technology, production, economic and other resources held by other actors. Table 2.5 presents the items used to capture the different underlying dimensions of networking activity, the relevant evaluations and t-test results.

Our empirical analysis suggests that, in general, there is no difference in terms of using networks for various firm activities across the two groups. This suggests the increased importance that founders attribute to networking, independently of sector classification. Nevertheless LMT firms state that networking has contributed more significantly to their advertising and promotion activities and assisted in arranging taxation and other legal issues. On the other hand, HMT firms use networking for developing new products and exploring export activities more than do LMT firms.

2.4.5 Formal Collaboration Agreements

Formal collaboration agreements and especially R&D and technical cooperation agreements have become a strategically important part of

Table 2.5   Contribution of networks to firm's various activities

Network's contribution to	HMT	LMT	t-value
contacting customers/clients	4.18	4.06	−1.90*
selecting suppliers	3.72	3.71	−0.21
recruiting skilled labor	3.50	3.35	−1.99*
developing new products/services	3.51	3.22	−4.01***
collecting information about competitors	3.29	3.27	−0.30
managing production and operations	3.33	3.32	−0.13
accessing distribution channels	3.09	3.11	0.29
advertising and promotion	2.83	2.98	2.09**
assistance in arranging taxation or other legal issues	2.76	2.94	2.47**
assistance in obtaining business loans/attracting funds	2.69	2.65	−0.40
exploring export opportunities	2.79	2.58	−2.58***

Note: ***, **, *, denote statistical significance at $p < 1\%$, $p < 5\%$ and $p < 10\%$ respectively. The values are mean average on a 1 (not important) to 5 (extremely important) Likert scale.
Source: AEGIS Survey, data processing by LIEE/NTUA.

business decision-making in many industries in recent years in both high- and low-tech sectors. The various types of technology collaborations are important for young firms in order to gain the knowledge necessary to develop or acquire the capabilities needed for new product development, R&D, innovation, design, manufacturing, or even technical services (Haeussler et al., 2012; Park et al., 2002).

Results (see Table 2.6) indicate that the majority of firms have rarely or never participated (extent of participation is assessed on a five-point Likert scale) in any type of agreement (not even any subcontracting agreement), thus confirming the non-collaborative trend in terms of participation in EU- or nationally funded research networks in Table 2.4. HMT firms seem to be slightly more active, becoming involved to a greater extent in all types of agreements, especially technical cooperation or R&D agreements. This finding may be also attributed to the fact of young firms developing early R&D cooperative strategies and continuing to have such agreements later on as well.

2.4.6   Innovation Performance

The definition and measurement of the innovation performance dimension is based on fairly standard variables similar to those of the Community Innovation Survey (CIS). Taken together they capture various aspects of innovation performance, including product, process and organizational

Table 2.6   Firm participation in various types of formal agreements

Company has participated in	HMT	LMT	t-value
strategic alliances	2.22	1.82	−5.56***
technical cooperation agreements	2.42	1.91	−7.18***
licensing agreements	1.84	1.70	−2.12**
R&D agreements	2.01	1.54	−7.21***
research contract-out	1.64	1.47	−3.03***
marketing/export promotion agreements	2.12	1.95	−2.39**
subcontracting agreements	2.61	2.26	−4.45***

Note: *** denotes statistical significance at $p < 1\%$. The values are mean average on a 1 (not important) to 5 (extremely important) Likert scale.
Source: AEGIS Survey, data processing by LIEE/NTUA.

innovation, and patenting as well as less formal methods of intellectual property protection.

Product innovation is measured by variables capturing both the presence and degree of novelty of product innovation that had occurred in the three years previous to the survey. Results reveal that overall there are significantly more HMT than LMT firms that innovate (see Table 2.7). This finding corroborates other studies, mainly based on CIS data, which suggest that product innovation plays a far greater role for HMT than for LMT firms (Heidenreich, 2009; Arundel et al., 2008). Product innovations demand specific technological competencies and R&D capabilities which LMT firms usually do not have or only have to a limited extent. What is more, many LMT firms focus on the continuous development of already existing products by improving product components incrementally or by upgrading the products' functional and technological characteristics. This is a way for non-research-intensive LMT firms to respond to changing customer preferences and attempt to create new sales segments.

On the other hand, in measures of process innovation as improvement in manufacturing methods, the performance of LMT firms is better: 56 per cent introduced new or significantly improved manufacturing methods during the last three years compared to 49 per cent of HMT firms. This finding is in line with other empirical studies stressing the much greater importance of technical process innovations in LMT firms than in high-to-medium-tech firms (Heidenreich, 2009; Rammer, 2010). Two factors are mentioned as important drivers of process innovations in LMT firms: first, process innovations can take place relatively smoothly, as their basic

Table 2.7   Innovation performance

		HMT	LMT
Product innovation	% of firms	71	63
	% of innovative firms with products new to the world	36	19
% of firms with process innovation	methods of manufacturing	49	56
% of firms with organizational innovation	at least one field where organizational innovation was introduced	71	71
	logistics, supply chain, delivery or distribution methods	39	46
	supporting activities for your processes	53	51
	knowledge management systems (KMS)	46	48
	changes in managing structure	29	33

Source: AEGIS Survey, data processing by LIEE/NTUA.

development is usually done by technology suppliers and typically do not require additional in-house R&D activities from the innovating firm (Hirsch-Kreinsen, 2013). Second, the substantial cost competition in LMT sectors forces firms to focus their innovation efforts on manufacturing processes as a means to cut costs rapidly, improve efficiency and ensure competitiveness (Cox et al., 2002; Kirner et al., 2009).

Our findings also show that firms do not differ in terms of organizational innovation: the same share of young ventures from both groups (71 per cent) introduced improvements in at least one type of the examined fields. In fact, LMT firms introduced innovations in logistics, supply chain, and delivery or distribution methods statistically more than did HMT firms. They also outperform HMT firms in making knowledge management system improvements and changes in managing structure, though not to a significant extent. These results suggest that organizational innovations such as the introduction of new forms of company organization or new logistics and distribution methods can be directly related to technical process innovations. Recent data largely corroborate our findings that for LMT firms this type of non-technical innovation is just as important as technically based process innovation activities.

Furthermore, firms do not differ in terms of the effect of product innovation on turnover, as on average 30 per cent of goods/services come from innovative products in both groups, though specifically the share of goods from high-tech firms is slightly larger than that from low-tech firms. They do differ, however, in terms of radicalness of innovation: 36 per cent of high-tech vs. 19 per cent of low-tech firms responded that some of their product innovations were new to the world and not just new to the market in which they operate or new to their portfolio of products.

Finally it should be stressed that the firms in our sample generally use more informal (secrecy) or semi-informal (confidentiality agreements, trademarks) than formal (patents and trademarks) methods of intellectual property protection.[5] Informal protection methods are often much simpler and faster to introduce than formal protection methods, and can be maintained with limited resources, which is very important especially for newly established firms. On the other hand, formal protection methods, mainly intellectual property rights, require major financial and human resources if they are to be exploited thoroughly in business. The HMT firms in our sample use patents, confidentiality agreements, secrecy, complexity of design, and lead-time advantage to a greater extent than LMT firms. For instance, 31 per cent of the HMT firms vs. only 16 per cent in LMT firms use patents. However, copyright is a more popular protection method among LMT firms (24 per cent vs. 16 per cent in HMT firms), whereas trademarks are used to the same extent by both groups, perhaps because they can be employed as a marketing tool so that customers can recognize the products of a specific trader.

Thus, a general conclusion that we make is that, at least in terms of innovative performance and the usual international definitions of the various types of innovation, the newly established LMT firms present in the survey do not lag behind their higher-tech counterparts, and in some cases they outperform them. But then the most crucial matter is to examine the inputs into this innovative performance to understand the mechanisms that these companies use.

The most common input indicator used in the literature is R&D intensity, which in the survey was measured as the percentage of turnover that has been spent on R&D during the last three years. Results show that HMT firms spend on average 16 per cent of their sales vs. only 10 per cent of sales for the lower-tech firms. Alternatively, some 30 per cent of the HMT firms that participated in the survey reported that they spent at least 20 per cent of their sales on R&D, whereas 19 per cent of the lower-tech firms spent that much.[6] Thus, as expected, higher-tech firms do spend a lot on R&D. The innovative performance of lower-tech firms, however, cannot be underestimated. Though R&D innovation is more important for HMT firms, our findings suggest that in the so-called traditional industries many of the activities that lead to innovative outcomes are not R&D based.

2.5   CONCLUDING REMARKS

This study is an exploratory exercise which uses data from the extensive AEGIS dataset to attempt to show – confirming recent empirical case-study work by Hirsch-Kreinsen and Schwinge (2011) – that opportunities for KIE may exist also in LMT sectors and firms. It does so by providing some meaningful comparisons between firms in HMT and LMT sectors. The empirical study identifies similarities which seem to stem mostly from the fact that the examined firms were newly founded ventures, that is, they have not yet been established in the field or not yet grown significantly in size. It also points out differences that can be characterized as sector-specific, rather to be expected and not surprising. In addition, our work provides some new reasons to call into question the traditional policy measures used to support entrepreneurship.

First of all, it should be stressed that the two groups surveyed were almost identical in terms of demographic characteristics. This indicates that there is no size discrimination that could largely explain some elements of the behavior of the different firms, although LMT firms seem to be affected by the crisis to a greater extent than HMT firms.

The two sectoral groups examined build more or less on the same factors during the formation phase. Due to sector-specific characteristics, however, technological opportunities appear to be more crucial for high-tech firms. Yet, the most interesting difference appears on the financing side: raising capital seems to be harder for LMT firms than for their HMT counterparts. What might be surprising is that during the formation process both groups mainly used the same funding mechanisms: their own savings or family members' support. This is an indication that in real life newly established firms find it difficult to raise significant capital, irrelevant of sector. But since during the last 20 years the overall funding environment has been more favorable towards HMT, new entrepreneurs in LMT sectors may perceive that their activity is less attractive than that of HMT firms to potential sources of business financing.

What is definitely worth noticing is that an almost equal share of firms in both groups shows innovative performance. Thus innovation can be considered a common element that may have contributed to firm survival so far. However, the examined firms differ in terms of the type of innovation across the two groups. Product innovation is more common in HMT firms; also more types of global innovation are attributed to them than to LMT firms. On the other hand, the fact that LMT firms show better performance in process innovation indicates that non-R&D innovation is important for them. A policy implication for this may be that new LMT ventures could be better supported in their technological upgrading by promoting investment in process technologies and networking with suppliers/customers, whereas developing formal R&D labs may not be an equally valuable option for them. HMT firms, on the other hand, could be more efficiently supported in their innovative performance if incentives for more formal R&D collaborations were developed.

Our findings suggest that policy-makers should improve their awareness of low-tech industries. We emphasize that measures to promote KIE should not only be focused on HMT industries, because LMT sectors and firms – contrary to established scientific and popular beliefs – appear routinely to become heavily involved in knowledge-seeking activities and exhibit innovation potential. Effective entrepreneurship and innovation policy needs to take into account the variety at the firm level and at the same time the specific environmental conditions in which companies operate. Because external knowledge sources appear to be conducive to the identification of new technology and market opportunities for LMT firms, policy measures should focus on the development of organizational capabilities and management skills that enable the companies to recognize important external knowledge, combine it with already existing internally generated knowledge and exploit it in a beneficial way (Hirsch-Kreinsen and Schwinge, 2011; Hirsch-Kreinsen, 2013) In practice, this can be achieved by introducing and promoting advanced management methods and work methods conducive to innovation, while upgrading already existing R&D-related activities or even introducing limited internal R&D capacity if it has not existed.

Furthermore, policy should promote networking activity that can facilitate the diffusion of globally produced knowledge (either in other industry sectors or in other markets) that is new to the LMT firms. This can be done by promoting cooperation relations of all types with both high-tech or scientific organizations and technology suppliers as well as with the demand side, such as lead customers. Policy measures should also promote more bridging institutions between LMT industries and science and the exchange of experiences with other networks. Trade fairs, one of the most important external information sources for firms, should be better further exploited for such bridging activities (Hirsch-Kreinsen and Schwinger, 2011; Hirsch-Kreinsen, 2013).

NOTES

1. The concept of the R&D intensity of different industrial sectors goes back to J.D. Bernal's lecture of 1947 in which he introduced the notion that the fastest-growing industries like electronics, pharmaceutical and aircraft were at that time also the most

      research-intensive industries (Chris Freeman, 'The Vega Lecture on Bernal and the Social Function of Science', available at http://vega.org.uk/video/programme/86, accessed 10 October 2013).
2. Advancing Knowledge-Intensive Entrepreneurship and Innovation for Economic Growth and Social Well-being in Europe (AEGIS), a project co-funded by the European Commission under the Theme 8 'Socio-Economic Sciences and Humanities' of the 7th Framework Programme.
3. KEINS – Knowledge-Based Entrepreneurship: Innovation, Networks and Systems – a project co-funded by the European Commission under the 6th Framework Programme.
4. They are measured on a five-point Likert scale ranging from one (not important) to five (extremely important).
5. Semi-formal protection methods are also based in law but do not entail any official registration. They are usually contracts (i.e. confidentiality agreements) that can be used similarly to formal protection methods (to protect knowledge and information) but can also be employed to formalize and legalize the relationships of a firm with its partners and employees.
6. Chi square analysis of independence shows that this difference is significant at the p < 1% level.

REFERENCES

Adams, P., R. Fontana and F. Malerba (2012), 'Spin-offs are Not the Only Story: Demand Start-ups in High-Tech Industries', paper submitted for selection to the EARIE 2012 Conference University of Tor Vergata, 2–4 September 2012.

Agarwal, R., R. Echambadi, A. Franco and M. Sarkar (2004), 'Knowledge Transfer through Inheritance: Spin-out Generation, Development and Survival', *Academy of Management Journal*, **47** (4), 501–22.

Arundel, A., C. Bordoy and M. Kanerva (2008), 'Neglected Innovators: How Do Innovative Firms that Do Not Perform R&D Innovate?' Results of an Analysis of the Innobarometer 2007 Survey No. 215, INNO-Metrics Thematic Paper, MERIT 31 March, available at www.merit.unu.edu/publications/wppdf/2010/wp2010-027.pdf (accessed 4 January 2014).

Audretsch, David B., Roy Thurik, Ingrid Verheul and Sander Wennekers (eds) (2002), *Entrepreneurship: Determinants and Policy in a European-U.S. Comparison*, Boston, USA: Kluwer Academic Publishers.

Autio, E. and Z.J. Acs (2007), 'Individual and Country Level Determinants of Growth Aspirations in New Ventures', paper presented at the Third Global Entrepreneurship Research Conference Washington, October 2007.

Bender, G. (2004), 'Innovation in Low-Tech – Considerations Based on a Few Case Studies in Eleven European Countries', Soziologische Arbeitspapiere, TU Dortmund University, available at www.wiso.tu-dortmund.de/wiso/is/Medienpool/Arbeitspapiere/ap-soz06.pdf (accessed 5 July 2013).

Brännback, M., A. Carsrud and M. Renko (2003), 'Knowledge Intensive Entrepreneurship: Networking within and across Boundaries', Frontiers of Entrepreneurship Research, vol. VIII, presented at Babson-College Kauffman foundation entrepreneurship research conference, 4–8 June 2003.

Breschi, S., F. Malerba and L. Orsenigo (2000), 'Technological Regimes and Schumpeterian Patterns of Innovation', *The Economic Journal*, **110** (463), 388–410.

Bröring, S., L.M. Cloutier and J. Leker (2006), 'The Front End of Innovation in an Era of Industry Convergence – The Case of Nutraceuticals and Functional Foods', *R&D Management Journal*, **36** (5), 487–98.

Caloghirou, Yannis, Anastasia Constantelou and Nicholas S. Vonortas (2006), 'By Way of an Introduction: Knowledge Flows: The Drivers for the Creation of a Knowledge-Based Economy', in Yannis Caloghirou, Anastasia Constantelou and Nicholas S. Vonortas (eds), *Knowledge Flows in European Industry*, Oxon, UK: Routledge, pp. 1–24.

Cox, H., M. Frenz and M. Prevezer (2002), 'Patterns of Innovation in UK Industry: Exploring the CIS Data to Contrast High and Low Technology Industries', *Journal of Interdisciplinary Economics*, **13**, 267–304.

Delmar, Frédéric and Karl Wennberg (eds) (2010), *Knowledge Intensive Entrepreneurship: The Birth, Growth and Demise of Entrepreneurial Firms*, Cheltenham, UK and Northampton, MA, USA: Edward Elgar.

Del Monte, A. and E. Papagni (2003), 'R&D and the Growth of Firms: Empirical Analysis of a Panel of Italian Firms', *Research Policy*, **32** (6), 1003–14.

Dosi, G. (1982), 'Technological Paradigms and Technological Trajectories: A Suggested Interpretation of the Determinants and Directions of Technical Change', *Research Policy*, **11** (3), 147–62.

Garavaglia, C. and D. Grieco (2005), 'Hand in Hand with Entrepreneurship – A Critical Overview from Entrepreneurship to Knowledge-Based Entrepreneurship', Cespri Working Paper, Bocconi University, Milan, available at www.kites.uni-bocconi.it/wps/allegatiCTP/July2005_WP0_Final.pdf (accessed 6 July 2013).

Garibaldo, Francesco and David Jacobson (2005), 'The Role of Company and Social Networks in Low-Tech Industry', in Gerd Bender, David Jacobson and Paul L. Robertson (eds), *Non-Research-Intensive Industries in the Knowledge Economy,* published in *Perspectives on Economic Political and Social Integration*, **XI** (1–2), special issue, 233–70.

Grimpe, C. and W. Sofka (2009), 'Search Patterns and Absorptive Capacity: Low- and High-Technology Sectors in European Countries', *Research Policy*, **38** (3), 495–506.

Haeussler, C., H. Patzelt and S.A. Zahra (2012), 'Strategic Alliances and Product Development in High Technology New Firms: The Moderating Effect of Technological Capabilities', *Journal of Business Venturing*, **27** (2), 217–33.

Hatzichronoglou, T. (1997), 'Revision of the High-Technology Sector and Product Classification', OECD Science, Technology and Industry Working Papers, available at http://dx.doi.org/10.1787/134337307632 (accessed 15 June 2013).

Heidenreich, M. (2009), 'Innovation Patterns and Location of European Low- and Medium-Technology Industries', *Research Policy*, **38** (3), 483–94.

Henderson, R.M. and K.B. Clark (1990), 'Architectural Innovation: The Reconfiguration of Existing Product Technologies and the Failure of Established Firms', *Administrative Science Quarterly*, **35** (1), 9–22.

Henrekson, M. and D. Johansson (2010), 'Gazelles as Job Creators: A Survey and Interpretation of the Evidence', *Small Business Economics*, **35** (2), 227–44.

Hirsch-Kreinsen, H. (2008), '"Low-Tech" Innovation', *Industry and Innovation*, **15** (1), 19–43.

Hirsch-Kreinsen, H. (2013), '"Low-Tech" Research Revisited', paper presented at the 35th DRUID Conference, Barcelona, 17–19 June 2013.

Hirsch-Kreinsen, H. and I. Schwinge (2011), 'Knowledge-Intensive Entrepreneurship and Innovativeness in Traditional Industries: Conceptual

Framework and Empirical Findings', Deliverable 1.3.1 AEGIS Project, available at www.aegis-fp7.eu/index.php?option=com_docman&task=doc_download& gid=64&Itemid=12 (accessed 6 June 2013).

Hirsch-Kreinsen H., D. Jacobson, S. Laestadius and K. Smith (2003), 'Low-Tech Industries and the Knowledge Economy: State of the Art and Research Challenges', EU 5th Framework Project PILOT, Policy and Innovation in Low-Tech, available at www.nifu.no/files/2012/11/STEPrapport2003–16.pdf (accessed 3 June 2013).

Ihrig, M., D. Zu Knyphausen-Aufseß and C. O'Gorman (2006), 'The Knowledge-Based Approach to Entrepreneurship: Linking the Entrepreneurial Process to the Dynamic Evolution of Knowledge', *International Journal of Knowledge Management Studies*, **1** (1/2), 38–58.

Kirner, E., S. Kinkel and A. Jaeger (2009), 'Innovation Paths and the Innovation Performance of Low-Technology Firms – An Empirical Analysis of German Industry', *Research Policy*, **38** (3), 447–58.

Kogut, B. and U. Zander (1992), 'Knowledge of the Firm, Combinative Capabilities, and the Replication of Technology', *Organization Science*, **3** (3), 383–97.

Langlois, R.N. (2003), 'The Vanishing Hand: The Changing Dynamics of Industrial Capitalism', *Industrial and Corporate Change*, **12** (2), 351–85.

Liebeskind, J.P. (1996), 'Knowledge, Strategy, and the Theory of the Firm', *Strategic Management Journal*, **17** (special issue), 93–107.

Malerba, Franco (2010), *Knowledge-Intensive Entrepreneurship and Innovation Systems: Evidence from Europe*, London, UK and New York, USA: Routledge.

Malerba, F. and M. McKelvey (2010), 'Conceptualizing Knowledge-Intensive Entrepreneurship: Concepts and Models', paper presented at the DIME – AEGIS – LIEE/NTUA Athens 2010 Conference, 29–30 April 2010.

McKelvey, Maureen and Astrid H. Lassen (eds) (2013), *Managing Knowledge Intensive Entrepreneurship*, Cheltenham, UK and Northampton, MA, USA: Edward Elgar.

Mendonça, S. (2009), 'Brave Old World: Accounting for "High-Tech" Knowledge in "Low-Tech" Industries', *Research Policy*, **38** (3), 470–82.

Mokyr, Joel (2002), *The Gifts of Athena: Historical Origins of the Knowledge Economy*, Princeton, NJ, USA and Woodstock, UK: Princeton University Press.

Ndofor, H.A. and E. Levitas (2004), 'Signaling the Strategic Value of Knowledge', *Journal of Management*, **30** (5), 685–702.

Park, S.H., R. Chen and S. Gallagher (2002), 'Firm Resources as Moderators of the Relationship between Market Growth and Strategic Alliances in Semiconductor Start-ups', *Academy of Management Journal*, **45** (3), 527–45.

Protogerou, A., Y. Caloghirou and E. Siokas (2013), 'Publicly-Funded Collaborative R&D Networks as Drivers for Promoting Knowledge-Intensive Entrepreneurship: An Exploratory Exercise', paper presented at the 35th DRUID Conference, Barcelona, 17–19 June 2013.

Rammer, C. (2010), 'Innovation and Systems: What are We Talking About?', in Deutsche Gesellschaft für Technische Zusammenarbeit (GTZ), Workshop Documentation Strengthening Innovation Systems in the Context of Development Cooperation, 5–8 October 2009, Dortmund, Germany, pp. 24–9.

Robertson, P. and P.R. Patel (2007), 'New Wine in Old Bottles: Technological Diffusion in Developed Economies', *Research Policy*, **36** (5), 708–21.

Robertson, P. and K. Smith (2008), 'Distributed Knowledge Bases in Low and Medium Technology Industries', working paper, Australian Innovation Research

Centre University of Tasmania, available at www.utas.edu.au/__data/assets/ pdf_file/0019/111178/Distributed-Knowledge-Bases-in-Low-and-Medium.pdf (accessed 16 July 2013).

Rodrigues, Maria J. (2002), *The New Knowledge Economy in Europe*, Cheltenham, UK and Northampton, MA, USA: Edward Elgar.

Rosenkopf, L. and A. Nerkar (2001), 'Beyond Local Search: Boundary-Spanning, Exploration, and Impact in the Optical Disk Industry', *Strategic Management Journal*, **22** (4), 287–306.

Santamaria, L., M. Nieto and A. Barge-Gil (2009), 'Beyond Formal R&D: Taking Advantage of Other Sources of Innovation in Low- and Medium-Technology Industries', *Research Policy*, **38** (3), 507–17.

Sciascia, S. and P. Mazzola (2008), 'Family Involvement in Ownership and Management: Exploring Nonlinear Effects on Performance', *Family Business Review*, **21** (4), 331–45.

Segarra-Blasco, A. and J.M. Arauzo-Carod (2008), 'Sources of Innovation and Industry–University Interaction: Evidence from Spanish Firms', *Research Policy*, **37** (3), 1283–95.

Smith, K. (2002), 'What is the "Knowledge Economy"? Knowledge Intensity and Distributed Knowledge Bases', working paper, United Nations University Maastricht, available at www.intech.unu.edu/publications/discussion-papers/2002–6.pdf (accessed 4 June 2013).

Stam, E. and K. Wennberg (2009), 'The Roles of R&D in New Firm Growth', *Small Business Economics*, **33** (1), 77–89.

Von Hippel, Eric (2005), *Democratizing Innovation*, Cambridge, MA, USA: MIT Press.

Von Tunzelmann, Nick and Virginia Acha (2005), 'Innovation in "Low-Tech" Industries', in Jan Fagerberg, David C. Mowery and Richard R. Nelson (eds), *The Oxford Handbook of Innovation*, New York, USA: Oxford University Press, pp. 407–32.

3. Patterns of knowledge-intensive entrepreneurship in low-tech industries[1]

Hartmut Hirsch-Kreinsen

3.1 INTRODUCTION

The starting point of this chapter is the recent discussion of 'knowledge-intensive entrepreneurship' (KIE) in innovation research (see the introductory chapter in this volume). The term 'knowledge intensive' points to the fact that entrepreneurial activity focuses not only on the use of existing knowledge, experience and skills, but also to a significant extent on the integration and coordination of different knowledge assets and the creation of new knowledge. Thus, the dimension of knowledge is primarily related to scientific, engineering and design knowledge, respective to systematic, problem-solving knowledge. In general, the term KIE is closely linked to the discourse on the growing significance of knowledge for societal development, i.e. the emerging 'knowledge economy' (Foray, 2002). The debate on KIE has thus far mainly focused on firms or start-ups in new technology-based, high-tech industries (Cohendet and Llerena, 2010; Malerba, 2010; Malerba and McKelvey, 2010; Audretsch et al., 2011). Unsurprisingly, in this discourse no attention has been paid to firms in the so-called low-technology industries.

This chapter, by contrast, examines KIE in low- and medium-low-technology (LMT) sectors and analyses the determining factors, mechanisms and paths associated with KIE in LMT sectors. Furthermore, it asks what theoretical and policy-oriented conclusions can be drawn from the empirical findings. Case studies of 27 industrial LMT companies revealed the four different patterns of KIE in LMT industries to be outlined here. These patterns represent the distinguishable constellations of opportunities and determining factors of KIE in LMT sectors which describe and explain the similarities and differences among KIE activities in LMT industries. They prove not only that KIE activities in low-tech industries are promising, but also have implications for understanding the sources and directions of KIE activities in mature industries, and make it possible to derive recommendations for innovation policy.

This chapter proceeds as follows: in Section 2 a conceptual framework as a guideline for the interpretation of empirical findings is developed. Section 3 deals with methodological questions and the empirical base of the investigation. Section 4 comprises the empirical findings, namely, the four patterns of KIE found in the LMT sectors. In Section 5 the findings are summarized, and theoretical as well as policy-oriented conclusions outlined. Generally, this chapter aims at a first understanding of this largely still uninvestigated issue, and at the development of hypotheses which should stimulate further research.

3.2 ANALYTICAL FRAMEWORK FOR THE EMPIRICAL ANALYSIS

As a basic definition, one can speak of KIE in LMT sectors only if significant growth of the knowledge base is occurring compared to the already existing knowledge base on the firm-specific as well as the sectoral level. The term 'significant growth of the knowledge base' refers to the development of technological innovations comprised of not only new combinations of existing available knowledge resources, but also of knowledge which is fundamentally new. Furthermore, the type of innovation indicating successful KIE activities in LMT industries should leave the path of the prevailing type of incremental innovation. As research shows, incremental innovation is typical and widespread in LMT industries but does not affect or overcome the established industrial situation (Hirsch-Kreinsen, 2008). In contrast, KIE innovations are far-reaching and disruptive in nature.

If such KIE activities are possible in LMT industries, they may be characterized by specific features that differ from those already discussed in the KIE debate, which is mainly focused on high-tech industries (see the introductory chapter in this volume). First, it must be strongly emphasized that KIE in LMT industries not only implies newly founded companies, but that it also takes place in the context of existing organizations and established companies. This perspective may apply particularly to LMT industries where competitive pressure can force existing firms and their managers to change their competitive position by adopting an increasingly reflective approach towards established practices and searching for breakthrough innovations. Second, it has to be assumed that the strong structural path-dependency of LMT industries can only be overcome by the activities of individual agents or firms. Third, these actors have to seize new technological, institutional and market opportunities and, in particular, knowledge which is new vis-à-vis the structures and knowledge of the already existing sectoral conditions. These considerations imply the following relevant dimensions of a *conceptual framework* for the empirical analysis of KIE in LMT industries.

First, the *level of generally available entrepreneurial opportunities* (see in particular Radosevic, 2010), which encompasses market, technological and institutional advantages beyond the specific and often restrictive situation of LMT industries; this level refers to conditions, practices, knowledge, etc. which exist beyond the boundaries of specific technological sectors and are of global character.[2] It can be assumed that these factors offer opportunities for KIE in LMT industries to overcome their strong path-dependency. In a general perspective, the LMT literature refers to global knowledge opportunities of LMT firms as the 'distributed knowledge base' (Robertson and Smith, 2008). It comprises different forms of knowledge held by actors who are independent of each other and often come from different industries and technology fields. LMT research suggests that the main source of knowledge generation in LMT companies lies here.

Second, the *level of the sectoral system*, characterized by the sectoral specifics and the established technological paths of the LMT sector, offers only limited opportunities for, and many constraints on, KIE. As outlined in the introductory chapter, the reason for this is that innovations in LMT industries are known to be path-dependent and based on a relatively slow accumulation of capabilities around a previously known technological specialization. This path-dependency is continuously stabilized by incremental innovation activities and the continuously optimized processes of the existing technologies – the basic emerging momentum of these developmental paths. However, strong economic competition at this level may put pressure on firms to overcome this position with the aid of KIE processes and opportunities offered elsewhere.

Third, the *local level of the individual firm and/or individual actor respective entrepreneur*, which embraces firm- or actor-specific features of KIE; in entrepreneurship research (Grichnik, 2006) this level may also constitute an important determining factor for KIE processes as the institutional and technological arrangements of a given sectoral system can only be changed by the knowledge and the competences of actors who leverage resources to create new knowledge and technologies. LMT research defines these capabilities more precisely as transformative capabilities, because the main requirement is to combine existing and new knowledge to create a new level of knowledge and conduct an innovation process successfully. The term 'capability' refers to the well-known 'resource-based approaches' of innovation research (Teece and Pisano, 1994). Capabilities are characterized by specific abilities to act that have developed through learning processes, including the attitudes, skills and experiences of decision-makers. The term capability should not be understood as a pattern of activities, but as a term to describe specific conditions for specific activities: a particular configuration and constellation in the company that in particular enables the deployment of the company's internal and external knowledge resources, which potentially constitute KIE for this organization (Bender and Laestadius, 2005).

Furthermore, *intervening factors* have to be taken into consideration. Though these factors cannot be regarded as important determining factors for KIE, they may modify the KIE process. In the literature on LMT, innovativeness factors like innovation policy and aspects of regional proximity are of rather minor significance for LMT activities (Jacobson and Heanue, 2005).

The interplay of these factors may take place in different ways and constellations to foster KIE in LMT industries. *Innovation* has to be regarded as the outcome of these KIE processes. In attempts to specify typical KIE innovations in the LMT sector, the innovation type 'incremental innovation' has already been excluded because it occurs routinely and is based on existing firm-specific or sectoral knowledge. It is typical for and widespread in LMT industries but does not overcome or affect the established sectoral firm-specific situation. By contrast, typical KIE innovations are far-reaching and disruptive in nature. Thus after the well-known taxonomy of Henderson and Clark (1990), one can conclude that 'architectural' and 'modular' innovations can be regarded as an indication of KIE in LMT sectors. But, because of the connotation of KIE, radical innovation cannot be completely excluded either.

Finally, the *impact* of these KIE innovation patterns on the local as well as global level of knowledge creation has to be taken into consideration. This aspect refers to the KIE-specific character of innovations, i.e. an innovation should not only be novel to the firm but also novel to the whole sector. This impact constitutes a feedback loop between the KIE process initiated by an individual firm or entrepreneur, changing local and global structures and, thus, creating new opportunities for further KIE activity. On the basis of the above considerations, a model of KIE in LMT can be graphically sketched as follows (see Figure 3.1).

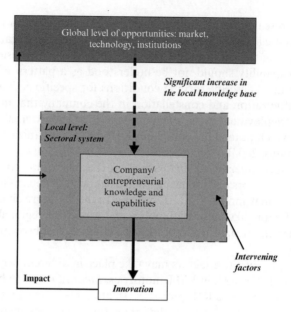

Figure 3.1   Model of KIE in LMT sectors

3.3   METHODOLOGY

3.3.1   Data Base

This chapter aims at a first understanding of a still uninvestigated issue and the development of hypotheses which should stimulate further research. The aim is to describe, understand and explain KIE processes in LMT industries. The appropriate methodology is 'qualitative case-study analysis' because it facilitates a greater flexibility, in-depth focus and completeness required for examining such dynamic and largely uninvestigated processes as KIE. 'Deep data' and 'thick description' are terms frequently used to differentiate the results of case studies from those of population or sample surveys. Therefore, case-study analysis leads to a deeper understanding of this empirical phenomenon and allows the development of hypotheses which should stimulate further research (see e.g. Yin, 1994).

The analysis is based on the results of 27 case studies conducted in selected LMT companies in 2009 and 2010 in the 'low-tech' work package of the AEGIS project.[3] The case studies were conducted in the LMT industries of food, beverages and tobacco, textiles, apparel and leather, and metalworking. Unlike the general debate on KIE, the focus on KIE in LMT has to include not only newly founded companies (start-ups and spin-offs) but also change processes in established companies. The reason for this extended perspective is that in traditional manufacturing industries with mature technologies, newly founded companies based on new technological knowledge may be more unusual than in high-tech industries with their technologically less established tradition. Therefore the case-study companies were either established or newly founded companies. The KIE process in established companies is termed 'corporate entrepreneurship'; in newly founded companies (including foundations by already existing companies or individual entrepreneurs) – 'industrial start-ups', and foundations undertaken by academic institutions – 'academic spin-offs'.[4]

The main selection criterion for the case-study companies was a significant rise in the knowledge level they reached through their activities, as indicated particularly by the following: first, the companies were to be evidently 'first-movers', i.e. among the most innovative companies in the market or product field. Second, the innovation implemented by the companies can be either a new product or a new, not previously applied process technology – that is, generally more than only incremental innovation activities. Additional selection criteria were: new companies founded between 2000 and 2006, or the implementation of innovations in established companies between 2000 and 2006; the case-study companies were to be SMEs, i.e. have less than 250 employees. The case-study companies were to be located in southern Europe (Greece) and Western Europe (Portugal, Denmark and Germany). However, the different national settings of the companies and sectoral differences were not considered systematically because this study was to be regarded as a first approach to the issue of KIE in LMT sectors.

To allow comparability of results, the common methodological basis of all case studies was a standardized questionnaire and structured interview guidelines. The items in the common interview guidelines included the following dimensions: general information about the entrepreneur and the firm; the entrepreneurial innovation process; the factors determining this process; and the outcome and performance of this process. On the basis of the structured interview guidelines, one or two interviews per case study were conducted with company experts at different hierarchical levels and in different functions. Normally the managing director or the founder, respective the owner of the firm, was interviewed. The expert interviews were often supplemented by a company tour and the analysis of accessible company documents. The data collected were summarized in case-study reports based on a standardized structure. These reports were evaluated systematically in a qualitative content analysis.

3.3.2   KIE Patterns

On the basis of the case-study results, four patterns of KIE processes in LMT industries are outlined below. These patterns represent the distinguishable types of opportunities and determining factors for KIE in LMT industries, which in turn describe and explain similarities and differences amongst KIE activities in industrial LMT industries. This typology leads to an understanding of the determining factors, the firms' behavior and the directions of KIE processes in LMT industries in this still uninvestigated field of innovation research. These patterns may stimulate further quantitatively based research. In particular, they yield implications that could be the basis for policy recommendations.

The generation of the patterns is based on the dimensions of the analytical framework. They differ in two respects: first, each KIE pattern represents a specific expression and combination of the various dimensions of the framework. Second, the patterns differ as to the most influential factor; that is, one of the dimensions of the analytical framework proves to be the main determining factor for the respective KIE pattern. Hence, the description of the different KIE patterns is centered on two features: first, the dominant determining factor guiding the KIE process, and, second, complementary factors which are – in comparison – of less importance. Third, further common intervening factors have to be taken into consideration. As remarked above, these intervening factors cannot be regarded as core dimensions of KIE, but they may influence the KIE process in a general way.

The estimation of the importance of the various influencing factors in the analysed KIE processes is based on a combination of several indicators corresponding to the conventional methodological steps of qualitative analysis (Kelle and Kluge, 2010). First, the direct statements of the interviewees and their self-assessments of their entrepreneurial activities were regarded as the main indicator. Second, a comparative 'cross-examination' of the various data from the entire case-study analysis (standardized data, interview results, and secondary sources as documents) and their 'plausible' interpretation was regarded as the second-most important indicator. Basically the KIE patterns have to be regarded as empirical types. Their development is data-driven but also guided conceptually by the analytical framework.[5]

3.4   EMPIRICAL FINDINGS: FOUR PATTERNS OF KIE IN LMT SECTORS

With this methodological approach in mind, four patterns of KIE in LMT sectors can be distinguished on the basis of the case-study findings:

Table 3.1   *Pattern and classification of KIE in LMT sectors: case studies*

KIE mode	KIE pattern			
	Market-driven	Science and technology-driven	Capability-driven	Competitive pressure
Corporate entrepreneurship	CMDK2	CFGE3	CFDK2	CMGE1
	CTGR1		CFGE1	CTGE3
	CFGR2		CTGE2	CTGR2
	CFGR3		CMP2	CFP2
Industrial start-up	CMDK1	CFP1	CTDK2	CMP1
	CFDK1		CFGR1	
	CMGR1		CMGE2	
	CTP2			
Academic spin-off		CTDK3		
		CFGE2		
		CMGE3		
		CTGE1		
		CTP1		
Total (N = 27)	8	7	7	5

market-driven pattern, a *science-and-technology-driven* (S&T) pattern, a *capability-driven* pattern and a fourth pattern termed *competitive pressure* (see Table 3.1). These four patterns are described in detail in the following sections.

3.4.1   Market-Driven

Market opportunities as determining factor
This KIE in LMT sectors pattern is mainly driven by market opportunities due to an increasing variety of customer demands or already existing and as yet unexploited market segments. Nine of the examined case-study companies belong to this pattern. Five of these are corporate entrepreneurships, i.e. enterprises with extended business activities, and four are start-up companies. They come from all three examined industries. There are no case-study companies which can be characterized as academic spin-offs. It may be assumed that the identification of new market opportunities is easier for established companies or industry-oriented entrepreneurs compared to entrepreneurs from academia who are only loosely familiar with markets and customer demand.

The common feature of these market opportunities is that they do not constitute an element of traditional LMT industries; instead they tend to be of global character and are sources of generally applicable knowledge and technologies. They offer new sales opportunities and high profits compared to the established restricted market position of the individual LMT firms. The empirical material shows that the new market opportunities often result from socio-structural changes, in particular, changed ways of life, new role structures and – hence – new customer preferences. Outstanding examples of this are changed customer preferences in foods and eating habits as well as a notable increase in demand for sophisticated convenience products or functionally sophisticated textiles (CFGR2; CTGR1). Moreover, in two cases the new market opportunities resulted from direct customer requests which prompted the firms to innovate. Thus, a Danish manufacturer of sintered components reported that the development process for the innovation was triggered by a customer who wanted to make wear plates from a new material. The customer's role in the development of the new product was to motivate the company to start testing and prototyping different materials blending (CMDK2). Additionally, the orientation towards new market opportunities is also prompted by the difficult economic position the enterprises need to overcome. Thus, one food producer pointed to the pronounced 'market bottleneck' in their situation: the existing domestic market was limited and the competition increasingly stiff. Therefore the management was convinced that the company's survival depended on finding new products and markets (CFGR3). All in all, the companies investigated are exposed to a significant 'market pull' – an excellent prerequisite for the successful market launch of new products.

Complementary factors: transformative capabilities of the firms
The existing stock of firm-specific knowledge and the set of capabilities needed for acquiring new knowledge and combining existing and new knowledge into a new level of knowledge plays an additional and indispensable role for this KIE pattern. These factors are essential for sensing and seizing diverse opportunities effectively. A key prerequisite for this is a broad firm-specific knowledge base including the specific position of the firm and its own achievement potential. In all the studied cases, this knowledge base comprised a high degree of accumulated knowledge of and manifold experiences in markets, management and organizational issues, as well as the potential of the given technology. This knowledge base is only to some extent the result of firms' own research efforts in in-house R&D departments (CFGR3). In fact, it is to a high degree of a practical nature. In the case of the established companies, it was acquired in the operations process, and in the case of new foundations, it is the result of previous business activities. A typical example of this is the founding of a food business in convenience and bread products (CFDK1). The founder

had acquired the necessary management and technology skills during his earlier business activities in industrial bakeries. The findings of two more case studies show that this knowledge of actors also explicitly reflects the restrictions and the lack of opportunities in the given sector. The research material points to the often strong conviction of management that the sectoral technological paths and existing market structures no longer offer adequate opportunities for economic development (CFGR3; CMGR1).

In all the examined cases belonging to the market-driven pattern, the capability of transforming and absorbing external knowledge proved to be of utmost importance. In other words, the company's ability to manage and effectively co-ordinate network relations with other companies within the value chain is a central precondition for successful KIE in LMT sectors. According to the research findings, cooperation with customers, potential customers and even with competitors was of great significance in these cases (CMGR1; CMDK1; CTGR2). Evidently, these cooperative relations are the precondition for the ability of enterprises and founders to gain the necessary knowledge about existing market opportunities and to analyse these in terms of their possible success. In addition, cooperative relations with technology suppliers from other industries such as machine manufacturers or research institutions also play a large role in the realization of planned innovations. These relations enable the companies to obtain the necessary additional technological and scientific knowledge, e.g. new machine designs, materials or design capabilities.

Additionally, the companies had to be able to synthesize and combine the past and new knowledge if they wanted to profit from the given opportunities. In this regard, the established firms show the importance of an established learning culture and open organizational routines that facilitate the integration and utilization of new knowledge (CMDK1; CTGR1). In another case, the specific capability of the actors can be termed 'bricolage' capability (CFGR3), i.e. the ability to synthesize knowledge from many fields. All in all, this KIE type is well illustrated by the example of one Greek start-up. The founder had investigated, learned from and interpreted both existing information and new data. He identified the role of telecommunications (and later, photovoltaics) as crucial for the development of his company. Rapid developments resulted in a need, as yet generally undetected, for the construction of smart installations and their further maintenance. He also had a clear picture of both the market and the technology, and profited from the fact that there was only one competitor, whom he knew very well. The founder had many years of field experience and developed the vision of building an organization that would be integrated across the products and services of this specific field with the primary goal of serving the customer in the best way possible (fast delivery, flexibility, total solutions). The new knowledge-based activity was carefully but rapidly planned (CMGR1). This specific capability of actors can be conceptually termed 'transformative capability', i.e. the ability to synthesize knowledge from many fields (Bender and Laestadius, 2005).

Outcome: architectural innovations
In a nutshell, knowledge intensification in the examined enterprises stands for a considerable expansion of the local knowledge base, primarily by using generally applicable knowledge about markets and knowledge of the possibilities of new products beyond sectoral constraints. This knowledge intensification leads to innovations that can mostly be called 'architectural' (Henderson and Clark, 1990). For established LMT industries, these innovations represent a new type of technology which has not been used by them so far. The new products or processes are based not only on new combinations of existing locally or sectorally available knowledge resources and technologies, but also on globally available technologies and corresponding components which are new to the local-level LMT firms and the sectoral level of LMT industries.

An example is the flexible process innovation of the Danish food industry start-up described here. Although this innovation is called 'unique' with regard to its flexibility, it is 'architectural' in nature, i.e. it is the development of new process design by a recombination of already available machine technologies and components (CFDK1). The innovation of the Greek metal company follows a similar mode: it features the redesign of an existing product technology to increase its functional efficiency. In doing so, the firm systematically made use of globally available technology components and changed their already existing ones, but without changing the products in their basic design (CMGR1).

3.4.2   Science-and-Technology-Driven

Science and technology as determining factors
Scientific and technological opportunities are the main driving factors in this KIE pattern. These opportunities facilitate the development of new products or processes that open up possibilities for overcoming the restrictive LMT situation and opening up new business perspectives. One can characterize this as 'technology push': the entrepreneurial activities in this pattern rely on technologies that are globally available, but their application is completely new to the LMT industry. Seven of the examined case-study companies can be assigned to this pattern category. A large majority (six companies) includes newly founded firms – some are start-ups but most are spin-offs of scientific research (Table 3.1). This distribution is

quite obviously no coincidence. Newly founded enterprises normally aim at the implementation of new technological opportunities that lie off the established technology paths. The empirical evidence shows that the examined enterprises drew on new and above all utilizable technological opportunities. Thus, the start-ups in the textile industry combined for example the new electronic fiber technologies with traditional textile and clothing concepts to develop smart textiles (CTDK3; CTGE1; CTP1). The case of food industry companies in the study was comparable: they drew on knowledge from globally available research findings on the use of edible films in foodstuffs (CFP1), and on fruit-drying methods for a specific drying technology (CFGE2). The importance of globally available technological opportunities is plainly demonstrated by the example of a German metal start-up. Its foundation was based on the application of a process technology already available for a long time to create a specific new welding technology in which the scope of applications of established welding technologies could be significantly extended (CMGE3).

Complementary factors: profound technological knowledge
The case-study results show that this KIE pattern is also based on a sound technological knowledge which the founders of the academic spin-offs acquired in their previous scientific fields of work. This factor can be classified as an important complementary factor. A German spin-off company that developed systems for drying fruit is a good example of this: both founders had gained great expertise and experience in fruit drying in general and solar drying systems in particular at a university (CFGE2). Similar evidence can be found in the case of a start-up metal company that developed new welding technologies. Here, their profound theoretical knowledge of welding technologies and their possibilities and limitations was cited as an essential precondition for the innovations (CMGE3). In the interviews, the established companies emphasized the importance of having qualified staff as well as specialists with an academic background. In particular the latter are considered of vital importance for evaluating new technological possibilities (CMGE3; CFP1).

Another essential complementary factor is the extension and intensification of this knowledge base by means of cooperative relations with external partners. The enhancement of application-oriented technological knowledge and a broadening of the product field-specific knowledge is an important objective of these cooperative activities in which the often technology-savvy founders are not well versed. The start-ups in particular cultivated close formal and informal cooperation relations with diverse organizations from various fields to obtain the necessary basic knowledge on running an active business. The lacking application-oriented competencies were obtained by, for example, the targeted recruitment of technology specialists such as electronic and software engineers. A prerequisite for this was the close contact with a scientific institute that trains such specialists (CTP1). Another case-study firm purchased the lacking process technology within the framework of close cooperation with a mechanical engineering company (CTGE1). Generally, the more practice-oriented business competencies were acquired within the scope of network relations with suppliers of primary products, future clients as well as industry associations (e.g. CMGE3; CFGE3; CFP1).

The above can be instructively demonstrated using the example of the German spin-off that markets food-drying systems (CFGE2). The founders were very well versed in technology but lacked organizational know-how in general and knowledge of markets, as well as of governmental regulations and food laws in particular. Therefore, stable cooperation relations with specialized advisors from the technology transfer office of their former university, and particularly with the suppliers of their raw materials, viz. the fruit, were essential. The situation in a textile spin-off examined here was similar: besides the technical knowledge and know-how to set up the production line it was also vital to collaborate with suppliers and users for information on the application of the fibers in the further processing along the supply chain (CTGE1). If one probes into how new knowledge stocks are employed in the operating process, and how they are combined with the hitherto existing knowledge, the answers all point to an interactive and dynamic process (e.g. CTP1; CFGE2) that takes place between the partners involved as well as within the enterprises.

Outcome: towards 'radical' innovation

To sum up, this KIE pattern is characterized by a process of knowledge intensification based on the expansion of the already available technologically oriented competencies by generally applicable, mostly scientifically created knowledge which is fundamentally new to the local and sectoral knowledge base. Therefore, the innovations implemented within this context have at least a partially more far-reaching character, or, putting it tentatively: measured against the traditional technologies of LMT industries, they approach the type 'radical innovation': often a new dominant design of a product or a process can be discerned that has resulted from the combination of various technological components. In the case of the technology-driven KIE pattern, this is highly plausible. It seems obvious that the use of globally available technological opportunities leads to completely new product and process technologies and that these are implemented especially in the context of academic spin-offs. Thus, this pattern is characterized by the use of technologies not used before by LMT firms.

As described above, this involved specific and newly developed information technology and software components, the use of completely new textile fibers and the deployment of new process technologies. Compared to previous technological development paths these innovations often have a fundamentally novel character.

3.4.3 Capability-Driven

Company capabilities as determining factors
A third pattern of KIE in LMT sectors can be termed 'capability-driven'. This pattern is not propelled by globally available market or technological opportunities; instead the driving forces behind the innovative process can be primarily found at the local level of individual companies. An entrepreneur or company, on the basis of its ability to extend systematically the available knowledge stock, implements an idea considered promising, thereby lastingly improving its economic situation. This is the classic Schumpeterian entrepreneur. Of course this KIE process cannot be seen in isolation from the overall situation, i.e. the given sector-specific constraints and opportunities. Seven of the examined case-study companies can be allocated to this KIE pattern category. Four of them can be termed corporate entrepreneurship and three have the character of industrial start-ups (Table 3.1). This latter empirical pattern is plausible because this KIE type is based on accumulated capabilities within an established company or based on the sector and product field-specific experience and knowledge of individual entrepreneurs. Entrepreneurs from academia by contrast usually lack such competences.

In all examined cases, the starting point of these KIE activities was a profound knowledge base in the given industrial structures and the development potential of the available technologies. In addition, the key actors had extensive management and organizational experience. Evidence shows that corporate entrepreneurships in particular profit from the accumulated knowledge of the established enterprises. The KIE activities of a Danish milk-products manufacturer are an instructive example. The precondition to these activities was a strong knowledge base in cream production dating back 20 years, and sound knowledge of and experience with competitors, suppliers and customers (CFDK2). The case of a brewery, an over 100-year-old family enterprise, was similar: it had outstanding local brewery knowledge at its disposal (CFGE1). Newly founded companies in their turn can profit indirectly from the knowledge base of other companies, as their founders often belong to the entrepreneurial milieu – either by birth or work history (CFGR1) – or have previously founded successful companies (CMGE2).

The interview partners from corporate entrepreneurships almost unanimously pointed to a long culture of innovation and an entrepreneurial tradition in their companies, expressed for example in interdisciplinary development teams that continually drive innovations. In the case of the Portuguese metalware manufacturer the innovation process was based on the existence of a qualified, interdisciplinary team embracing the commercial, marketing, design, engineering, production, procurement and quality departments which acted in consultations with clients (CMP2). These activities were accompanied by continuous internal learning and training in the workforce. The interview results point to a similar situation in one of the two spin-offs. Here the typically low-tech innovation culture of 'tinkering around' is highlighted by the founder (CMGE2). These organizational processes, routines and practices evidently facilitate a constant recombination of in-house knowledge and thus the creation of a new and expanded local knowledge base.

In addition, new external knowledge is acquired by means of strong cooperative relations with customers and specialized technology suppliers as well as in some cases also with scientific institutions, with the objective of quickly identifying market needs but also special application requirements (CMP2; CFDK2; CFGR1). An example was the close cooperation between a textile company and a producer of conveyor belts. The goal of this cooperation was to use the conveyor belts as advertising vehicles by printing logos on them (see below). Further evidence that this company's KIE was capability-driven was the impression in the interviews that the company had initiated the inter-sectoral cooperation – very untypical for enterprises in the textile sector (CTGE2).

Complementary factors: mainly market opportunities
Knowledge of market opportunities has to be regarded as an important complementary factor. These are often market niches that the companies find by means of their KIE activities and that exist beyond the product field-specific structures that develop in the context of changing market structures and demand preferences. Among the opportunities to be mentioned is, first, the growing demand for high-quality products. In the cases of a foodstuff manufacturer and a textile manufacturer, this trend opened up the possibility of actively creating new market segments (CFGR1; CFDK2; CTDK2). Second, the opportunity of expanding given markets plays an important role. In one of the examined cases, the company's objective was to expand its regional market outlet in order to reach the national market (CFGE1), and in another case the company aimed at entering foreign markets (CMP2). Third, the innovation of the aforementioned textile manufacturer was aimed at the creation of a new market

segment: the conveyor belts with advertisements printed on them were intended for supermarket checkouts and thus were created for a field of application non-existent until then.

Additionally, technological opportunities play an important role. These include globally available technologies, e.g. packaging (CFGR1), material (CMP2; CMGE2) and transport technologies (CTGE2), which enterprises can use. In the case of the already mentioned brewery, the local knowledge and technology base had not yet been fully tapped, which demonstrates how the recombination of available knowledge elements opens up promising innovation perspectives (CFGE1).

Outcome: mostly modular innovations
In this KIE pattern, knowledge intensification signifies the expansion of the accumulated firm-specific knowledge base by a recombination of the elements on hand with the systematic integration of pertinent, generally available knowledge of market opportunities. The innovations pursued by firms exhibiting this KIE pattern are mostly of modular nature. They make systematic use of globally available technological components and change already existing ones without changing the products in their basic design. Examples of this are a new label for children's fashion (CTDK2), high-quality, health-oriented food and beverages (CFGR1; CFDK2; CFGE1) and new metal and textile products (CMP2; CTGE2; CMGE2).

3.4.4 Competitive Pressure

Competitive pressure as determining factor
A fourth pattern of KIE in LMT sectors can be termed 'competitive pressure'. The innovation driver of this type is the particularly strong competitive pressure in the specific sectoral environment. The representatives of the companies in this pattern category have a pronounced awareness of the economically and technologically severe condition of their firms. This knowledge is of firm-specific and sector-specific nature. The interviewees convincingly emphasized that if the enterprises were not successful in their innovation efforts, their existence could be in jeopardy. Five of the examined case-study companies belong to this KIE type. Four of them can be referred to as corporate entrepreneurships; one can be regarded as an independently founded start-up (Table 3.1). Similar to the demand-driven pattern of KIE, the identification of a severe industrial situation is more likely for established companies or industry-oriented entrepreneurs than for entrepreneurs from academia who are only weakly familiar with the industry situation.

To summarize the research findings, two basic aspects of competitive pressure can be distinguished: first, the very difficult overall economic situation of the whole LMT sector with its mature technologies is due to the growing cost pressure from competitors in low-cost countries. As shown, this central feature is particularly pressing in the examined enterprises. Second, technological product or process bottlenecks are a weak point for companies, frequently resulting from new requirements on them that thwart attempts to increase efficiency and lower costs. Or, they hamper the further incremental development of products which is needed just to maintain the company's market share. Both aspects have to be resolutely tackled to avoid existential risk.

An example of a difficult economic situation is that of a German manufacturer of specific steel ware (CMGE1). The market was described as 'becoming thinner and thinner'. There was increasing competition from abroad, and from bigger firms in general who were able to make cheaper products through scale economies for this relatively simple kind of product, which, according to the interviewed manager, 'anyone can build'. The company depended on occasional orders from customers needing products at short notice. However, these orders are subject to high volatility and the firm has been in a permanent state of hustling for customers, with management systematically seeking possibilities to become more independent of this market segment. A further example is the very difficult situation of a Greek textile manufacturer (CTGR2) confronted with a highly internationalized and fragmented market and high competitive pressure. Apparently there are hardly any opportunities for innovations in specific market niches. The enterprise is, however, an exceptional case within its sector as it is actively addressing the problem. Within the framework of a corporate entrepreneurship a new process for dyeing and finishing textiles is being developed. The process is vertically integrated into the whole value chain. Thereby the company could achieve a good competitive position despite the difficult sectoral situation.

An instructive example of a bottleneck is an enterprise in the food industry that processes fruit and vegetables for wholesale trade. Because of the growing quality requirements in wholesale trade, the company was confronted with a high number of 'rejects', i.e. unmarketable apples. To avoid the associated losses, the idea arose to use the apples of lesser quality for the production of apple juice and establish a new product line. This situation is succinctly described in the report on the case study: 'Of course, the rationalization of the company's resources – namely, the fruit that couldn't be commercialized – was the underlying motivation for the new business' (CFP2). Another example of a bottleneck is a textile manufacturer who has been producing elastic thread for surgical stockings for 50 years (CTGE3). However, this primary product is at a very advanced stage of its product life cycle and thus yields very little profit. This situation is being taken into account in the planning stage of new product innovations with management initiating a systematic search for new products with a greater value creation.

Complementary factor: specific innovation culture
A distinct knowledge base and the specific innovative capabilities of the companies have to be interpreted as complementary factors important to the success of initiatives to overcome competitive pressure. In one of the examined cases (CMGE1) the interviewees pointed to a 'typical low-tech innovation culture', on which these capabilities are based. It is characterized by innovation activities occurring during and besides daily work. Furthermore, innovative ideas are often developed by individual actors; structured and systematic search processes seem to be less common.

For all the examined companies, the case-study findings moreover make the point that their management or founders have a sizeable stock of knowledge accumulated over the course of many years – knowledge of the technological opportunities, sales markets as well as management requirements. This knowledge stock enabled them to systematically and purposefully establish cooperative relations with, for example, machine manufacturers, suppliers, marketing experts and other external partners, as well as to integrate and use new knowledge. Additionally, the companies were able to identify new market opportunities. According to the research material, these opportunities were solely due to generally emerging market trends. By means of their KIE activities, the enterprises tapped these markets. A typical example for this is a German metal company (CMGE1): the firm benefited from a discernible shift in the interest of society towards environmental issues in general and green technologies in particular. With its early focus and knowledge of these issues, the company had a head start over competitors. Making the most efficient and environmentally friendly product has been a major sales argument for the firm. The situation of the earlier mentioned apple juice producer was comparable (CFP2). On the one hand, the company reacted to a generally growing demand in Europe with this innovation. On the other, it was the first Portuguese company to actively market such a product at home and abroad. And finally, the above-mentioned yarn manufacturer systematically pursued a strategy of substituting old yarn products with new composite yarn materials which were much more flexible and above all electrically conductive, thus opening up completely new application possibilities in the field of functional textiles (CTGE3).

Outcome: far-reaching innovations

In summary, knowledge intensification in this KIE pattern signifies the use and expansion of the firm-specific and product field-specific knowledge base, most notably by purposefully rounding it off with generally applicable knowledge of new technologies and market opportunities. The innovations pursued by the firms in this KIE pattern aim at innovations of a far-reaching or even radical nature. In doing so, they attempt to overcome strong sectoral pressure. Empirical examples among the case-study companies are a completely new production facility for apple juice based on a likewise new process (CFP2), the development of an elastic and conductive textile fiber based on completely new materials (CTGE3), or the development of a purlin not only having a completely new design but also made of new materials (CMP1).

3.4.5   Intervening Factors

As outlined above (Section 3), additional intervening factors have to be taken into consideration in order to analyse a KIE process as completely as possible. However, the empirical material shows no clear correlation between certain intervening factors and the various patterns of KIE in LMT sectors. Intervening factors can be identified only in a general perspective, i.e. they prove to be occasionally important for individual KIE cases. According to the empirical material, there are several factors of major significance.

First, new policy regulations and institutional opportunities indirectly affect KIE processes. Thus, one of the companies examined profited from the liberalization of the national telecommunications market that opened up a completely new market segment for newly developed technical components of communication systems (CMGR1). In other cases, stricter environmental protection regulations indirectly influenced customer preferences and new market opportunities could thereby emerge (e.g. CMDK2). Most notably, stricter EU standards regarding the shelf life of food has led to a growing demand for new preservation methods.

Second, new customer preferences – generally due to changed lifestyles and higher disposable incomes – lead to new market opportunities which can be taken up by KIE activities. For textile sector start-ups these changes entail a growing demand for sophisticated and functionally enhanced clothing; for the food industry, the growing popularity of healthy and high-quality products plays an important role. For the German metal start-up, the increasing use of aluminum as a basic material is of importance, as it opens up application opportunities for new welding techniques (CMGE3).

Third, the issue of funding and financing KIE processes proved to be of great importance in nearly all cases and independently of the KIE pattern. Most of the KIE companies and start-ups investigated used internal funds to finance their activities. Some of the companies took out loans for smaller parts of the required funding (e.g. CMGE2). Only a few successfully applied for funding from the state or public support programs. In contrast, many company representatives interviewed emphasized that such programs are not attractive for the companies because of the bureaucracy and program managers' lack of knowledge of the specific situation of LMT firms (e.g. CMP1; CTP1). These and similar comments referred to both national as well as European funding programs.

Fourth, regional embeddedness seems to be beneficial to some KIE cases independently of the specific pattern. Local proximity to, for example, suppliers, scientific organizations or banks and investors makes it easier to gain new technological knowledge, additional capacities or financial resources. An example is the Portuguese metalworking firm and its network with local 'rivals' (CMP2). This local network had two functions: for one, the production capacities were leveled out between the different metalware manufacturers; for another, this cooperation facilitated the opening up of 'unfriendly' markets such as China.

Fifth, there are also constraining conditions on KIE processes. The interviewees, often from Southern Europe, referred to an 'unfriendly environment for entrepreneurial activities' and the lack of a recognizable institutional framework promoting such activities, as well as to many political and institutional obstacles (e.g. CTGR2). They also mentioned lack of support from industry associations and the poor professional guidance of consultants (CMGE3). Furthermore, they criticized the limited or even absent venture capital especially needed in the high-risk initial phases of company foundations (e.g. CFP1).

3.5 CONCLUSION: SOME THEORETICAL AND POLICY IMPLICATIONS

To sum up, four patterns of KIE in LMT sectors can be distinguished: the market-driven, science-and-technology-driven, capability-driven and competitive pressure-driven patterns. These patterns differ with the configuration of the most important determining factor, complementary factors (which step up the effects of the determining factors) and the innovation modes resulting from the KIE processes. The main features of these four patterns are summarized in Table 3.2.

The value of this typology is, first, of a theoretical nature because it advances the theoretical understanding of the opportunities for KIE

Table 3.2   Main features of KIE in LMT sectors

Factors	KIE pattern			
	Market-driven	Science and technology-driven	Capability-driven	Competitive pressure
Determining factor	New global market segments	New global technology opportunities and corresponding knowledge	Broad and profound local knowledge base and an outstanding entrepreneurial and innovation culture	Severe sectoral situation: cost and competition pressure; technological bottlenecks
Complementary factors	Outstanding transformative capabilities of firms	Sound local technological knowledge, close relations with external organizations	Local knowledge about new market opportunities	Accumulated local knowledge base and an outstanding entrepreneurial and innovation culture
Innovation	Mostly architectural innovations	Radical innovations	Modular innovations	Far-reaching innovations
Moderating factors	- Policy regulations and institutional opportunities - New customer preferences - Available financial resources, mostly internal sources and loans - Regional embeddedness as an advantage - Unfriendly environment to entrepreneurial activities as constraints			

activities in a technologically restricted industrial sector like LMT. Overall, these findings widen the positions of mainstream research and overcome the concept of KIE as exclusively linked to high-tech and knowledge-intensive industries and start-up firms. As the findings show, entrepreneurial activities can go beyond the borders of a highly path-dependent system; it may be that a majority of the actors involved view new ideas and inventions as a cul-de-sac whereas for a minority of economic actors a situation of stable path-dependency offers opportunities with a high potential of economic success. The intense competitive pressure in LMT industries may force actors to adopt not only cost-cutting and routine-optimizing managerial strategies but also a reflective stance towards established practices. Especially because of the great persistence and stability of LMT industries, entrepreneurial activities and successful deviation from established practices and technological paths promise competitive advantages and a high profitability. As the findings show, such activities are based on two distinct capabilities: that of taking up given opportunities for KIE activities on the basis of existing information about these opportunities, and that of looking actively for possible opportunities for KIE based on a specific 'alertness' of the entrepreneurial actor.[6]

However, the findings also show that KIE activities can only be understood as a nexus of entrepreneurial activities on the micro-level of individual companies and valuable opportunities on the macro-level of economic, institutional and technological structures. An indispensable factor influencing KIE activities is overcoming the restrictions inherent in the established LMT tradition. The strong path-dependency of LMT industries means that firms and individual entrepreneurs cannot be the drivers of KIE processes if they rely only on their specific sectoral or local knowledge; instead they have to connect with actors, resources and opportunities from outside the sector. Furthermore, this argument can be linked to conceptual findings in LMT research which emphasize the particular relevance of a 'distributed knowledge base' for the innovativeness of LMT companies, i.e. the relevance of sector-external knowledge stocks, especially scientifically created knowledge in high-tech industries, for the innovativeness of LMT firms (Robertson and Smith, 2008).

This typology has also a practical political value because the study findings point to several possibilities for policy measures which could foster KIE activities in LMT. These are for example:[7]

- improving access to globally available knowledge, especially for existing LMT firms and individual entrepreneurs with their often limited resources;
- promoting processes of the transfer of globally available knowledge to the local knowledge stock of individual LMT firms and entrepreneurs;
- enhancing local and firm-specific capabilities to integrate and utilize new knowledge by e.g. improving management competence, especially in cooperation and networking in a global direction;
- consideration of the framework conditions, i.e. the moderating factors that should be the object of policy measures, in particular with respect to regional proximity and networking, as well as the terms of corporate financing.

Without question, these policy recommendations should be considered of major relevance to entrepreneurial activities in LMT industries.

However, they need to be made more specific by future broad-based research on these activities. The KIE patterns outlined here may be the starting point and hypothesis for such research. Additionally, a systematic comparison between KIE in low-tech industries and KIE in high-tech industries will be of particular importance. The assumption is plausible that these differences may be only a matter of degree. One could also speak of a spectrum with at one extreme KIE in low-tech and at the other KIE in high-tech industries, with a smooth transition of types between the two poles. However, this comparative perspective has not yet been systematically applied and thus may also be a major topic in future research.

NOTES

1. I thank our project partners Ioanna Kastelli, Manuel Mira Godinho, Ricardo Mamede and Rick Woodward (University of Edinburgh Business School) for comments and suggestions on draft versions of this chapter.
2. Concerning the distinction between global and local levels of social and economic orders and interlinked actors, see in particular Disco and van der Meulen (1998).
3. I thank our AEGIS work-package partners Bram Timmermans, Christian Østergaard, Eun Kyung Park and Kenney V. Christiansen from Aalborg University (AAU), Glykeria Karagouni, Ioanna Kastelli and Yannis Caloghirou from National Technical University of Athens (LIEE-NTUA), Guido Bünstorf, Christina Guenther and Matthias Geissler from Max Planck Institute of Economics (MPI), Isabel Schwinge from TU Dortmund University (TUDO) and Alexandra Rosa, Manuel Mira Godinho and Ricardo Mamede from Technical University of Lisbon (UECE) for their case-study research.
4. As entrepreneurship literature stresses, these three entrepreneurial modes should be treated as basically different (Stam and Noteboom, 2011). However, because this chapter presents only first findings on an as yet uninvestigated issue, the differences between these modes have not been taken into consideration. The possible differences could be the topic of future research.
5. This methodological approach is known as 'abduction', i.e. to make new discoveries in a logically and methodologically ordered way which follows neither a theoretically grounded deductive approach nor an exclusively empirically based inductive approach (Reichertz, 2009).
6. The first aspect refers to Schumpeter's notion of innovative opportunities (Schumpeter, 1997), the second to Kirzner who emphasized the discovering of opportunities (Kirzner, 1997).
7. For a more detailed discussion of policy recommendations to promote KIE processes in the industrial LMT sector, see Chapter 10 in this volume.

REFERENCES

Audretsch, David, Oliver Falck, Stephan Heblich and Adam Lederer (eds) (2011), *Handbook of Research on Innovation and Entrepreneurship*, Cheltenham, UK and Northampton, MA, USA: Edward Elgar.

Bender, Gerd and Staffan Laestadius (2005), 'Non-Science Based Innovativeness: On Capabilities Relevant to Generate Profitable Novelty', in Gerd Bender, David Jacobson and Paul L. Robertson (eds), *Non-Research-Intensive Industries in the Knowledge Economy*, published in *Perspectives on Economic Political and Social Integration*, **XI** (1–2), special issue, 123–70.

Cohendet, Patrick and Patrick Llerena (2010), 'The Knowledge-Based Entrepreneur: The Need for a Relevant Theory of the Firm', in Franco Malerba (ed.), *Knowledge-Intensive Entrepreneurship and Innovation Systems: Evidence from Europe*, London, UK and New York, USA: Routledge, pp. 31–51.

Disco, Cornelius and Barend van der Meulen (eds) (1998), *Getting New Technologies Together: Studies in Making Sociotechnical Order*, Berlin, Germany and New York, USA: de Gruyter.

Foray, D. (2002), 'The Knowledge Economy and Society', *International Social Science Journal*, **54** (171), 1–169.

Grichnik, D. (2006), 'Die Opportunity Map der internationalen Entrepreneurshipforschung: Zum Kern des interdisziplinären Forschungs-programms', *Zeitschrift für Betriebswirtschaft*, **76** (12), 1303–33.

Henderson, R.M. and K.B. Clark (1990), 'Architectural Innovation: The Reconfiguration of Existing Product Technologies and the Failure of Established Firms', *Administrative Science Quarterly*, **35** (1), 9–30.

Hirsch-Kreinsen, H. (2008), '"Low-Tech" Innovation', *Industry and Innovation*, **15** (1), 19–43.

Jacobson, David and Kevin Heanue (2005), 'Policy Conclusions and Recommendations', in Gerd Bender, David Jacobson and Paul L. Robertson (eds), *Non-Research-Intensive Industries in the Knowledge Economy*, published in *Perspectives on Economic Political and Social Integration*, **XI** (1–2), special issue, 359–416.

Kelle, Udo and Susann Kluge (eds) (2010), *Vom Einzelfall zum Typus*, Wiesbaden, Germany: VS Verlag.

Kirzner, I. (1997), 'Entrepreneurial Discovery and the Competitive Market Process', *Journal of Economic Literature*, **35** (1), 60–85.

Malerba, Franco (2010), *Knowledge-Intensive Entrepreneurship and Innovation System: Evidence from Europe*, London, UK and New York, USA: Routledge.

Malerba, F. and M. McKelvey (2010), 'Conceptualizing Knowledge-Intensive Entrepreneurship: Concepts and Models', paper presented at the DIME – AEGIS – LIEE/NTUA Athens 2010 Conference, 29–30 April 2010.

Radosevic, Slavo (2010), 'What Makes Entrepreneurship Systemic?', in Franco Malerba (ed.), *Knowledge-Intensive Entrepreneurship and Innovation Systems: Evidence from Europe*, London, UK and New York, USA: Routledge, pp. 52–76.

Reichertz, J. (2009), 'Abduction: The Logic of Discovery of Grounded Theory', *Forum Qualitative Social Research*, **11** (1), available at www.qualitative-research.net/index.php/fqs/article/view/1412 (accessed 30 May 2013).

Robertson, Paul L. and Keith Smith (2008), 'Technological Upgrading and Distributed Knowledge Bases', in Hartmut Hirsch-Kreinsen and David Jacobson (eds), *Innovation in Low-Tech Firms and Industries*, Cheltenham, UK and Northampton, MA, USA: Edward Elgar, pp. 93–117.

Schumpeter, Joseph (1997/1934), *Theorie der wirtschaftlichen Entwicklung*, Berlin, Germany: Duncker & Humblot.

Stam, Erik and Bart Nooteboom (2011), 'Entrepreneurship, Innovation and Institutions', in David B. Audretsch, Oliver Falck, Stephan Heblich and Adam

Lederer (eds), *Handbook of Research on Innovation and Entrepreneurship*, Cheltenham, UK and Northampton, MA, USA: Edward Elgar, pp. 421–38.

Teece, D. and G. Pisano (1994), 'The Dynamic Capabilities of Firms: An Introduction', *Industrial and Corporate Change*, **3**, 537–56.

Yin, Robert K. (1994), *Case Study Research: Design and Methods*, 2nd edn, Newbury Park, CA: Sage Publications.

4. The impact of knowledge-intensive entrepreneurship on the growth and competitiveness of European traditional industries[1]

Ioanna Kastelli and Yannis D. Caloghirou

4.1 INTRODUCTION

In this chapter, European traditional industries are identified with low- and medium-low-technology (LMT) sectors. More precisely, an attempt is made to examine the role of knowledge-intensive entrepreneurial ventures in fostering the competitiveness of these industries in Europe and thus improving their position in the international division of labor.

The considerable specific weight of LMT industries in Europe is clearly shown by their large share in the manufacturing sector in terms of value added. In particular, LMT industries contributed approximately 55 per cent of the value added of total manufacturing in the EU-25 before the current economic crisis (European Commission, 2011). However, in the literature as well as in the public debate on growth, these important industries of modern economies are largely ignored, as the focus has almost exclusively been shifted to the high-technology industries and environments. In addition, LMT sectors have been ignored in policy discussions for a long time or considered 'archaic hangovers from an earlier era of capitalism' (Scott, 2006).

It is widely accepted that European firms operating in traditional industries are facing increasing competitive pressure in globalized markets from companies in emerging countries (e.g. China, India, Brazil), as well as from firms in developing economies. As the low-cost option based on low wages is mainly pursued by firms in developing and emerging economies, European firms need to ensure their long-term competitive position in the global market by putting emphasis on innovative activities, creation of high added-value, exploitation of complementarities with technological advancements in high- and medium-high-technology (HMT) sectors, as well as on the recognition and quick response to new market needs and market opportunities. Furthermore, the economic crisis has accentuated the pressure imposed on European firms and made more urgent their need to shift towards more knowledge-intensive and innovative activities.

In this respect knowledge-intensive entrepreneurship (KIE) can be considered a transformative mechanism able to convert new knowledge – whether originating in R&D or other (non-R&D) activities (i.e. professional or business practice) – into innovations, new business activities and sustainable corporate growth.

As shown in the PILOT project (Bender, 2006), LMT industrial sectors can be very innovative and, as Keith Smith argued (2002: 27), 'low tech industries are knowledge intensive and are frequently part of high tech systems'. This approach challenges the conventional wisdom stating that the high-tech, science-based sector is the key driving force behind the transformation of the European Union to a knowledge-based economy.

Taking into consideration the above issues, this chapter intends to shed light on the relation of KIE to the growth and competitiveness of European traditional industries. We argue that KIE in LMT sectors can (a) contribute to overcoming competitive pressures from low-wage economies as it builds on knowledge-intensive assets, promotes innovation and continuous technological upgrading, and (b) create new economic value by exploiting knowledge bases 'belonging' to other industries (chemicals, information and computer technologies (ICTs), new materials, etc.) or scientific fields with widely applicable knowledge (molecular biology, genetics, etc.).

With this objective in mind we first highlight the specific dimensions of KIE that are relevant to the growth and competitiveness of traditional industries in Europe. Having identified KIE ventures in a number of EU countries (from the AEGIS field research survey and case studies), we assess the extent to which such ventures have characteristics and performance in terms of growth and competitiveness that are different from those of other ventures with more conventional and 'traditional' characteristics.

Policy implications stemming from the above-mentioned line of argumentation can be significant, first, by enriching the ongoing debate which is mainly based on the assumption that scientific knowledge, new technologies and innovations in the context of the high-tech sector are more important for social and economic development in Europe, and second, by feeding evidence and arguments into the design of specific policy measures that could be integrated into the formulation of a 'European Industrial Policy'.

The chapter is divided into three sections. The first section reports on the main challenges that European traditional industries are facing:

economic crisis, globalization and technological transformations. In the second section are presented empirical findings – based on the AEGIS survey results and the relevant case studies – related to the nature and the impact of KIE in the LMT sectors. In the final section the findings and their policy implications are discussed.

4.2 CHALLENGES AND TRANSFORMATIONS IN EUROPEAN LMT INDUSTRIES IN THE CONTEXT OF THE ECONOMIC CRISIS

4.2.1 Economic Crisis

The economic crisis has affected LMT sectors in terms of output, investment and employment.

The impact of the current crisis varies significantly across manufacturing industries and among LMT sectors. Food and beverages as 'necessity goods' were not severely hit by the financial crisis, as demand was expectedly less affected. Intermediate-goods industries such as wood, paper and metals faced a severe contraction in final demand although they seem to be starting to recover. Finally, textiles, clothing, leather and furniture were already undergoing restructuring before the crisis that accelerated or accentuated negative changes in terms of output and employment (output initially contracted by 15–22 per cent, although these industries have recently experienced some recovery) (European Commission, 2011).

However, productivity growth, measured as production per hours worked, showed an improvement following the general increase in manufacturing labor productivity over the period 2000–10. This productivity performance reflects rationalization efforts (with negative implications for employment), but also process and product innovation, a better qualified industrial workforce and outsourcing of non-core manufacturing business activities such as logistics or ICT (European Commission, 2010a, 2012a).

One of the drivers of sector growth and competitiveness is investment, and in times of crisis it can be affected in the long term, the same as employment and technology. Investment ratios in all LMT sectors presented a slight decrease over the period 1995–2009, but the crisis is evident as there was a steep drop from 2008 to 2009.

In general, after a contraction in output, LMT sectors need to ensure future growth and for this they need to specialize in more technologically advanced solutions, address niche markets and undergo further modernization of products and processes. This strategy is also relevant in the context of two main issues that shape opportunities and constraints for traditional industries, namely globalization and technological transformations (European Commission, 2009, 2011).

4.2.2   The Process of Globalization

In the context of the current economic crisis the process of globalization presents opportunities and threats for the competitiveness of European Union manufacturing industries. The new industrial economies can be major drivers of the recovery of industrial demand for the European firms but at the same time they increasingly compete with Europe in traditional and knowledge-intensive exports.

In particular, European traditional industries remain strong players in terms of their share in world trade despite losses in some of these industries (e.g. textiles, clothing, leather and footwear and fabricated metal products lost considerable shares in world markets). In addition, gains were recorded in food and beverages, tobacco, wood and wood products and paper and paper products. However, according to the 'revealed comparative advantage' in trade (RCA), the EU does not present a high relative performance in any of the four technology groups (see Table 4.1). More precisely, in LMT sectors, the EU performs below its main international competitors.[2] This picture points to the importance of long-term factors that can ensure future growth and competitiveness improvement; specialization in more technologically advanced niche markets, and product, process and organizational innovations can improve the competitive position of European firms in these industries.

In general, achieving a better position in global value chains should be considered a way to tap gains in the context of globalization. European

Table 4.1   RCA by technology category in 2009

	HT	MHT	MLT	LT
EU-27	0.84	1.14	0.89	1.03
Japan	0.81	1.49	0.97	0.18
USA	0.93	1.25	0.89	0.68
Brazil	0.39	0.71	0.95	2.45
China	1.49	0.67	0.88	1.30
India	0.41	0.51	2.06	1.33
Russia	0.08	0.46	2.97	0.60

Note: HT: high-tech; MHT: medium-high-tech; MLT: medium-low-tech; and LT: low-tech.

Source: 'European Industrial Structure', European Commission (2011).

firms active in traditional industries can pursue specialization strategies against their competitors by targeting the high added-value segments of specific global value chains. Moving along the value chain and climbing upstream on the value-added ladder (e.g. from production to the design of clothing and wearing-apparel materials) has proved in most cases to be the key to circumventing cost competition. The role of suppliers in creating new value for LMT producers is vital, as by creating new solutions they contribute to the increase in their clients' productivity. For instance, in the food and beverage industry suppliers put science to work on improving the nutritional value of food, ensuring food safety and finding smart, sustainable solutions to feeding a growing population. The value chain is then reformulated to include all the vital actors who respond to problems related to nutrition, safety, health or environment.

Other examples are the furniture and textile industries, where manufacturing is combined with creative activities. In this respect, a greater variety of actors are involved in the value chain covering a wider range of activities, from the primary material manufacturers to high-end industries such as design and fashion.

These transformations are not new. They started with the 'functionalization' of productive systems, meaning that production is related to functions and not simply to products. In addition, upgrading[3] is not related solely to the functional part, but often aims to deepen specific capabilities required to explore new opportunities opening up 'on the side' of the value chain stage where the firm is currently engaged (Morrison et al., 2008).

As a consequence, in LMT industries production processes are becoming more complex and the role of technology more vital in responding to new competitive challenges.

4.2.3   Technological Transformations

Unlike in high-tech industries, the nature of technological change in traditional industries is characterized by established developmental paths and fixed technological trajectories that are dominated by incremental innovations (Hirsch-Kreinsen and Schwinge, 2011). Because of the high persistence and stability of these industries, entrepreneurial activities and a successful deviation from established practices and technological paths can open appreciable opportunities for building competitive advantage and gaining profitability (ibid.). At the same time competitive pressure and strong path-dependency stimulate the innovative behavior needed to overcome these constraints.

An important consideration should be made regarding the technological development of traditional industries; they are conventionally LMT sectors. This is based on the standard classification of industries based on their average R&D intensity (R&D/total output). According to this classification, sectors with R&D intensity less than 3 per cent are considered low- and medium-low-tech (LMT) (Hatzichronoglou, 1997). However, the exclusive use of this classification is being challenged; LMT sectors might in fact be intensive in their use of knowledge, though the complexity and depth of their knowledge base does not result from their R&D activities (Smith, 2002). In addition, they can rely on high technologies to develop new products or processes.

In this respect, the key drivers of innovation in LMT sectors are identified instead as new technological developments related to general-purpose technologies or, equivalently, to key enabling technologies. The required knowledge base is a combination of specific, practical, in-house knowledge together with complex knowledge inputs created in the high-tech sector or embedded in high-tech networks.

This means that there are important applications of new and advanced technologies in traditional industries. As examples we can mention nanotechnologies in textiles and clothing (e.g. nanosilver for antibacterial textiles and aero gels for thermal protection), photonics in systems for commercial printing, or biotechnology in producing enzymes for the production of foodstuffs.

At the same time, new entrants (either firms or countries), having followed a process of competence-building, can challenge established actors. A few examples spring to mind. First, the Chinese textile and clothing sector is aiming to become the dominant world industrial actor by creating a number of advantages in terms of both price and quality (including technical textiles) (Peeters et al., 2007). Second, in the pulp and paper sector, non-EU competitors do not have the high costs of compliance with the strict environmental regulations as in the EU, and at the same time they are more and more able to supply low-cost, high-quality commodity-grade papers (here again China is one of the main threats) (European Commission, 2012b).

The above considerations point to the importance of innovation and the use of external technological knowledge in LMT sectors to ensure competitiveness, growth and the upgrading of the position of European industries in the international division of labor. In this respect knowledge-intensive entrepreneurship (KIE) could constitute for European traditional industries the driver of improvement in their competitive position globally.

But what are the main features of KIE? The concept of KIE takes into account four main characteristics of entrepreneurial ventures (Malerba and McKelvey, 2010). They are new innovative firms that have significant knowledge intensity in their activity and exploit innovative opportunities that are generated in different industries (high-, medium- and low-tech manufacturing and knowledge-intensive services). In addition, the definition adopted in this chapter can also be extended to cover new ventures initiated by already established corporations (i.e. corporate entrepreneurship). Moreover, it should be stressed that this approach focuses on the new firm or new venture as the unit of analysis and emphasizes the importance of context (comprising systems of innovation, networks, industries, socioeconomic configuration, etc).

This concept is particularly wide in order to cover new entrepreneurial ventures in LMT sectors – it does not restrict the 'know-vative' (knowledge and innovation) content of entrepreneurship to high-tech start-ups. In addition, it is relevant to LMT entrepreneurial ventures, as recent empirical findings show, that LMT industries are mostly characterized by process, organizational and marketing innovations, weak internal innovation capabilities, and a strong dependency on the external provision of machines, equipment and software (Heidenreich, 2009). In fact, low-tech firms use advances occurring in other (mostly high-tech) industries to cope with competition especially from low-wage countries. In this respect, this finding points to 'exploitative' rather than 'explorative' learning, to follow the distinction made by March (1991).

In the following section we investigate the impact of KIE on the growth and competitiveness of European LMT firms and draw upon the results of extensive field research to highlight the opportunities and strategic options created through the development of KIE ventures in LMT sectors.

4.3 THE IMPACT OF KIE ON GROWTH AND COMPETITIVENESS – AN EMPIRICAL ANALYSIS

In this section we use evidence from extensive field research in European firms[4] to investigate whether KIE ventures perform better than conventional non-KIE ventures in terms of growth and competitiveness and to analyse the way KIE ventures relate to the creation and sustainability of competitive advantage.

To operationalize KIE ventures we took into consideration innovativeness and human resources attributes. Especially for the knowledge-intensity of human capital, labor skills have been associated with industry performance in previous research (O'Mahony and van Ark, 2003). More precisely, there is evidence for a positive correlation of skilled labor with industry performance and, in addition, evidence of declining performance in low-skill-intensive industries, including many mature manufacturing industries subject to product-cycle influences arising from strong competition with low-wage economies in the developing world and Central and Eastern Europe (ibid.: 10).

To relate KIE to the impact on growth and competitiveness as measures of industry performance, we used a mix of indicators. The term competitiveness is used here with reference to firms and industries. In that sense, what matters is whether the firm or the sector deals successfully with international competition by making profits and increasing its market shares. In addition, there is a distinction made between the *ex post* and *ex ante* evaluation of competitiveness (Hatzichronoglou, 1996; Aiginger, 2006). The former is related to the results obtained (production, profits, sales, exports, market shares) whereas the latter is to the ability to achieve a certain competitive position and the underlying drivers of competitiveness. This approach is at variance with the concept of price competitiveness. We use thus: (1) an *ex post* evaluation of firm performance in terms of growth and competitiveness based on sales, exports and international exposure and openness; and (2) an *ex ante* evaluation of competitiveness based on the drivers of competitiveness.

For business performance, we used information on sales and exports over time as collected from the survey. Exports can also be considered a proxy for competitiveness. In the context of the case-study analysis we focus more on the notion of competitiveness, while making a distinction between cost and quality competitiveness. Academic research since the mid-1980s has pointed to the need to shift attention from the cost- and price-related factors of competitiveness, to technology, innovation and non-price factors of competitiveness. It is in that direction that we look for the opportunities opened through KIE in shaping quality competitiveness.

The underlying hypothesis is that KIE ventures should perform better than non-KIE ventures, presenting a better competitive position sustained by qualitative elements – not only low wages and cost.

In our empirical research we used two sources of information:

1) Data from the AEGIS large-scale survey on newly (in the 2000s) established entrepreneurial ventures in ten European countries, namely Croatia, the Czech Republic, Denmark, France, Germany, Greece, Italy, Portugal, Sweden and the UK. The survey collected 4004 responses from several groups of sectors (high-, medium- and low-tech) including 1456 questionnaires from LMT firms.
   The information collected from the AEGIS survey is used in order to distinguish KIE from non-KIE ventures and to evaluate the potential of KIE firms in terms of their growth and competitiveness.
2) Twenty-seven case studies conducted in the context of the AEGIS project. Both newly established firms and business ventures of exist-

ing firms were included in three LMT industries – food and beverages, metal and textile – in four European countries, namely Denmark, Germany, Greece and Portugal. The analysis of the case studies is used to highlight the drivers of competitiveness and the role of KIE in shaping quality competitiveness.

4.3.1 The Survey Analysis

The aim of the survey analysis is to characterize KIE in low-tech industries and show that within LMT sectors there is a significant differentiation between KIE and non-KIE firms in terms of their performance. To do this we intend to present some key indicators for KIE in low-tech industries and try to relate these indicators to competitive performance.

The survey was conducted in the first half of 2011. An extensive questionnaire was circulated to a large number of firms from different industries and 4004 responses were obtained, of which 36.4 per cent represents firms in LMT sectors. All the LMT-sector firms were newly established during the period 2001–07.

The distribution of firms in terms of LMT subsectors is shown in Table 4.2.

The questionnaire included general information about the firm, the founder and founding team, the firm's formation process, its market environment and strategy, innovation activity and some information on firm performance.

In order to address the issue of KIE in LMT we constructed a new variable that takes into consideration not only innovativeness but also labor skills. Educational intensity is positively associated with available

Table 4.2 Selected sectors for AEGIS survey

Selected Sectors	NACE rev. 1.1 code	No. of firms
Low-tech manufacturing sector		
Paper and printing	21,22	472 (32.5%)
Textile and clothing	17, 18, 19	203 (14%)
Food, beverages and tobacco	15,16	291 (20%)
Wood and furniture	20, 36.1	217 (14.9%)
Medium-low-tech manufacturing sector		
Basic metals	27	35 (2.4%)
Fabricated metal products	28	238 (16.3%)
Total		1456 (100%)

Source: AEGIS Survey, data processing by LIEE/NTUA.

productive capabilities and reflects the labor-skill requirements of firms, which in part depend on the characteristics of markets and industries (Peneder, 2007). Although formal education is only one of several elements characterizing employee skills (experience, on-the-job training, etc. being additional elements of skills), it is, however, an accepted and easily available measure for evaluating the educational intensity of industries or firms (ibid.). In addition, this measure is sector-specific. Our sample contains LMT firms, which points to the lower level of skills required, according also to the labor-skill taxonomy (O'Mahony and van Ark, 2003). According to this taxonomy, all selected LMT sectors are classified in low- and low-to-intermediate-skilled groups.

We defined as knowledge-intensive entrepreneurial ventures within our low-tech sample the cases where more than 10 per cent of the employees[5] have a university degree and at the same time introduced a product or process innovation during the period 2008–11. Of the firms giving valid answers, 35.2 per cent satisfy these criteria. The rest of the sample can be considered non-KIE – they do not satisfy the criteria.

Taking into consideration this distinction, we further compared these two groups on the basis of other characteristics relevant to the distinction of KIE and non-KIE firms. These characteristics refer to the sources of knowledge used by the two groups, their appropriability methods and factors enabling or constraining their growth and expansion. The statistical tests for the differentiation of the two groups in terms of these factors are presented in Tables 4.3 and 4.4.

A first observation is that there are statistically significant differences between the two groups. KIE firms focus more on exploiting external sources of knowledge such as public or private research institutes, journals and trade and technical publications, and they implement more in-house R&D to explore knowledge internally. They also use formal intellectual property protection methods such as patents, copyright and trademarks. In terms of capabilities that contribute to their competitive advantage, they reveal a greater focus on elements related to higher added-value solutions (innovative products/services, R&D activity and networking with scientific organizations).

Interestingly, firms in both samples are not much concerned with obstacles to their growth and expansion and there is no statistically significant differentiation of the two groups on these issues.

In general, the low level of concern with specific constraints might have two explanations: either the firms do not face these obstacles because they are well established, or they are not exposed to these problems because of a more conservative attitude towards competitive challenges.

The above findings confirm the relevance of the distinction already made between KIE and non-KIE firms in our sample.

Table 4.3 Differentiation of some characteristics of KIE and non-KIE firms

Important sources of knowledge	Non-KIE sample Mean	KIE sample Mean	Levene's test
Clients or customers	4.41	4.46	2.485
Suppliers	3.80	3.68	0.713
Competitors	3.40	3.45	2.367
Public research institutes	2.06	2.19	4.023***
Universities	2.01	2.16	2.439***
External commercial labs/R&D firms/technical institutes	2.06	2.26	5.467**
In-house (R&D laboratories in firm)	3.10	3.42	10.145***
Trade fairs, conferences and exhibitions	2.98	3.30	0.503
Scientific journals and other trade or technical publications	2.61	2.91	4.427**
Participation in nationally funded research programs	1.87	1.99	1.049
Participation in EU-funded research programs (Framework Programmes)	1.87	2.04	3.117*
Contribution in creating and sustaining competitive advantage	**Non-KIE sample Mean**	**KIE sample Mean**	**Levene's test**
Capability to offer novel products/ services	3.61	3.82	14.089***
Capacity to adapt the products/ services to the specific needs of different customers/market niches	4.11	4.18	0.140
Capability to offer expected products/ services at low cost	3.37	3.37	4.750
R&D activities	2.84	3.07	6.293***
Establishment of alliances/ partnerships with other firms	2.60	2.89	1.193
Capability to offer high quality product/services at a premium price	3.73	3.77	0.648
Networking with scientific research organizations	2.06	2.32	5.247**
Marketing and promotion activities	3.16	3.58	2.720*
Obstacles to growth and expansion	**Non-KIE sample Mean**	**KIE sample Mean**	**Levene's test**
Technology risk-uncertainty	2.30	2.35	0.102
Market risk-uncertainty	3.27	3.38	0.480

Table 4.3   (continued)

Obstacles to growth and expansion	Non-KIE sample Mean	KIE sample Mean	Levene's test
Difficulty finding necessary funding	3.29	3.32	0.220
Difficulty finding business partners	2.64	2.73	0.000
Difficulties recruiting highly skilled employees	3.04	3.00	10.930
Lack of technological know-how	2.27	2.38	0.678

Note: ***, **, *: 1%, 5%, 10% level of statistical significance respectively.

Source: AEGIS Survey, data processing by LIEE/NTUA.

Table 4.4   *Differentiation in formal appropriability methods (in %)*

Use of appropriability methods		KIE	Non-KIE	Total
Formal methods of protection	No	35.3	56	47
	Yes	64.7	44	53
Total (N=915)		100	100	100

Notes: Pearson Chi-Square 38.736***, Likelihood Ratio 39.129***, Phi -0.206***, Cramer's V 0.206***.
***, **, *: 1%, 5%, 10% level of statistical significance respectively.

Source: AEGIS Survey, data processing by LIEE/NTUA.

Growth and competitiveness of knowledge-intensive entrepreneurial ventures in LMT industries

In order to investigate the performance of KIE in LMT firms in terms of growth and competitiveness we used the following variables:

- Growth in sales and exports during 2007–09;
- Estimate of growth in sales and exports for 2010;
- Exposure and openness to the international market and the percentage of sales on the international market during 2007–09.

The growth in sales is a good proxy for a firm's growth and expansion, whereas the growth in exports over time demonstrates whether the firm can compete internationally. In addition, the estimated growth in sales and exports for 2010 is expected to capture the deterioration in production due to the economic crisis. The exposure and openness to the international market is another proxy for the competitive position of the firm. We used two variables to measure this characteristic: first, a variable taking value 1 when the firm is only present in the local and/or national market, and value 2 when the firm exports to foreign markets; second, we also used export intensity (exports/total sales), in the sense that firms with higher export intensity are expected to address the competitive challenges better.

We distinguish between two groups of firms, KIE and non-KIE, and investigate whether there are statistically significant differences in their performance in terms of sales, exports and international exposure and openness. We would expect these two groups to perform differently and show a different competitive potential. More precisely, we expected that those firms that are classified as KIE would have a better performance in terms of sales and exports, and a higher export intensity.

Comparing statistical means for KIE and non-KIE groups in regard to the variables described above, the following results reveal a significant differentiation between KIE and non-KIE firms:

1. As shown in the cross-tabulation that follows (see Table 4.5), KIE firms tend to show increases in sales and exports during the period 2007–09. Non-KIE firms to a larger extent show decreases

Table 4.5   Differentiation in firms' performance (in %)

		KIE	Non-KIE	Total
Sales 2007–09* KIE	increase	71.5	61.2	64.8
	decrease	28.5	38.8	35.2
Total (N=1296)		100	100	100

Notes: Pearson Chi-Square 13.743***, Likelihood Ratio 13.979***, Phi 0.103***, Cramer's V 0.103***.

		KIE	Non-KIE	Total
Exports 2007–09* KIE	increase	30.6	18.4	22.6
	decrease	69.4	81.6	77.4
Total (N=1290)		100	100	100

Notes: Pearson Chi-Square 25.081***, Likelihood Ratio 24.369***, Phi 0.139***, Cramer's V 0.139***.

Source: AEGIS Survey, data processing by LIEE/NTUA.

Table 4.6　Differentiation in predicted performance (in %)

		KIE	Non-KIE	Total
Sales 2010	increase	62.9	55.8	58.3
	decrease	37.1	44.2	41.7
Total (N=1297)		100	100	100

Notes:　Pearson Chi-Square 6.126***, Likelihood Ratio 6.164***, Phi 0.069***, Cramer's V 0.069***.

		KIE	Non-KIE	Total
Exports 2010	increase	26.6	18.1	21.2
	decrease	73.4	81.9	78.8
Total (N=1426)		100	100	100

Notes:　Pearson Chi-Square 16.645***, Likelihood Ratio 16.210***, Phi 0.114***, Cramer's V 0.114***.

Source:　AEGIS Survey, data processing by LIEE/NTUA.

    in sales and exports during the period 2007–09. These results are statistically significant.

2.　The same applies to estimated sales and exports for 2010 as shown in Table 4.6. KIE firms tended to expect an increase in sales and exports in 2010, whereas non-KIE firms tended to expect a decrease in sales and exports in 2010.

3.　As is shown in Table 4.7, KIE firms tend to be more present on the international market, while non-KIEs tend to be active only in local and national markets.

4.　For the ranges of export intensity we get similar results pointing to the better positioning of KIE firms on the international market as shown in Table 4.8. By contrast non-KIE firms are mostly present in the category 'no exports'.

    The above evidence supports two hypotheses: first, that it is justified to make a distinction between KIE and non-KIE firms, and second, that the KIE group of firms performs better in terms of sales and exports and the estimate for 2010 was definitely better for both variables. In addition, KIE firms tend to be more export intensive than non-KIE firms.

    We may argue on this evidence that KIE in LMT firms, even during a period of serious economic crisis, outperform non-KIE firms because of a wider scope of action, a capability to compete by offering attractive

Table 4.7   Differentiation in terms of openness to international market(in %)

	KIE	Non-KIE	Total
Local/national market	45.6	62.7	56.7
International market	54.4	37.2	43.3
Total (N=1602)	100	100	100

Notes: Pearson Chi-Square 39.877***, Likelihood Ratio 39.768***, Phi -0.155***, Cramer's V 0.15.

Source: AEGIS Survey, data processing by LIEE/NTUA.

Table 4.8   Differentiation in export intensity

		KIE %	Non-KIE %	Total %
Export intensity %	0	45.6	62.8	56.7
	0.1–10	23.8	13.9	17.4
	11–25	10.1	6.2	7.6
	26–50	9.6	8.2	8.7
	>50	10.9	9.0	9.7
		100	100	100
Total (N=1456)		513	943	1456

Notes: Pearson Chi-Square 80.121***, Likelihood Ratio 84.732***, Phi 0.235***, Cramer's V 0.235***.

Source: AEGIS Survey, data processing by LIEE/NTUA.

new products or services, exploit knowledge and technologies developed elsewhere and respond to market demand. It should be noticed, however, that the effects of the crisis, although not the same across industries, were expressed by a high drop in output in Europe (European Commission, 2010a). In this context, more dynamic firms with more knowledge-intensive characteristics seem to perform better during crises.

4.3.2   The Case-Study Analysis

In the previous section we demonstrated a significant difference in performance of KIE and non-KIE firms. In the present section we focus on the type of impact KIE has on performance, especially competitiveness, and investigate the opportunities and strategic options created through the evolution of knowledge-intensive entrepreneurial ventures in LMT industries.

The analysis is based on the results of 27 qualitative case studies conducted in selected established or newly founded LMT companies, as presented in our earlier section. The selection criteria for the case-study companies were: new innovative companies founded between 2000 and 2006; implementation of innovations between 2000 and 2006 in established companies; and status as SMEs, i.e. firms of fewer than 250 employees. The innovations implemented by the investigated companies could be either a new product or a new, i.e. not previously applied, process technology.

The field research investigated, among other things, the impact of the knowledge-intensive ventures on two levels of analysis – the firm level and the meso-level (sector and market dynamics). The evidence presented below can be related directly or indirectly to growth and competitiveness as they are at the core of the creation and sustainability of competitive advantages.

The type of impact of KIE on LMT performance is investigated by looking at four dimensions of structural competitiveness analysed by Fagerberg et al. (2004). They developed a framework addressing the different aspects of a country's competitiveness focusing on four dimensions: cost, technology, capacity and demand. While Fagerberg et al. applied this framework at the country level, we believe that these four dimensions can be relevant at the sectoral and firm level as well.

Price or cost competitiveness is the aspect of competitiveness that economists have long focused on. It relates mainly to unit labor cost.

Technology or technological competitiveness refers to the ability to compete successfully in markets for new goods and services. This type of competitiveness is closely related to innovativeness.

Capacity competitiveness is distinct from technological competitiveness in the sense that, even in cases where no new technologies are developed, the capacity for exploiting new technologies developed by third actors might be crucial for sustained performance. This capacity relates thus to a number of requirements for 'getting the most out' of opportunities for imitating more advanced technology in use elsewhere. Such requirements relate to absorptive capacity and, more precisely, to physical capital and infrastructure (such as capital equipment and ICT infrastructure), human capital, R&D efforts and social capital.

Demand competitiveness relates to the ability to exploit the changing composition of demand by offering attractive products that are in high demand at home and abroad. In the context of globalization, this dimension assumes a prominent role as it relates to the capability to exploit demand booms.

As already pointed out in the previous section, European firms active in low-tech industries are on new 'playing fields' and face different challenges from those of only a few decades ago. In this respect the search for market segments that do not pose the same constraints as the respective sector as a whole is a crucial strategy for new entrants as well as for established firms needing sustainability. There is a wider context of evolving markets driven by new technologies (such as ICTs or biotechnology) or societal needs (such as environmentally friendly solutions, healthy nutrition, etc.) that presents new challenges and opportunities. The LMT firms in our case studies show an interesting exploitation of opportunities arising either from technological developments that go beyond developmental paths of the specific industries, or from new market needs that are being recognized and commercially exploited and require new concepts for products and different ways of production (e.g. offering higher flexibility or quality control).

Initial conditions for the investigated case firms reveal some similarities. These firms present some 'provisions' at the first place that relate to: (a) the founder or founding team and their educational attainment and expertise; (b) their innovation capability, as these firms were established on the basis of the introduction of some new applied knowledge (new product, process or service); and (c) the social capital of the founder(s).

Once established, these firms developed their activities in a way that differentiated them from firms following established development patterns in LMT sectors. Their innovative potential spurred the accumulation of organizational knowledge and competencies out of which they created a development process which could enable further innovation, initiating the dynamic process of KIE.

It is obviously critical that the path from the initial conditions to a sustained KIE process is not mechanistic but strongly dependent on endogenous capability-building. The firms investigated exhibited a continuous effort at developing skills in various functions of the entrepreneurial activity: in assessing the technological and market opportunities, mastering and assimilating technologies developed by external actors, operating efficiently with a given technology, managing and coordinating production stages and operations, and establishing linkages with other organizations (suppliers, customers, science and technology institutions).

Looking at the impact of the investigated KIE ventures, we identify four different types of effects relating to competitiveness at the *firm level*.

1) Creation of new, innovative products, whereby firms:
   Discover new and better ways to address old/existing needs;
   Increase their market share by offering new products or creating totally new business lines;

Create new market segments.

In most of the cases, as start-ups or established companies, they exploited their internal knowledge base (especially the founder's in the case of start-ups) in combination with knowledge and techno-logical know-how from different scientific fields to introduce new solutions to their customers. These solutions were either responses to already existent and recorded needs, or in anticipation of new demand trends.

2) Creation of new processes, whereby firms:
    Use known processes to produce new products with higher added-value (better quality and attributes);
    Introduce new innovative ways to produce existing products;
    Establish new systems of production.
    These new processes either resulted in better quality and attributes or made the production process more flexible and effective, or made it possible to expand the production spectrum.

3) Competence-/capability-building:
    a) The entrepreneurial ventures in our field research are strong in the creation of new technological capabilities, as many of the firms started producing and commercializing innovative products that constituted for them totally new business activities;
    b) In many cases these technological capabilities represented certain potential for new applications in the near future;
    c) Learning and experimenting established an absorptive poten-tial that ensured further exploitation of external knowledge. At the same time, working on a specific application deepened the knowledge related to the field, opening new possibilities for technological advancement and market exploitation;
    d) As the cases studied were innovative, most of the time they also involved new managerial and organizational capabilities required to manage more complex business systems and relations with customers or suppliers;
    e) Last but not least, firms expanded their market knowledge through the exploitation of new market opportunities and through responding to customers' new needs.

4) Cost reduction
    This aspect relates mainly to process and organizational innovation.
    There were few cases of process innovation or reorganization which resulted in cost reduction. However, even in those cases entrepreneur-ial activity focused at the same time on the improvement of quality. For example, a new plastic bag for packaging olives in a Greek food company resulted in the reduction of transportation costs, but at the

same time improved the quality, image and attributes of the company's product, leading to the capability of its sale at premium prices.

At the *sector level*, some interesting features have been identified relating to the issue of competitiveness:

1) Expansion of the sectoral knowledge base
   This is the result of either:
   a) The combination of knowledge and technologies generated in different fields, but not necessarily in the same field as the firm's activity; or
   b) The development of totally new know-how.
   An example is the transformation of electrocardiography monitoring equipment into a wearable device, opening up new opportunities for electronics and software engineering in biomedical applications. Another example is clothing items using bioactive fiber incorporating algae and silver which were targeted at the medical care market and respective patients with dermatological problems.

2) Diffusion into the value chain
   New knowledge developing in the context of KIE diffuses and affects the value chain backwards and/or forwards, by:
   a) Adding value to customers offering improved solutions;
   b) Improving the customers' effectiveness, and
   c) Creating new opportunities for them to innovate, especially in cases (b) and (c) for intermediate products;
   d) Opening up new market opportunities for suppliers, and
   e) Deploying suppliers' knowledge base through feedback and interaction.
   Some examples are illustrative. In the case of a manufacturer of metal structures, the introduction of a system of cold-formed metallic structures in galvanized steel saves time and cost (in terms of transportation, assembly and dismantling) in construction activities. In textiles, the introduction of a new technology that integrates additives of different substances into cellulosic fibers from a German start-up added-value to the textile products of customers (through material effectiveness, better input quality and environmental compatibility) and contributed to further product innovations and new fields of application.
   The use of high-pressure processing in beverages and food processing in a Portuguese firm resulted in products with superior attributes for final consumers.
   The case of a Greek company producing stuffed natural Greek agricultural products points to the opening of new market opportunities

for suppliers of raw materials and the knowledge feedback to suppliers of packaging through the setting of specifications.

3) Expansion of the market and sector

The expansion of the knowledge base and the diffusion of knowledge resulted in many cases in new opportunities for new entrants/competitors, and in the development of new technological paths also related to new market segments. In this respect other manufacturers could be encouraged to try to develop new products. For instance: (i) in the food industry the combination with know-how from the health sector related to nutrition issues; and (ii) in textiles and clothing the creation of a new business activity relating clothing items with bioactive fibers targeting the medical care market.

A common feature in all 27 cases was innovation and innovation strategy as the way to circumvent the limits of sector development and expansion. Their strategy was not mainly based on formal internal R&D efforts (though R&D was not absent in all cases). External sources of knowledge instead – various actors, mainly suppliers and customers – played a decisive role and in some cases cooperation with universities and research institutes were vital. In this context, another very important element at the firm level was the capability to transform the market/customer need into a business concept, and the capability to understand and apply the supplier's knowledge and solutions to new product solutions. This absorptive capability was embedded both at the individual and organizational level. Expectedly, in the early phases of the start-up, the founder's or founding team's capability was prevalent. In the case of established firms this capability takes the character of an organizational capability that sustains organizational change and transformation through learning. Firms need to identify the most promising external knowledge sources and align their absorptive capacities accordingly. Hence they also need search strategies that provide direction and priorities (Laursen and Saulter, 2006).

While the study firms succeeded in capturing a market segment, at the same time they developed a capability to exploit new knowledge and technology developed elsewhere, and thus created a dynamic state of sustained performance. Technologies can be 'out there', but firms, either new or established, need to be able to improvise to use these technologies in ways that create new value. As 'first movers' in fields where competition is not intense or non-existent, they establish a potential to exploit new market opportunities either locally or internationally. For example, the case firms in the textile industry exploited what was on the market, merging it with high- or medium-high technologies (e.g. electronics, chemicals or new materials). Such firms' new products are then new to the market and therefore their company portfolios of innovative products may be considered somewhere between radical and incremental. The main focus of their strategy is technology, capacity and demand competitiveness as described at the beginning of this section. Although cost competitiveness might be affected as well (e.g. by process innovations that reduce production costs or increase productivity), their innovative strategy focuses on avoiding established patterns of competition (e.g. based on economies of scale, concentration, cost reduction, etc.) by departing onto new development paths.

4.4   DISCUSSION AND POLICY IMPLICATIONS

Today, the European LMT industries' competitive position is challenged by the emergence of new competitors from countries of lower production cost.

There is a debate concerning whether economic growth and employment is mostly the result of research-intensive industries or if excluding LMT sectors from the policy agenda on promoting a knowledge-based European economy is a 'high-tech myopia'. The question is whether, in a context of competitive deterioration as described in the first section of the report, LMT industries could play the role of an alternative, autonomous specialization pattern and be a source of competitive advantage (Heidenreich, 2009).

Our field research provides some interesting results that point to the innovative potential – based on exploitative learning processes – of LMT industries and firms.

We identified in the survey an important number of newly established LMT firms that can be characterized as KIE because they are knowledge intensive, innovative and highly skilled. These KIE firms seem to be positively differentiated from non-KIE firms in terms of their growth and export intensity, even during the period of the current crisis.

In KIE firms of LMT sectors competitive advantage is mainly based on qualitative aspects rather than on cost aspects. It relies on their ability to introduce innovative products or processes, to exploit and integrate the technological advancements of other sectors (mainly HMT) and to respond to new demand conditions.

At the *firm level*, there is a clear indication that knowledge-intensive activities bring new market opportunities for the firm, as well as technological development and capability building.

Particularly for the established case firms, it seems clear that combining new production processes with the conceptualization of new products opened totally new areas of activity and operation for both the firm and sector. This brought new market opportunities, mainly through the exploitation of niche markets and new market segments, mostly for high value-added products displaying unique characteristics. Moreover, in some cases there is the possibility of international market penetration. In addition, we can make the case for KIE firms as agents supporting growth and competitiveness based on quality and technologically complex characteristics. The competition pattern traditionally followed by companies in low-tech industries, i.e. protection by barriers to entry for long periods, was based on established advantages of scale and scope economies (Chandler, 1990).

The impact of KIE can be relevant to the whole value chain, from suppliers to customers. Market opportunities are created for suppliers, but also added-value and new opportunities are offered to customers (especially in terms of quality improvement or responses to specific needs not met until then). Learning in new areas of expertise can result in better service to customers and thus raise their competitiveness as well. It might also create new market opportunities for industrial customers – e.g. in cases where innovation and KIE activity affect an intermediate input.

KIE can also change the way of competing by opening new options for competitive strategies; some firms can become first movers in industries where there are established competitors by introducing innovative solutions.

The creation of new fields of activity leverages the development of new technological capabilities (e.g. the establishment of a totally new and modern plant or the initiation of an innovative process that gives rise to differentiation), but also managerial capabilities, as KIE very often causes changes in the established value chain or depends on different types of suppliers or customers from previous regimes. In addition, one innovation may serve as the basis for the development of further innovations. For established companies, KIE is a way to differentiate themselves from established competitors and assure themselves the possibility of growth in times when competition squeezes out players in standard activities.

Another characteristic of KIE is visibility. Very often these ventures subscribe to best practices and this has a positive effect on their accessibility to banks, politicians and so on.

At the *sectoral level*, the impact of KIE activities relates to the development of the sectoral knowledge base, the nature of competition, the generation of new opportunities for new entrants and the diffusion of knowledge to the whole value chain, with positive effects sometimes for supplier's or customer's competitiveness.

Many of the case studies of KIE were the outcome of a combination of technologies or activities (e.g. biochemistry and biotechnology in food technology, or food production or textile manufacturing in the health sector, etc.). This expanded the sectoral knowledge base and had positive effects on competition as it created business opportunities for new entrants.

Taking into consideration the above points one can assume that, for countries whose specialization pattern is based on LMT industries, it is a reasonable strategy to look at the growth prospects of these industries and promote their transformation by supporting KIE activities.

However, to address this issue two more points that emerged from the case studies should be taken into account:

- KIE in LMT firms presents some similarities to high-tech firms: they use higher-skilled personnel than traditional LMT firms; though not performing formal R&D, to a large extent they intensively use knowledge from external sources to produce innovative solutions that go beyond established technological regimes; and they need a high level of technological, production and organizational capabilities to effectively exploit the external knowledge. In that sense one may argue that LMT industries constitute an engine for growth and competitiveness if subjected to a transformation process moving them towards knowledge-intensive activity.
- There is, however, a matter of complementarity with high-tech industries, as initially pointed out by Heidenreich (2009). Innovation and growth in LMT industries is largely shaped by technological advancements of suppliers, many of them in high- or medium-high-tech (HMT) industries. In addition, technological change proceeds faster but also tends to be more expensive (capital intensive), especially for high-tech (HT) industries (Strange, 1998), with the pace of change leaving less time for amortization of the innovation costs from profitable sales. Here KIE low- and medium-tech industries can open new market opportunities for high-tech industries. In that sense one might argue for the desirability of a more balanced pattern of specialization and development.

A question to be answered, however, is whether and to what extent in the context of globalization, international cooperation and proliferation of technological transfer mechanisms – it is relevant to raise this issue of complementarity at the national level. At the European level, however, it is definitely relevant.

The above discussion points to the need to address these issues in the context of the European industrial policy. In this context the European Commission has called for the reinforcement of certain 'Key Enabling Technologies' (KETs) such as ICTs, electronics, biotechnology and nanotechnologies. Although they present smaller direct returns on investment,

KETs are expected to have important indirect effects on job creation and growth and wealth in the economy and to boost competitiveness through their application (European Commission, 2010b). Some of the areas of application of key enabling technologies relate to LMT sectors (food, textiles, pulp and paper, fabricated metal products, etc.).

In the context of this policy framework it is important to promote interactions between developers and users of these technologies. In that way innovation could be facilitated.

There is also another important issue that relates to the capability of users to assimilate and exploit these technologies: Because LMT sectors are characterized as low-skilled, there is a need to promote improvement of absorptive capacity and technology management capability in these sectors. This might be done by intermediate organizations that could offer their services to low-tech firms to help them deal adequately with more complex techno-economic systems.

We believe that the above discussion is particularly relevant to countries that are highly specialized in LMT industrial activities. For countries where traditional industries dominate in terms of production value, exports and value added, the transformation towards knowledge-intensive activities should have important multiplier effects. It is crucial that firms in these industries develop their managerial and technological capabilities to increase productivity and profitability and thereby overcome competitive pressure from low-wage economies. Thus firms should adopt an 'open industrial model' of active adaptation to changing economic conditions while taking advantage of local assets, scientific and technological advancements in different domains and the expansion of external markets. Creating new economic value by exploiting knowledge bases already developed in other sectors and industries is the key to sustainable competitive advantage in LMT firms.

NOTES

1. The authors wish to thank Evangelos Siokas at LIEE/NTUA for data processing.
2. The 'revealed comparative advantage indicator' compares the share of a given sector's exports in the country's total manufacturing exports with the share of the same sector's exports in the total manufacturing exports of a group of reference countries. Values higher (lower) than one mean that a given industry performs better (worse) than the reference group and are interpreted as a sign of comparative advantage (disadvantage).
3. Upgrading is here defined as innovation producing an increase in the value added and not the result of cost reductions through e.g. 'squeezing wages'.
4. The field research was carried out in the context of the AEGIS project funded by the 7th Framework Programme of the European Commission.
5. The cutoff point of 10 per cent was chosen as it is very close to the median (6.7 per cent) of the LMT sample and there were no firms in the range from 6.7 to 10 per cent.

REFERENCES

Aiginger, K. (2006), 'Competitiveness: From a Dangerous Obsession to a Welfare Creating Ability with Positive Externalities', *Journal of Industry, Competition and Trade*, **6** (2), 161–77.

Bender, G. (2006), 'Peculiarities and Relevance of Non-Research-Intensive Industries in the Knowledge-Based Economy', final report of the project PILOT, Policy and Innovation in Low-Tech, available at http://citeseerx.ist.psu.edu/viewdoc/download?rep=rep1&type=pdf&doi=10.1.1.134.743 (accessed 23 May 2013).

Chandler Jr., Alfred D. (1990), *Scale and Scope: The Dynamics of Industrial Capitalism*, Cambridge, MA, USA and London, UK: Harvard University Press.

European Commission (2009), 'Report on the Competitiveness of the European Agro-Food Industry', vol. HLG.007, available at http://ec.europa.eu/enterprise/sectors/food/files/high_level_group_2008/documents_hlg/final_report_hlg_17_03_09_en.pdf (accessed 24 March 2013).

European Commission (2010a), 'EU Manufacturing Industry: What are the Challenges and Opportunities for the Coming Years?', available at http://ec.europa.eu/enterprise/policies/industrial-competitiveness/economic-crisis/files/eu_manufacturing_challenges_and_opportunities_en.pdf (accessed 15 March 2013).

European Commission (2010b), *European Competitiveness Report*, vol. III, available at www.uni-mannheim.de/edz/pdf/sek/2010/sek-2010-1276-3-en.pdf (accessed 20 March 2013).

European Commission (2011), 'European Industrial Structure: Trends and Performances', available at http://ec.europa.eu/enterprise/newsroom/cf/_getdocument.cfm?doc_id=7066 (accessed 3 April 2013).

European Commission (2012a), 'Reaping the Benefits of Globalization, European Competitiveness Report', available at http://ec.europa.eu/enterprise/policies/industrial-competitiveness/competitiveness-analysis/european-competitiveness-report/files/ecr2012_full_en.pdf (accessed 15 April 2013).

European Commission (2012b), 'Pulp and Paper Competitiveness', DG Enterprise and Industry, available at http://ec.europa.eu/enterprise/sectors/wood-paper-printing/paper/competitiveness/index_en.htm (accessed 1 October 2013).

Fagerberg, Jan, Mark Knell and Martin Srholec (2004), 'The Competitiveness of Nations: Economic Growth in the ECE Region', paper presented at the UNECE Spring Seminar on Competitiveness and Economic Growth in the ECE Region, 23 February 2004, available at www.unece.org/fileadmin/DAM/ead/sem/sem2004/papers/Fagerberg.pdf (accessed 24 September 2013).

Hatzichronoglou, T. (1996), 'Globalization and Competitiveness: Relevant Indicators', OECD Science, Technology and Industry Working Papers, available at http://dx.doi.org/10.1787/885511061376 (accessed 24 September 2013).

Hatzichronoglou, T. (1997), 'Revision of the High-Technology Sector and Product Classification', OECD Science, Technology and Industry Working Papers, available at http://dx.doi.org/10.1787/134337307632 (accessed 15 June 2013).

Heidenreich, M. (2009), 'Innovation Patterns and Location of European Low- and Medium-Technology Industries', *Research Policy*, **38** (3), 483–94.

Hirsch-Kreinsen, H. and I. Schwinge (2011), 'Knowledge-Intensive Entrepreneurship and Innovativeness in Traditional Industries: Conceptual Framework and

Empirical Findings', Deliverable 1.3.1 AEGIS Project, available at www.aegis-fp7.
eu/index.php?option=com_docman&task=doc_download&gid=64&Itemid=
12 (accessed 6 June 2013).

Laursen, K. and A. Salter (2006), 'Open for Innovation: The Role of Openness
in Explaining Innovation Performance among UK Manufacturing Firms',
Strategic Management Journal, **27** (2), 131–50.

Malerba, F. and M. McKelvey (2010), 'Conceptualizing Knowledge-Intensive
Entrepreneurship: Concepts and Models', Deliverable 1.1.1. AEGIS Project,
available   at   www.aegis-fp7.eu/index.php?option=com_docman&task=cat_
view&gid=93&Itemid=12 (accessed 13 August 2013).

March, J. (1991), 'Exploration and Exploitation in Organizational Learning',
Organization Science, **2** (1), 71–87.

Morrison, A., C. Pietrobelli and R. Rabellotti (2008), 'Global Value Chains and
Technological Capabilities: A Framework to Study Learning and Innovation in
Developing Countries', *Oxford Development Studies*, **36** (1), 39–58.

O'Mahony, Mary and Bart van Ark (eds) (2003), 'EU Productivity and
Competitiveness: An Industry Perspective – Can Europe Resume the
Catching-Up Process?', available at http://ec.europa.eu/enterprise/newsroom/
cf/_getdocument.cfm?doc_id=1752 (accessed 24 August 2013).

Peeters, A., B. Boussemart, F. Bruggeman and D. Paucart (2007), 'Report for the
European Textile and Clothing Social Partners to Secure Better Anticipation
and Management of Industrial Change and Sectorial Restructuring',
CÉDAC and Syndex seminars, available at www.mire-restructuring.eu/docs/
RapEuratexFSETHC%20En.pdf (accessed 26 September 2013).

Peneder, M. (2007), 'A Sectoral Taxonomy of Educational Intensity', *Journal of
Applied Economics & Economic Policy*, **34** (3), 189–212.

Scott, A. (2006), 'The Changing Global Geography of Low-Technology: Labor-
Intensive Industry – Clothing, Footwear and Furniture', *World Development*, **34**
(9), 1517–36.

Smith, K. (2002), 'What is the "Knowledge Economy"? Knowledge Intensity and
Distributed Knowledge Bases', Discussion Paper, United Nations University
Maastricht,   available   at   www.intech.unu.edu/publications/discussion-
papers/2002–6.pdf (accessed 4 June 2013).

Strange, S. (1998), 'Who are EU? Ambiguities in the Concept of Competitiveness',
Journal of Common Market Studies, **36** (1), 101–14.

PART II

Strategies and development prospects

Strategic and development prospects

5. Patterns and determinants of trademark use in Portugal[1]

Ricardo P. Mamede, Teresa F. Fernandes and Manuel M. Godinho

5.1 INTRODUCTION

A trademark is a sign used in economic activities by a producer or vendor to identify a particular product or service, enabling consumers to differentiate between the goods or services offered in the market and recognize their origins (Ramello, 2006). Even though a trademark is not directly informative about the quality of a product, it often provides this type of information by referring to consumers' own, or others', past experience (Economides, 1988). The economic value of trademarks, therefore, derives from the fact that they can be a solution (even if an incomplete one) to the problems of asymmetric information. On the other hand, as consumers' trademark loyalty also works as a barrier to the entry of new competitors in a market, it may also cause adverse effects by supporting existent oligopolistic advantages (ibid.).

Beyond their economic relevance to social welfare, trademarks have been a major focus of attention by their strong association with innovation activities. Because they are a source of visibility and reputation, trademarks become a strategic asset to firms that compete on the basis of product differentiation and customer loyalty. When successful, trademarks become associated with high perceived value to consumers and, consequently, they are a source of higher margins for the firms that register them. To the extent that trademarks help firms appropriate the returns on investments in product quality, they constitute an incentive for the introduction of new or improved goods and services in the economy (Landes and Posner, 1987; Economides, 1988). In other words, by contributing to the distinctiveness of firms' offers, trademarks give them an additional incentive to innovate.

In fact, trademarks seem to be strongly related to firms' innovation activities. Mendonça et al. (2004) find that innovative firms are more intensive users of trademarks and use trademarks more often than patents. This does not mean, however, that every new trademark is necessarily related to a new or improved product, nor do trademarks provide any measure of the degree of innovativeness of a new product. Still, firms that apply for a trademark are willing to pay the cost of obtaining and maintaining the exclusive right to use that trademark – which would hardly be the case if they did not believe that new trademarks allow customers to attach a distinct value to the associated products.

Consequently, the use of trademarks as indicators of innovation – or at least of some sort of entrepreneurial drive – has been growing in recent years. For example, Schmoch (2003) and Schmoch and Gauch (2009) have used trademarks to study innovation in services. Krasnikov et al. (2009), Greenhalgh and Rogers (2007) and Griffiths et al. (2005) have taken trademarks as a measure of innovativeness and assessed the impact of trademarking on firms' performance. And Mangani (2007) has used trademarks to measure the variety and quality of products.

Millot (2009) suggests that trademarks, taken as indicators, can be particularly suited to capture the presence of non-technological innovations and innovation activities in low-tech and service industries – cases in which the availability of innovation indicators is typically poor. In this sense, trademarks can be used to deepen our knowledge about innovation dynamics, especially in the context of less knowledge-intensive economic structures. The analysis of trademarks in the context of the so-called low-tech or low knowledge-intensive industries has become more relevant as many firms in these industries have been adopting complex innovative strategies based on the combination of knowledge inputs from many diverse sources. Some empirical studies have underscored the fact that firms in industries such as clothing or footwear, agro-food, or the paper and wood industries – often seen as 'old-fashioned' (Robertson et al., 2009) – have been quite innovative, despite the low R&D intensity of this sector (Hirsch-Kreinsen, 2008). The increasing interest in analysing innovation in the low-tech industries has also been justified both by the fact of these industries having a significant weight in the industrial structure of the advanced economies, and by the permanency of a high-tech 'bias' in the industrial policies of those economies (von Tunzelmann and Acha, 2005; Bender and Laestadius, 2005). The analysis of inter-sectoral variation in trademark use in relation to innovation may thus have relevant implications for the strategies of the innovative firms operating in the lower-tech or less knowledge-intensive industries.

The recent rise in the use of trademark statistics in innovation and marketing studies is partly explained by the increasing availability of and reliance on official databases, both at the national and international levels. However, those databases typically include very little information about the trademark holders (e.g. legal status, size, age, industry, and so on), making it necessary for researchers to match the information from trademark databases with other sources of micro-data in order to analyse the use of trademarks at the firm level. Also, different kinds of constraints (unavailability of extensive micro-databases, difficulties in matching different datasets, and so on) restrict micro-level analyses of trademarking usually to a relatively small sample of firms.

This chapter analyses the patterns and determinants of trademarking on the basis of a newly created dataset that combines the information provided by the Instituto Nacional de Propriedade Industrial (INPI) on national trademark applications in Portugal from 1995 to 2006, with Quadros de Pessoal micro-data, which contains relevant information on all the firms with employees that were active in the country in the same period. We describe the main patterns of trademark use in Portugal, and identify the characteristics of firms that are typically associated with trademark use.

The chapter is organized as follows. In the next section we describe the data. Section 3 presents the basic descriptive statistics of trademarking, and Section 4 puts the relevant variables into a multivariate framework (a logistic regression) in order to analyse the determinants of trademark use at the firm level. Section 5 concludes our contribution.

5.2   DATA

The integrated database used in this study was constructed by crossing two main sources of data. One is the Quadros de Pessoal (QP) database, which contains information on Portuguese employers and employees collected by the Portuguese Ministry of Employment on a yearly basis.[2] The QP questionnaire includes questions on the characteristics of both firms (e.g. total employment, industry classification, location, legal status, and so on) and their employees (gender, date of birth, educational background, professional category, type of contract, and so on). Both firms and workers are identified by their social security or fiscal numbers, making it possible to follow them over time and cross the QP database with other databases. In order to study the patterns and determinants of trademarks in Portugal, we combined the QP data with trademark data collected by the National Institute of Industrial Property (INPI).

The INPI data used in this chapter include the identification of the main applicant in every trademark application in Portugal since 1995. They do not, however, include any detailed information about the applicant, limiting the scope of economic analyses that can be carried out with those data. By crossing the QP and the INPI databases we were able to unequivocally identify the main applicants in about 52 per cent of the trademark applications between 1995 and 2006.[3] Since the QP includes all firms employing paid labor in Portugal, we believe that the remaining applications (that is, those for which we could not identify the owner) were submitted mainly by sole-proprietorship firms, foreign firms without employees operating in Portugal, and non-corporate public entities. Therefore we did not consider these types of entities for this chapter.

Moreover, we restricted the scope of the analysis to market-oriented industries. These are manufacturing, electricity, gas and water supply, construction, wholesale and retail trade, hotels and restaurants, transport and communication, financial intermediation, and real estate, renting and business services. We also excluded firms of only one employee.[4]

5.3   PATTERNS OF TRADEMARKING

The yearly percentage of firms applying for trademarks since 1995 (Figure 5.1) remained low over the period analysed, increasing slightly from 0.7 per cent (out of 141 438 firms) at the beginning to 1 per cent in 2006 (out of 214 540 firms). The percentage of existing firms that have applied for at least one trademark up to a certain year increased from 3.5 per cent in 1995 to 5.6 per cent in 2006. The increase is especially notable from 2002 onwards, which is explained by a higher incidence of trademark use among newer firms.

The use of trademarks varies widely across industries. Retail and wholesale trade, hotels and restaurants, and business services accounted for more than half the firms applying for trademarks in 2006. However, these are also industries with a high number of total firms, so in relative terms their trademark use is not particularly intense.

By contrast, the proportion of firms applying for trademarks is more noticeable in financial services, chemical products, R&D, ICT services, publishing and printing, basic metals, and food and beverage products (Figure 5.2).[5] In other words, among the industries that use trademarks most intensively we find many knowledge-intensive services, but also manufacturing industries with varying levels of knowledge intensity. In any case the proportion of firms applying for trademarks has always been modest (never above 9 per cent).

Several factors may account for the different intensities of trademark use by firms across industries. On one hand, the conditions that lead to competition being based on product differentiation and customer

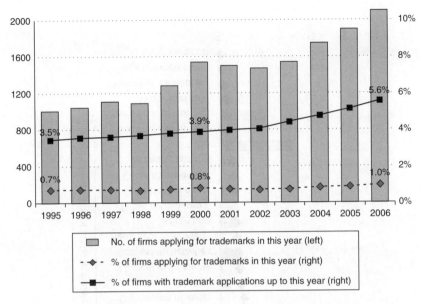

Figure 5.1   Evolution of the number and percentage of firms applying for trademarks

loyalty – features that create incentives for protecting a brand name and image, as discussed above – are unevenly distributed among industries. On the other, given the heterogeneity of productivity, industries also differ in their capacity to pay high wages and, therefore, to recruit more competent managers and employees, which may translate into the adoption of more sophisticated business strategies by a larger proportion of firms in some industries (more on this below).

Such features can be proxied by two types of variables for which data is available: the qualification of the workforce (proxied by the proportion of workers holding a university degree) and, to a lesser extent, the industry's marketing intensity (proxied by the average expenditures on publicity of firms). Both variables are positively related with the proportion of firms applying for trademarks. Figure 5.3 illustrates that relationship for human capital.

At the industry level, trademarking seems to be determined by the value assigned to visibility and reputation by more sophisticated firms, at least as much as by the structural features of each industry. This idea is confirmed by the analysis of the relation between firm size and the frequency of trademark use. As Figure 5.4 shows, the proportion of firms applying for trademarks is larger for larger firms. To some extent, this

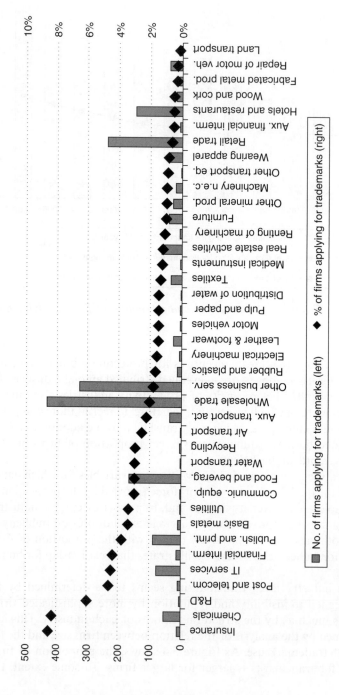

Figure 5.2   Firms applying for trademarks by industry

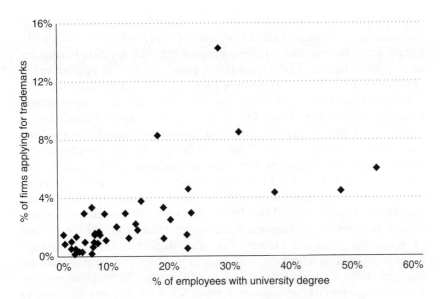

Figure 5.3 *The relation between the proportion of firms applying for trademarks and the industries' human capital*

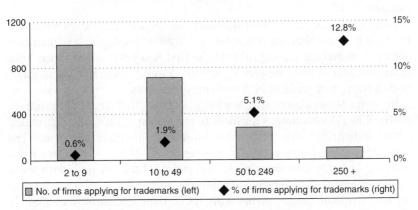

Figure 5.4 *Firms applying for trademarks by firm size in number of employees (2006)*

suggests that either the use of trademarks is associated with more professional management structures, or the net benefits of trademarking are proportional to the scale of operations (which is reasonable, given that the cost of registering a trademark is the same regardless the size of the company), or both.

If that is the case, one could expect that in regions which concentrate a larger proportion of firms with more sophisticated management structures and wider scale of operations, the intensity of trademarking is also greater. Figure 5.5 confirms this intuition by showing that the two Portuguese metropolitan regions, Lisbon and Porto, stand out both in relative and in absolute terms in their proportion of firms applying for trademarks.

Interestingly, trademarking is also relatively intense in some manu-facturing regions (e.g. Entre Douro e Vouga and Baixo Vouga) and in regions with highly characteristic and well-known consumer products (e.g. Serra da Estrela, home of the most famous Portuguese cheese, and Douro, where the legendary Port wine is produced). This suggests that the use of trademarks may be a rather localized phenomenon, which may be explained by at least two factors. In the case of regions with typical, well-known consumer products, firms often compete by signaling to con-sumers the genuine and unique character of their products (in the face of imitations and other brands); this often implies a strong investment in both product development and branding, which can be protected (at least partially) through trademarks. Additionally, the regional concen-tration of trademarking firms may result from the attempt to replicate the business strategies of successful local firms, possibly with the help of business consultants specializing in intellectual property rights (IPR) management.[6]

Finally, the frequency of trademark use is also related to firm age. Figure 5.6 shows that the percentage of firms applying for trademarks is higher than average among firms in the first two years of existence, both in relative and in absolute terms, suggesting that trademarks are in many cases a relevant ingredient of firms' entry strategies.

In sum, these descriptive statistics suggest that trademark use in Portugal is: (1) uncommon for most firms; (2) asymmetrically distributed across industries, with both more knowledge-intensive and some less knowledge-intensive industries displaying greater-than-average use of this IPR; (3) strongly concentrated in the metropolitan regions (with some smaller regions also showing a relatively intensive use of trademarks); (4) less frequent among firms with fewer than ten employees than in those with more, and disproportionally frequent among large firms; and (5) more common among new firms than in older ones. In what follows we put these and other variables in a multivariate regression framework in order to identify the most relevant determinants of trademark use in Portugal.

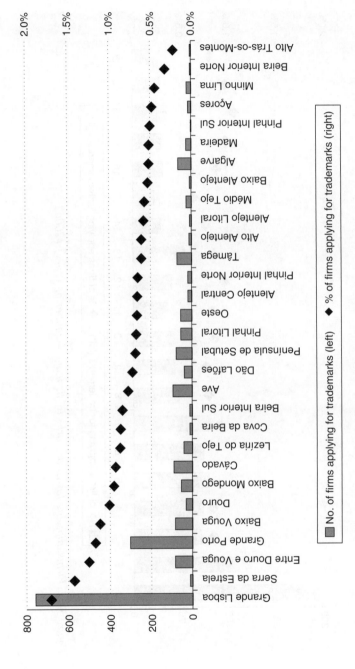

Figure 5.5   Firms applying for trademarks by region NUTS 3 (2006)

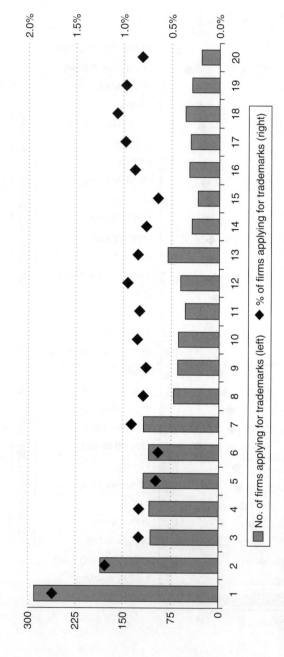

Figure 5.6 Firms applying for trademarks by firm age (number of years) (2006)

5.4 DETERMINANTS OF TRADEMARK USE AT THE FIRM LEVEL

5.4.1 Estimation Method

To identify the structural determinants of trademarking we used a simple Logit Regression Model. This well-known method describes the relationship between a binary dependent variable and one or more explanatory variables, accounting for the relative probability (odds) of obtaining a given binomial result category. Hosmer and Lemeshow (2000) use the following specific form of the logistic regression model

$$\pi = \frac{e^{\beta_0 + \beta_1 x}}{1 + e^{\beta_0 + \beta_1 x}}$$

which is bounded between zero and one, and whose errors follow a binomial distribution (Bernoulli) instead of a normal distribution as in a Linear Regression Model.

Basically, the logit transforms the previous equation into

$$g(x) - \ln \left[\frac{\pi(x)}{1 - \pi(x)} \right] = \beta_0 + \beta_1 x$$

so that it has many of the desirable properties of a linear regression model: it is linear in its parameters and, depending on the range of x, it may be continuous and range from $-\infty$ to $+\infty$.

Usually the coefficients in the logistic model describe the variation in the log-odds when the regressor x increases by one unit, *ceteris paribus*. The interpretation of those parameters is given by the anti-log of each coefficient, e^{β}, which is the change in the adjusted odds-ratio. One can also compute $1 - e^{\beta}$ to obtain the percentage increase (or decrease) in the adjusted odds-ratio for every unit increase in the regressor. Thus in the present case the adjusted odds-ratio is the variation in odds of a firm applying for trademarks when the value of the regressor increases by one.

Although it is easy to move from odds to probabilities, we will present the results in odds, since the interpretation of the coefficients is then more straightforward.

5.4.2 Hypotheses

Following the introductory literature review and the discussion in Section 3, we analyse the determinants of trademarks by testing the following hypotheses.

Hypothesis 1: The use of trademarks is more frequent among new firms, after controlling for industry effects.

In the descriptive section we showed that the percentage of firms applying for trademarks is higher among new firms. We suspect that this is related to the fact that some entrants use trademarks as part of their entry strategies to signal the distinctiveness of their offers or to protect their initial investments from future imitators. However, in order to test this hypothesis it is important to control for industry effects. Since industries display significant differences in both trademark use by firms (Section 3) and in entry rates (e.g. Geroski, 1995), without control for industry effects, the correlation between the propensity for trademark use and being a new firm could result from a greater number of firms in the database that are simultaneously more intensive users of trademarks and are new firms.

Hypothesis 2: The use of trademarks is more frequent in locations with a higher density of trademark users, and especially if they belong to the same industry, after controlling for metropolitan regions, industry effects, and firm size.

Firms with a wider geographical range of operations tend to locate their headquarters in metropolitan regions. Since those firms tend to pursue more sophisticated strategies and have more professional management structures, one should expect more propensity for trademark use in firms located in such regions than in those located elsewhere. Therefore, it is reasonable to include location in metropolitan regions as a control variable in our regressions. However, there are reasons to believe that location matters beyond the aforementioned factors. On the one hand, some territories may have a disproportionate amount of firms in specific niche activities that are particularly active in trademarking. On the other hand, trademark use by firms may be partly explained by imitative behavior at the local level: direct contact with firms that have benefited from registering and maintaining their trademarks may create extra incentives for neighboring firms to follow the same strategy; alternatively, one may assume that a relevant underlying cause for trademark use by firms is the influence exerted by local business consultants that particularly favors trademarks as a business strategy. This explanation is all the more reasonable in light of the relative ignorance of firms regarding the use of trademarks. For example, in their survey on the use of IPR by Portuguese firms, Godinho et al. (2003) showed that the relatively low levels of IPR use in the country is largely determined by the firms' lack of knowledge about the costs and benefits of these instruments. Therefore if we control for other relevant factors, we expect the propensity of a firm to use trademarks to be greater in regions where the level of use of trademarks is high.

Hypothesis 3: The use of trademarks is more frequent among firms with a higher level of human capital, after controlling for size, industry, and regional effects.

It is shown above that the industries with the highest percentage of firms applying for trademarks are typically characterized by high levels of human capital (proxied by the proportion of employees with an academic degree). Regardless of industry (that is, after this factor is controlled for), we expect firms which are managed by more highly qualified staff to have a greater propensity to use trademarks, since the latter is most probably related to more sophisticated management practices. However, since the presence of highly qualified managers is related to size and location factors (highly educated people often prefer to live in metropolitan regions where they benefit from better amenities), we should include such factors as controls in our regressions.

Hypothesis 4: The use of trademarks is more frequent among multi-establishment firms, after controlling for size, industry, and regional effects.

We also expect multi-establishment firms to display a higher propensity to trademark, regardless of their size, industry, and location. Especially in the case of business strategies encompassing the direct sale to end-users in different locations, trademarks are often necessary to protect the value of substantial fixed investments in both infrastructure and branding.

Hypothesis 5: The use of trademarks is highly idiosyncratic, with some firms being recurrent users of trademarks.

While we expect all the above factors to influence the firms' propensity for trademarking, the very small number of firms which actually use this IPR mechanism suggests that a substantial part of the explanation for trademark use at the firm level is not captured by the diversity of variables mentioned above. In other words, the propensity for trademark use may be largely due to unobservable, idiosyncratic characteristics of firms, which lead them to consider trademarks as a valuable practice in their business strategy. We attempt to partly capture such characteristics by including in our regressions the occurrence of trademark applications of the firm in previous periods. After controlling for all the other meas-urable features, we expect the probability of applying for a trademark in a certain year to be greater in firms that have previously applied for trademarks.

5.4.3   Variables Used in the Regression

Our dependent variable is the binary variable *Trademark (TM) Applicant*, which equals one if the firm i applied for trademarks in 2006 (the last year for which we had data from the two sources used in this chapter), and zero otherwise.

Among the explanatory variables we used the following control variables:

Industry effect, for each firm i, is the percentage of firms (excluding the firm i) in the same sector as the firm i (NACE Rev. 2 at three-digit level) that applied for trademarks in the last three years;

Metropolitan center is a dummy variable that assumes the value one if the firm i is from Lisbon or from Porto (NUT 3), and zero otherwise;

Size 10 to 49 and *Size 50 or more* are dummy variables for firms' size groups, respectively, ten up to 49 employees, and more than 49 employees, assuming the value one if the firm i is included in the size group, and zero otherwise.

In order to test the hypotheses listed above, we computed the following variables:

For Hypothesis 1, *New firm* is a dummy variable that assumes the value one if the firm i is in its first or second year of existence in 2006 and zero otherwise;[7]

For Hypothesis 2, *Regional effect*, for each firm i, is the percentage of firms (excluding the firm i) in the same region as the firm i (municipality level) that applied for trademarks in the last three years; and *Regional-industry effect*, for each firm i, is the percentage of firms (excluding the firm i) in the same region and in the same industry (municipality level and NACE Rev. 2 at two-digit level) that applied for trademarks within the last three years;

For Hypothesis 3, *Employer with university degree* is a dummy variable which assumes the value one if the firm i has one or more employers with a university degree and zero otherwise; and *Employee with business studies degree* is a dummy variable which assumes the value one if the firm i has one or more employees with an academic degree in business sciences and zero otherwise;

For Hypothesis 4, *Multi-establishment firm* is a dummy variable which assumes the value one if the firm i has two or more establishments and zero otherwise.

Finally, for Hypothesis 5, *Recurrent TM applicant* is a dummy variable which assumes the value one if the firm *i* applied for trademarks in 2004 or 2005 and zero otherwise.

The bivariate correlations between the variables used in the regressions and the basic descriptive statistics are presented in Tables 5.1 and 5.2.

5.4.4   Regression Results

Table 5.3 displays different specifications of our model, all of which confirm the hypotheses listed above.

In the first regression we included only the control variables – the industry effect, the dummy for firms located in one of the two metropolitan centers, and the size dummies. Without consideration of other explanatory variables, the results show that for each 1 per cent increase in the proportion of firms applying for trademarks in the same industry, the likelihood of being a trademark user goes up by 10 per cent; since the value of this variable spans 0–75 per cent (Table 5.2), this confirms that the industry effect has a substantial impact on the probability of trademarking. The results also show that medium and large firms have more than seven times the odds of applying for trademarks than very small firms (the benchmark), while firms located in a metropolitan area have nearly twice the odds of trademarking.

Regressions 2 to 6 include alternately the variables we chose to test the five hypotheses put forward in this chapter.

In regression 2 we do not reject the hypothesis of a positive impact of being a new firm on the probability of trademarking. From the results of this regression, compared to other firms entrants have a 2.7-times higher probability of applying for trademarks. Interestingly, the odds-ratios for other than very small firms increase after we consider the effect of entrants. This may be due to the fact that a substantial part of the very small firms applying for trademarks do it soon after they enter the market.[8] In regression 3 we consider the effect on trademarking of being in a location where a large proportion of firms also apply for trademarks, as well as the effect of being both in a location and in an industry in which a large proportion of firms also apply for trademarks. The results confirm that, even after the effect of being located in a metropolitan region is controlled for, co-location seems to be a relevant determinant of trademarking, especially in the case of co-location of firms in the same industry. The probability of trademarking increases 23 per cent for each percentage point change in the proportion of firms applying for trademarks in the same region, and 3 per cent for each percentage point change in the proportion of firms in the same industry and located in the same region that apply for trademarks. Note, however, that the variability

Table 5.1 Bivariate correlation matrix

Variables	TM applicant	Industry effect	Metropolitan center (dummy)	Size 10 to 49 (dummy)	Size 50 or more (dummy)	New firm (dummy)	Regional effect	Employer with university degree (dummy)	Employee with business studies degree (dummy)	Recurrent TM applicant (dummy)
TM applicant	1.00									
Industry effect	0.13	1.00								
Metropolitan center (dummy)	0.04	0.07	1.00							
Size 10 to 49 (dummy)	0.04	0.07	0.01	1.00						
Size 50 or more (dummy)	0.09	0.12	0.03	−0.08	1.00					
New firm (dummy)	0.02	−0.01	−0.02	−0.06	−0.04	1.00				
Regional effect	0.05	0.12	0.61	0.02	0.06	−0.02	1.00			
Employer with university degree (dummy)	0.04	0.10	0.11	0.04	0.01	0.02	0.13	1.00		
Employee with business studies degree (dummy)	0.10	0.17	0.10	0.14	0.29	−0.03	0.14	0.22	1.00	
Recurrent TM applicant (dummy)	0.19	0.18	0.05	0.06	0.11	−0.02	0.07	0.04	0.13	1.00

Note: All coefficients are significant at 5% level.

Table 5.2   Basic descriptive statistics for the variables used in the regressions

Dummy variables	Yes cases	
	N.	%
TM applicant	2102	1%
Metropolitan center (dummy)	70050	33%
Size 10 to 49 (dummy)	37005	17%
Size 50 or more (dummy)	6304	3%
New firm (dummy)	20893	10%
Employer with university degree (dummy)	18841	9%
Employee with business studies degree (dummy)	16575	8%
Recurrent TM applicant (dummy)	3477	2%
Continuous variables	average	sd
Industry effect	2.0	2.8
Regional effect	2.0	1.1
Regional-industry effect	2.0	2.5

Note: Total number of observations: 214540.

of the *regional-industry effect* variable is substantially *greater* than that of the *regional effect* variable. In other words, the high concentration of trademarking firms in the same industry in a specific region can have a relevant impact on the probability of using trademarks, even after control for industry effects and regional effects. As expected, after introducing those two region-related variables in the regression, the odds-ratio of being in a metropolitan area decreases considerably. Still, being in one of the two metropolitan regions increases the odds of trademarking by nearly 30 per cent.

Regression 4 includes the variables related to human capital. On the basis of these results we do not reject the hypothesis that the use of trademarks is more frequent among firms with more skilled employees. According to these results, having at least one academic degree-holder on the management team increases the probability of trademarking by 2/3. More expressively, having at least one employee holding a degree in business studies increases such probability by 2.5. It is worth noting that the odds-ratio for medium-size and large firms decreases considerably in this regression, confirming the notion that bigger firms typically have more access to human capital.

The results of regression 5 show that, if only the control variables and the multi-establishment dummy variable are considered, the probability

Table 5.3 *Regression results*

Variables	Coefficients for each regression*						
	1	2	3	4	5	6	7
Industry effect	1.10	1.10	1.10	1.10	1.10	1.08	1.07
Metropolitan center (dummy)	1.93	1.95	1.31	1.70	1.85	1.78	1.19
Size 10 to 49 (dummy)	2.95	3.21	2.91	2.48	2.68	2.53	2.29
Size 50 or more (dummy)	7.57	8.43	7.03	4.69	5.88	5.03	3.27
New firm (dummy)		2.67					2.99
Regional effect			1.23				1.14
Regional-industry effect			1.03				1.03
Employer with university degree (dummy)				1.67			1.59
Employee with degree in business studies (dummy)				2.46			1.96
Multi-establishment firm (dummy)					1.82		1.54
Reccurent TM applicant (dummy)						10.43	9.03
Model Summary							
-2 Log likelihood	21218	21003	21082	20859	21124	20103	19943
Cox & Snell R Square	1.1%	1.2%	1.2%	1.3%	1.4%	1.7%	1.9%
Nagelkerke R Square	10.7%	11.7%	11.3%	12.3%	11.1%	15.6%	18.3%

Note: * Results presented in odd ratios; all coefficients are significant at 1% level; number of observations: 214 540.

of trademarking is 82 per cent higher for multi-establishment firms. Introducing this dummy reduces to some extent the size effect (especially for firms with over 50 employees), suggesting that the greater incidence of multiple-establishment firms among larger firms is one of the reasons why the frequency of trademarking is greater in this size group.

In regression 6 we consider the effect of having been a trademark applicant in previous years. The results of this regression seem to confirm the notion that the use of trademarks is a somewhat idiosyncratic feature of firms: for reasons that are not captured by the basic control variables, nor by the other available explanatory variables, some firms display a recurrent tendency to trademark. Using only the control variables and a dummy that identifies firms that have applied for trademarks within the previous two years, we conclude that recurrent trademark users have 7.5 times more probability of applying for a trademark in a given year than other firms. Once we consider the effect of recurrent trademark applications, the odds-ratios related to size dummies is somewhat reduced with regard to the previous regressions.[9]

In general, the results presented above remain valid when all the explanatory variables are included simultaneously, as in regression 7.

The fact that our dependent variable has a very reduced proportion (about 1 per cent) of 'yes cases' affects the overall predictive capacity of our models (which, accordingly, fail the Hosmer and Lemeshow test). Notwithstanding, the variables in the regressions always provide a good joint fit (passing the Omnibus Tests of Coefficients), and all the coefficients are statistically significant, with p-values near or equal to zero, allowing us to conclude that, both jointly and individually, all the explanatory variables used here are relevant to understanding the still little-studied phenomenon of trademarking.

5.5   CONCLUSIONS

In this chapter we provide the first results drawn from an integrated database that combines information on national trademark applications with micro-data on all firms with employees in Portugal. We describe the main patterns of trademark use in the country and identify the characteristics of firms that are typically associated with trademark use.

The descriptive analysis leads to the conclusion that trademark use in Portugal is: (1) uncommon for most firms; (2) asymmetrically distributed across industries, with both more knowledge-intensive and some less knowledge-intensive industries displaying greater than average use of this IPR; (3) strongly concentrated in the metropolitan regions (though some smaller regions also show a relatively more intensive use of trademarks); (4) less frequent among firms of fewer than ten employees than in those of larger firm size, and disproportionally frequent among large firms; and (5), more common among new firms than in older ones.

Our regression results largely confirm the notion that firm-specific variables are very relevant predictors of trademark use, even after control for industry effects. In particular, new firms reveal a greater propensity for trademarking, while trademark use is more probable among bigger firms than in smaller ones. Also human capital – in particular, business degree-holders in firm management – is a relevant determinant of trademarking. Even more importantly, the probability of applying for trademarks is to a high degree determined by the previous use of this IPR mechanism.

The regression results also show that geographical proximity plays an important role in explaining trademark use by firms – even after control for the greater propensity for trademarking of firms located in metropolitan centers. This is especially the case of neighboring firms that belong to the same industry, suggesting that trademarking is a characteristic feature of some local clusters.

These conclusions indicate, therefore, that the use of trademarks is not primarily dependent on the knowledge intensity of the industries the firms belong to, but rather on certain individual characteristics of the firms. A relevant implication for the more innovative firms operating in the so-called low-tech and less knowledge-intensive industries is that the use of trademarks may thus be a valid option for reinforcing their strategies, as much as it is for the innovative firms operating in the more knowledge-intensive industries.

NOTES

1. This research was conducted within AEGIS ('Advancing Knowledge-Intensive Entrepreneurship and Innovation for Economic Growth and Social Well-being in Europe'), a project co-funded by the European Commission under Theme 8, 'Socio-Economic Sciences and Humanities', of the '7th Framework Programme for Research and Technological Development'.
2. This annual reporting is mandatory for all firms employing paid labor in Portugal.
3. The number of trademark applications recorded by INPI each year has varied between 8306 in 1995 and 12 894 in 2006, totaling 102 833 applications over the period.
4. In many firms the only employee is the firm owner. However, there are instances of sole-proprietor firms in which the owner does not declare him- or herself as an employee. The reasons that lead a firm owner to register him- or herself as an employee are rather arbitrary. However, only those firms declaring at least one employee are registered in the QP database.
5. These results largely converge with those of Baroncelli et al. (2005) who find that, at the world level, trademarks are mostly concentrated in research- and development-

intensive industries (pharmaceuticals, scientific equipment, and the chemical industry), in advertising-intensive industries (clothing, footwear, detergents, and food products), and also in the service sector.

6. Godinho et al. (2003) find that firms often lack knowledge regarding the costs and benefits, as well as the administrative procedures involved in trademarking. This creates a situation of asymmetric information, increasing the capacity of consultants to influence the decisions of firms regarding the use of trademarks.

7. In order to compute the age variable we considered the administrative records. In most cases, since reporting to the QP database is mandatory, the first year of activity of a firm must match its first year in the administrative register. We ran several quality checks in the data in order to minimize the possibility of errors in the age variable.

8. Although we do not deal with this issue in the present chapter, it can be shown that bigger firms that apply for trademarks in a given year tend to have already applied for trademarks in previous years.

9. This happens mainly because the size distribution of firms that apply for trademarks for the first time is different from the size distribution of firms which are recurrent applicants. Although this issue is beyond the scope of this chapter, it can be shown that firms applying for trademarks for the first time in 2006 are mostly very small firms (62 per cent), while firms that have multiple applications are mainly small, medium-size or large firms (jointly 72 per cent).

REFERENCES

Bender, G. and S. Laestadius (2005), 'Non-Science-Based Innovativeness: On Capabilities Relevant to Generate Profitable Novelty', *Perspectives on Economic Political and Social Integration*, **11** (1/2), 123–70.

Economides, N. (1988), 'The Economics of Trademarks', *Trademark Reporter*, **78** (July–August), 523–39.

Geroski, P.A. (1995), 'What Do We Know about Entry?', *International Journal of Industrial Organization*, **13** (4), 421–40.

Godinho, M.M., T.S. Pereira, V.C. Simões, S. Mendonça and V. Sousa (2003), 'Estudo Sobre a Utilização da Propriedade Industrial em Portugal', vol. 1, available at www.marcasepatentes.pt/files/collections/pt_PT/1/8/65/Vol.%20I%20-%20Estudo%20sobre%20a%20utiliza%C3%A7%C3%A3o%20da%20PI%20em%20Portugal.pdf (accessed 23 August 2013).

Greenhalgh, C. and M. Rogers (2007), 'Trade Marks and Performance in UK Firms: Evidence of Schumpeterian Competition through Innovation', Economic Series Working Paper, University of Oxford, available at http://economics.ouls.ox.ac.uk/13545/1/Item.pdf (accessed 5 August 2013).

Griffiths, W.E., P.H. Jensen and E. Webster (2005), 'The Effects on Firm Profits of the Stock of Intellectual Property Rights', working paper, Intellectual Property Research Institute of Australia, available at www.ipria.com/publications/wp/2005/IPRIAWP05.2005.pdf (accessed 2 August 2013).

Hirsch-Kreinsen, H. (2008), 'Low-Technology: A Forgotten Sector in Innovation Policy', *Journal of Technology Management & Innovation*, **3** (3), 11–20.

Hosmer, David W. and Stanley Lemeshow (2000), *Applied Logistic Regression*, 2nd edn, New York, USA: John Wiley & Sons.

Krasnikov, A., S. Mishra and D. Orozo (2009), 'Evaluating the Financial Impact of Branding using Trademarks: A Framework and Empirical Evidence', *Journal of Marketing*, **73** (6), 154–66.

Landes, William M. and Richard A. Posner (eds) (1987), *The Economic Structure of Intellectual Property Law*, Cambridge, MA, USA: Harvard University Press.

Mangani, A. (2007), 'Measuring Variety and Quality of Products with Trademarks', *International Economic Journal*, **21** (4), 613–31.

Mendonça, S., T. Pereira and M. Godinho (2004), 'Trademarks as an Indicator of Industrial Change', *Research Policy*, **33** (9), 1385–404.

Millot, V. (2009), 'Trademarks as an Indicator of Product and Marketing Innovations', OECD Science, Technology and Industry Working Papers, available at www.oecd-ilibrary.org/docserver/download/5kskrw3cq036.pdf?expires= 1381221173&id=id&accname=guest&checksum=19E4A3ED452A7AD99F11 CAAD0DD62DFE (accessed 4 August 2013).

Ramello, G. (2006), 'What's in a Sign? Trademark Law and Economic Theory', *Journal of Economic Surveys*, **20** (4), 547–65.

Robertson, P., K. Smith and N. von Tunzelmann (2009), 'Introduction: Innovation in Low- and Medium-Technology Industries', *Research Policy*, **38** (3), 441–6.

Schmoch, U. (2003), 'Service Marks as a Novel Innovation Indicator', *Research Evaluation*, **12** (2), 149–56.

Schmoch, U. and S. Gauch (2009), 'Service Marks as Indicators for Innovation in Knowledge Based Services', *Research Evaluation*, **18** (4), 323–35.

Von Tunzelmann, Nick and Virginia Acha (2005), 'Innovation in "Low-Tech" Industries' in Jan Fagerberg, David C. Mowery and Richard R. Nelson (eds), *The Oxford Handbook of Innovation*, New York, USA: Oxford University Press, pp. 407–32.

6. High-growth LMT firms and the evolution of the Russian economy[1]

Andrei Yudanov

6.1 INTRODUCTION

Joseph Schumpeter was among the first to distinguish the innovative activity of an entrepreneur from technological innovations – and much more so from inventions. He stated that the main task of the entrepreneur is to carry out new combinations which might be not just technological but also marketing-oriented (new markets for existing goods) or managerial (new forms of industrial organization) in nature (Schumpeter, 1951: 131–5). At the time of writing, the best-known reference work about tracking innovative processes with such a broad understanding is the *Oslo Manual: Guidelines for Collecting and Interpreting Innovation Data* (OECD, 2005a; see also the theoretical concept of KIE: Malerba, 2010).

In practice, however, innovations are often considered almost exclusively to consist in the development of new technologies. Moreover, the degree of innovativeness of a firm or a branch tends to be reduced to easily measurable aspects of their technological activity: the level of R&D expenditures, the number of research personnel, or the number of registered patents. The emergence of concrete quantitative recommendations of the OECD (1996; 2002; 2005b) which divides various industries of the economy into categories of 'high-tech', 'medium-high-tech', 'medium-low-tech', or 'low-tech', derived as the ratio of R&D expenditures to the output value of a branch, could be considered as the logical conclusion of this tendency.

Nevertheless, the R&D-oriented approach never found substantial support in at least two spheres of research, specifically, low-tech industries and high-growth firms. Thus with reference to the low-tech sector it has been shown that the basic volume of innovation used in a finished product often does not come from a firm's own technological achievements but from the achievements of other industries and their adaptation to the concrete requirements of consumers (Hirsch-Kreinsen and Jacobson, 2008; Kirner et al., 2009). It has also been discovered that in this sector 'formalized processes of knowledge generation and use only play an insignificant role' and that innovation is based on practical knowledge, which 'is generated in application contexts of new technologies and obeys validity criteria such as practicability, functionality, efficiency and failure-free use of a given technology' (Hirsch-Kreinsen, 2008: 27).

Independent of the above, research on high-growth firms, also called 'gazelle-firms', comes to similar conclusions about the importance of informal innovations. David Birch coined the expression 'gazelle' in his 1987 study of the job-generation process in the USA (Birch, 1987). Birch's empirical research shows that most large and small firms make a very modest contribution to job creation and gross domestic product (GDP) growth. But there is a small group of firms, which he called 'gazelles', that are distinguished by their long-term dynamism. In his initial estimates, gazelles, while constituting only 4 per cent of the total number of firms, created about 70 per cent of all new jobs in the American economy in 1988–92 (Birch and Medoff, 1994).

The discovery of a special type of firm with exceptional value for the development of the economy could not but attract steadfast attention. Despite some outspoken criticism (e.g. Davis et al., 1996), Birch's conclusions have received considerable international acknowledgement (Kirchhoff, 1994; Delmar et al., 2003; Mitusch and Schimke, 2011; NESTA, 2011). One of the most-cited reviews of the literature devoted to gazelles says:

> A few rapidly growing firms generate a disproportionately large share of all new net jobs compared with non-high-growth firms. This is a clear-cut result. All studies find Gazelles to generate a large share, all or more than all net jobs (in the case where employment shrinks in non-Gazelle firms taken as a whole). (Henrekson and Johansson, 2010: 240)

While certainly establishing a fact, the research on gazelles also produced an unexpected result, showing that they do not necessarily operate in the high-tech sector. On the contrary, the majority of gazelles are concentrated in mature, low- and medium-low-tech (LMT) sectors (for a collection of modern international data, see Mitusch and Schimke, 2011). As a rule, the R&D expenditures of gazelles are not high. Yet a more detailed analysis in almost every case revealed a 'highlight', a certain informal innovation that guaranteed the success of a gazelle.

With reference to modern Russia, to consider innovative activity in the full variety of its manifestations (and not just R&D-intensive innovations) is especially valuable and timely, as it creates adequate instruments to study the extremely unusual processes that began to develop in the country after the fall of the Soviet Union. Crucially, the former, centrally planned

National Innovation System (NIS) of the Soviet Union not only ceased to exist but practically all R&D activities in the country collapsed. The complete cessation of state orders for scientific research rendered most state-owned centers for science and research unviable.

Against this background the R&D activities of newly established private companies amounted to almost zero. The Russian economy was being transformed from a planned economy into a market economy under extremely liberal conditions of international openness. Consequently, the qualitative superiority of imported products proved itself so vividly as to cause the mass replacement of domestic high-tech production. Instead of pursuing their own R&D activity, Russian firms received and copied foreign technology. In other cases, national R&D activity was not even replaced with analogous foreign technologies but with directly imported products embodying foreign knowledge.

At the same time the country's high educational and scientific potential has appeared more resistant to shocks than other elements of the Russian NIS. Despite the menacing brain drain, millions of highly qualified specialists have remained in the country. Despite changed conditions, these people have found their place in business (for the latest review of the literature devoted to Russian entrepreneurship, see Chepurenko and Yakovlev, 2013). In Russia, cases such as a successful shoe firm headed by a trained nuclear physicist or a confectionery firm run by a group of former military engineers have been the rule rather than exceptions. It is no wonder that the combination of extensive educational backgrounds among the leaders of Russian business and the low commercial return from formal R&D expenditures stimulated and promoted the large scope of informal innovative activity.

Knowledge-intensive entrepreneurship (KIE) in Russia began to develop mainly with LMT-type (or gazelle-type) innovation activities rather than R&D-intensive innovation activities. Gazelles became initiators of the major structural transformations in the Russian economy. In areas where gazelles began to operate, the innovations introduced by them changed the profile of the corresponding industries within a few years.

Accordingly, this chapter is structured as follows: Section 2 gives a short overview of the dramatic decrease in R&D activity as a result of a transition to the market economy. Section 3 describes the Russian gazelles and their importance for the national economy. And Section 4 discusses the role of gazelle-type LMT firms as agents of the rapid evolution of the Russian economy.

6.2   BACKGROUND: COLLAPSE OF THE NATIONAL R&D SYSTEM

In the first decades of post-Soviet development, the R&D-oriented method of developing KIE practically ended for Russian firms, first of all because of the catastrophic decrease in state demand for high-tech production and scientific development. Expensive research equipment was written off as waste for the sake of ridiculously meager benefits from renting out the emptied premises (after destruction of their equipment, laboratory buildings were often used as warehouses). Even current research expenses (purchase of reactants, accounting materials, and so forth) were no longer financed. Highly skilled experts left the country or for decades were compelled to reconcile themselves with a meager salary.

As a result there was a collapse of all national innovative activity indicators (Table 6.1). The number of researchers decreased almost threefold in comparison to the late Soviet period (1985–90) and twofold over the first year of Russia's independent existence (1992). R&D expenditure as a percentage of GDP was about the same. It is characteristic that both indicators, after a sharp decrease, were stabilized, but they have not returned to their initial level, despite the fact that in 2000–08 the country had an unprecedented period of strong economic growth.

The curtailing of the state's innovative activity could have in principle been compensated for by the private sector. But this did not happen, either at the moment of the state's leaving the innovative sphere or years later. Total R&D expenditures of Russian firms (even including state-owned enterprises and non-commercial organizations) have still yet to surpass the measly level of 0.2 per cent of GDP (Table 6.1).

Where do the causes lie of the low R&D activity in Russian private business? In my opinion, the main causes can be classed into three groups. First, interest in R&D activity was undermined by a short time-horizon in the planning of Russian companies. Up to the mid-2000s the planning time-horizon did not often exceed one year and, less often, three years. Under the institutional instability of the emerging economy, combined with the availability of quick enrichment, interest in long-term projects of any kind was rather limited. This pertained equally to long-term investments, loans for a term of over one year, and the establishment of long-term partner contacts. But it was R&D activity that suffered most of all, as it relates not only to long terms of return on investment, but also significant risks.

Second, the autarchic, vertically integrated structure of the Soviet NIS made it extremely vulnerable to any withdrawal of certain elements from the system – exactly what happened in the post-Soviet epoch. The first wave of the system's decomposition was provoked by the disintegration

Table 6.1   Number of researchers and R&D intramural expenditures in Russia

Year	Number of Researchers*	R&D expenditures			
		Total		Including entrepreneurial sector organization funds**	
		Rbl.Bln (at constant 1989 prices)	Percentage of GDP	Rbl. Bln (at constant 1989 prices)	Percentage of GDP
1985–90***	1100	–	3.5–4.0	–	–
1991	–	7.3	1.43	–	–
1992	804	3.2	0.74	–	–
1995	518.7	2.5	0.85	0.4	0.15
2000	425.9	3.3	1.05	0.5	0.17
2005	391.1	4.5	1.07	0.9	0.22
2010	368.9	5.9	1.16	1.0	0.19
2011	374.8	5.9	1.12	1.0	0.18

Notes: * In thousands of persons at year-end. ** All organizations with main activity associated with production of goods or services for sale, including state-owned enterprises and non-commercial organizations. *** Our estimate for Russia as a part of the USSR.Rbl. Bln = billions of rubles.

Source: Author's estimate based on Rosstat (2012: 393/398; 2013: 377/382).

of the Soviet Union. Enterprises and laboratories, which previously functioned as a single mechanism, found themselves assigned to different states and quickly lost contact with each other (Yudanov, 2000). Inside Russia, similar processes were also underway: some enterprises existing earlier in a common technological chain were closed or changed their industrial profile, the state's scientific institutes were sold off, and prominent experts died or left for the West without leaving any replacements. As a result not only the demand but also the supply of R&D-intensive products was radically reduced.

Whole industries disappeared or switched over to assembling foreign models from foreign components, among them the manufacture of computers, household electronics, photo equipment, civil aircraft, microprocessors, industrial robots, and others, as well as many subsectors in engineering. Accordingly, semi-finished goods from industries that ceased to exist also lost their markets. Sadly, many industries in today's Russia would be unable to solve problems less complex than those encountered in Soviet industry 25 years ago.

Both of the above-mentioned reasons, however, could hardly predetermine such a low level of R&D activity in Russian private business as we observe in reality, without a third reason – foreign competition. From the point of view of consumer interest in a liberal economy, all of the described difficulties could be solved more easily and profitably by applying the achievements of NIS of other countries and in many cases paying for this additional comfort with the loss of Russia's own NIS capability.

It is true that Russian consumers of high-tech products would much rather buy not Russian but foreign equipment. In contrast to new domestic designs, foreign equipment is repeatedly tested and has guaranteed good service, financial schemes that are profitable, and is very often cheaper than what Russian manufacturers offer (Medovnikov et al., 2009).

In recent years, after decades of neglect, the problem of modernizing the Russian economy has moved to the center of public attention and policy initiatives. At present in Russia practically all the institutions of development known to world practice are in place. The main emphasis is placed on stimulating the creation and early growth of high-tech companies. This is undoubtedly an important task, because entrepreneurs building innovative companies in Russia without help and support face huge difficulties and various obstacles. However, we still do not see a noticeable increase in innovation. The problem of restoring the NIS has proven to be more complex than it seemed at first. The main hurdle is that innovative companies simply lack sufficient demand. In the simplified Russian economy, which shifted its focus to primary products, sophisticated high-tech products have drifted into a limbo status despite the fact that they could unquestionably be built to outstanding product standards.

6.3   SHORT DESCRIPTION OF THE POPULATION OF GAZELLES IN RUSSIA

As the R&D disaster unfolded in Russia, the high educational level of the population as a whole, and in particular of those who acted as founders and top managers of the new private enterprises, created the precondition for informal innovation. The broad worldview of these people objectively promoted entrepreneurial alertness, as it is called in the terminology of the neo-Austrian school. By that is meant that innovation is perhaps to a lesser degree connected with persistent inventive activity, rather than with the ability to notice something that is lying practically under one's nose – but has not as yet been used by other firms (Kirzner, 1997).

Noticeably, the matter regards the fulfillment of preconditions for KIE that are rather similar to those observed in developed countries among high-growth gazelles. It is true that about innovative activity it is usually said that 'with regard to gazelles in particular, innovation is understood in a broad sense, i.e. managerial, organizational and technological'; moreover, 'innovation in gazelles is more remarkable in the new applications of resources and in new organizational structures than in the generation of new technologies'; and finally, 'contrary to popular perception, only around one-third of gazelles are "high-tech" companies. Fast-growing firms whose success comes from innovative approaches to marketing, organization or distribution can be found across a wide range of activities' (Rigby et al., 2007: 18).

But are there actually any gazelles in the Russian economy today? Until recently there was no answer to this question, and not only for Russia but also other post-Soviet countries. One of the most-cited works recorded only 20 empirical studies throughout the entire history of research on gazelles (Henrekson and Johansson, 2010). But all of them concerned 11 developed market economies in North America and Western Europe. Only the most recent research has confirmed the existence of gazelles in new EU member states (Hölzl and Friesenbichler, 2010; Mitusch and Schimke, 2011).

Empirical studies of gazelles in Russia began at the Financial University in Moscow in 2003 (Yudanov, 2007a). In 2006 our group joined a group from *Ekspert*, a leading Russian business weekly, and proceeded with a systematic analysis of large databases compiled by this same weekly (Yudanov, 2007b; 2009). We had at our disposal information on all Russian enterprises that for at least one year in the period 1999–2011 had revenues of over $10 million and had existed for at least three years. The initial list of companies was narrowed down by discarding all non-market enterprises, such as companies in 100 per cent state ownership and non-commercial partnerships. The total number of remaining firms ranged per year from 25 to 65 thousand. We singled out permanent firms (firms that existed for the entire period under review, 1999–2011) into a special group. For that entire period the number of permanent firms ranged between 6.5 and 21.5 thousand (per different five-year periods used for identifying gazelles).

In the literature there is no generally accepted technique for identifying gazelles. As a basis we took David Birch's original algorithm, according to which any company that has grown at a rate of 20 per cent or more each year for at least five years is considered a gazelle. A significant amendment to this was that the revenue time series were deflated to remove the effect of high Russian inflation, which varied in different years from 10 per cent to 15 per cent. After making a list of gazelles, we compiled dossiers on many of them (about 800 firms). The top executives of 42 gazelles responded to a questionnaire, and 24 firms gave in-depth interviews.

Table 6.2   Number of gazelles in Russia

Period	Number of permanent firms	Number of gazelles[a]	Percentage of gazelles among permanent firms
1999–2003	6 524	484	7.4
2000–04	7 348	527	7.2
2001–05	8 244	587	7.1
2002–06	9 381	744	7.9
2003–07	10 174	830	8.2
2004–08	12 911	916	7.0
2005–09	10 080	199	2.0
2006–10	18 164	445	2.5
2007–11	21 530	532	2.5

Notes: a. Including subsidiaries of large corporations (including foreign).

Source: Financial University – Expert Database.

According to direct estimates (Table 6.2), before the crisis gazelles made up 7–8 per cent of the number of permanent firms. This figure is large by international standards: Birch's algorithm is sufficiently rigorous, and in developed countries its requirements are usually met by only 3–5 per cent of firms. The peculiarities of Russian accounting lead us to believe that even these high figures dramatically underestimate the 'historically normal', non-crisis number of gazelles, and that the correct assessment should be 12–13 per cent of all companies (for details, see Yudanov, 2009: 12–13).

We provide in Table 6.2 the latest available data for 2009–11. The impact of the 2008–09 crisis proved to be exceptionally severe. In contrast to the UK, for example, where the number and share of gazelles remained unchanged during the recession (NESTA, 2011: 5), the Russian population of gazelles proved to be highly vulnerable to the crisis and both indicators significantly decreased. A high number of firms have already experienced fast growth in the post-crisis period, but they have not demonstrated such growth long enough to be considered gazelles according to the strict requirements of Birch's algorithm. The high number of such firms allows us to make the following prediction: the large share of gazelles in the population of Russian companies should for the most part be restored by 2013–14.

Other than their high numbers, the second peculiarity of Russian gazelles is that they are all LMT firms (Table 6.3). Among Russian gazelles we identified only 1 per cent in the information technology and research

Table 6.3   The sectoral structure of the gazelle population

	Percentage of revenue	
	2007	2011
Wholesale and retail trade	37.8	49.4
Construction and building materials industry	4.3	11.3
Extractive industry	2.7	9.6
Machine building	5.7	6.9
Transportation	5.4	4.5
Chemicals	2.4	4.1
Finance, real estate	31.0	3.2
Services	2.5	2.8
Consumer goods	3.8	2.7
IT and research industry	1.2	0.8
Other	3.2	4.7
Total	100	100

Source: Financial University – Expert Database.

industries. Most are found in low-technology and mature industries. This is seen, for example, in the large share of such firms operating in wholesale and retail trade (49 per cent in 2011), construction (11 per cent), extractive industries (10 per cent), and traditional manufacturing industries.

Despite belonging largely to LMT industries (but also, thanks to the fact that they belong to LMT, as discussed below), gazelles proved to be the most important agents for modernizing the Russian economy. Let us ask a question: what is the fundamental difference between the modern Russian banking system and the banking system in 1999? Skipping over the details, the answer is obvious to all Russian citizens: the main difference is the creation of a consumer lending industry. If we ask the same question regarding retail trade, then the answer is the domination of retail chains that are well-established in the market. In the communications sector, the main innovation is that mobile telephony has turned into a mass phenomenon that has greatly changed the lives of entire social strata and improved business conditions in many regions of Russia. If we look for the pioneering firms that have carried out these revolutionary changes, it will turn out that they are on our lists of gazelles for the respective years.

Some of the most significant changes in the Russian economy and the names of the gazelles that initiated them are given in Table 6.4. Notably great success was achieved in manufacturing technologically simple products such as beer, shoes, candy, toothpaste, cable management systems, power tools, and agricultural machinery. In all of these, practically the

Table 6.4   Gazelles and some structural changes in Russia

Gazelle name	Period of rapid growth	Changes in Russia
Baltika	1991–2001	First Russian beer meeting world standards
1S	1991–2007	Automated accounting and enterprise management for SMEs
Ralf Ringer	1995–2005	Competitive footwear manufacturing in Russia
VimpelCom	1999–2007	Widespread use of mobile telephones
X5 Retail	1999–2007	Retail chains in democratic formats
Kaspersky Lab	1999–2007	Antivirus software competitive on the world market
NFC	1999–2005	Factoring in Russia
Tonar	2000–2007	Competitive manufacturing of tippers, trailers, and agricultural machinery in Russia
Yandex	2000–2007	First Russian search engine on the Internet
Korkunov	2000–2005	Premium domestic sweets
RBC	2000–2007	Internet advertising, TV business channel
Russian Standard Bank	2001–2006	Consumer lending
Interskol	2001–2008	Manufacturing of power tools
Polymerteplo Group	2002–2008	Manufacturing of polymer pipes for district heating and hot water distribution
SPLAT Cosmetica	2001–2011	Competitive oral care items manufacturing in Russia
SKB-Contour	2003–2011	SaaS (Software as a Service) in Russia
DKC	1999–2008 2010–2012	Modern cable management systems and enclosures
TechnoNICOL	1999–2008 2010–2012	The largest European manufacturer of roofing and water/heating insulation materials

Source: Financial University – Expert Database.

same basic development of events repeated itself. The commercial success of an entrepreneurial idea created a point of reference for a new process or approach.

For example, the firm Ralf Ringer began manufacturing shoes for consumers willing to pay for higher quality but unable to pay even more for the prestige of a well-known brand. In a comparatively modest country with highly educated and demanding consumers, this became a driver for rapid growth in shoe sales. TechnoNICOL offered people an alternative to the widespread practice at that time in the USSR of roofing houses with carcinogenic asbestos board. DKC solved the problem of providing buildings under construction with a modern system of electric communications. Polymerteplo Group, a producer of flexible pre-insulated polymer pipe systems for district heating and hot-water networks, offered a solution to one of Russia's most troublesome problems – how to repair at low cost the run-down central heating systems in apartment buildings.

The history of many gazelles began with importing advanced Western goods. The experience acquired in trading these goods gave firms a deeper understanding of the peculiarities of the Russian market and nudged them towards the creation of in-country production. They had competitive advantages over the traditional Russian manufacturers, while localized production added cost advantages over imports. All this significantly expanded the circle of potential consumers and quickened firm growth. The next step was usually in modifying products in consideration of the particularities of their use in Russia. Gazelles often undertook the function of being integrators by including in their products the most useful components for the Russian market and, if needed, by ordering necessary engineering refinements from around the world. Finally, proprietary R&D departments arose which usually brought about original engineering developments and the search for, or adaptations of, the successful ideas of others. Rising demand for the products of gazelles and the strengthening of the innovativeness of these businesses went hand in hand and each strengthened the other.

In a word, the commercial success of gazelles played a fundamental role in modernizing the Russian economy. In this catch-up modernization, the demand for innovation does not arise on its own, nor does it always arise where the supply-driven logic of the innovator expects to find it. The objective merits of a new and revolutionary product are perhaps undervalued in any country, but in the Russian economy with its distinctively weak demand for innovation, this undervaluation occurs often. And the assistance that the state can provide to innovators in firm creation – important as it is – cannot at all solve the basic problem of the market not having enough demand.

In Russia, demand for innovation rises when the end-products that include these innovations become successful. That is to say that it rises not when, for example, we are able to spread fluoropolymer covering on a metal roof without using poisonous chemicals, but rather when people stand in lines to buy safe non-stick frying pans with this same type of covering (a product of a real-life Russian gazelle – Neva-Metall Posuda Ltd). This occurs especially often in low-tech or medium-to-low-tech firms that are close to end-users and thus know better what qualities are capable of increasing demand among consumers.

To make a broader generalization: what kind of qualitative improvements have taken place at the micro-level of the Russian economy? In our opinion, positive changes are mostly observed in the two sectors with the highest concentration both of gazelles and effective demand. Namely, where (1) the infrastructure for doing business has been upgraded and (2) lines of production have appeared that target the consumers of the 'lower-middle' or 'upper-low' social strata who are the agents – the 'workhorses' – of market reform.

The transition economy in Russia presented a very strange picture in the 1990s. The normal business support infrastructure that exists all over the world was absent in Russia. There was no leasing, factoring, automation of everyday enterprise activities, or recruiting. There were not even normal distribution channels. Firms were prepared to pay for normalizing the conditions of conducting business, but there were no suppliers of these services. At the same time, there were no goods for the key personnel of the lower and middle echelons – the backbone of companies. The people who performed the major part of the skilled work in companies could not properly spend their moderate, but already not meager, salaries. They were offered either very cheap articles or good products at prohibitively high prices. These realities destroyed the motivation of skilled labor. This kind of economy could be compared to an organism without a digestive tract: the country swallowed, without digesting, various import products purchased with petrodollars and sold to customers from the backs of trucks at bazaars.

Gazelles have done a great deal to end this intolerable state of affairs. In a very short time the country has organized a basic infrastructure for business activity and has at least started producing the most needed consumer goods for average-income Russians.

6.4   EXPONENTIAL GROWTH OF GAZELLES AND THE MECHANISM OF RAPID EVOLUTION

Why do high-growth firms play such a great role in the general flow of qualitative changes in an economy? In our view, a gazelle's conscious choice of its field of activity is highly important in this respect. The future niche is selected in a purposeful, deliberate way that is based on the prospects it opens and the absence of competitors. It is no wonder that when a company finds such a niche, it can lead to explosive growth which not only has a significant effect on the company itself, but also may change the very structure of the whole industry concerned.

It can be said that gazelles convert their advantage of knowing the real requirements of the market into fast sales growth. But this growth, it was discovered, is of a rather unusual character: an unexpected phenomenon

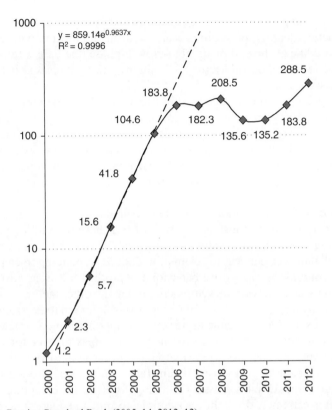

$$y = 859.14e^{0.9637x}$$
$$R^2 = 0.9996$$

Source: Russian Standard Bank (2005: 14; 2012: 12).

Figure 6.1 *Total assets of Russian Standard Bank (billions of rubles at year-end)*

revealed by our study of Russian gazelles is that the growth of most is practically exponential. And, as known, this exponential growth has the tendency to accelerate in time in absolute terms. It is no wonder that the moment an exponentially growing gazelle appears, the corresponding branch becomes unrecognizable within a few years.

We begin our discussion of this phenomenon with a case study of the Russian Standard Bank, a pioneer of consumer lending in Russia (Figure 6.1). In 1999, Russian Standard, a small bank by industry standards, whose total assets in 2000 amounted to 1.1 billion rubles, or $41 million, became the first in Russia to offer point-of-sale (POS) consumer lending, providing Western-style consumer loans upon the purchaser's presenting basic documents such as a passport or driver's license and a completed application form. Consumers, extremely weary of previous bureaucratic lending procedures, welcomed this innovation with enthusiasm. In 2006, at the end of its high-growth phase, the bank's total assets reached 183.8 billion rubles (or $6.8 billion), having increased it 157-fold in only six years.

The semi-logarithmic scale used in Figure 6.1 clearly demonstrates that this growth in its avalanche phase resembles an almost perfect exponential curve. Indeed, on this scale exponential curves look like straight lines. And, as the graph shows, the rate of growth in Russian Standard's assets falls on a straight line, as if the data for each year were artificially adjusted to this function. More properly, the accuracy of the approximation is incredibly high ($R^2 = 0.9996$).

This case, in our opinion, is of great heuristic importance. Even if we consider it an isolated instance, it is hard to believe it could be random. The thing is that the sales volume of a typical firm (or the total assets of a 'normal' bank) are subject to strong fluctuations responding to changes in macroeconomic activity, price behavior, the product life cycle, advertising campaigns, sales network development, and many other factors.

Normally it is impossible to find a regression equation to describe actual data with such inconceivable accuracy, not only by using a simple exponential function, but even with the help of complex multifactor models. Quite simply, actual sales keep 'jumping' and deviating from theoretical values under the impact of significant factors not taken into account by the model. Incidentally, Russian Standard itself is no exception in this sense: it is extremely difficult, for example, to find an equation describing the fluctuations in its total assets after it ceased to be a gazelle (for 2006–12 we have $R^2 = 0.1315$). But as a gazelle it grew at a strictly exponential rate and, as it turns out, this bank was not alone.

The exponential growth of Russian Standard is not an isolated artifact, but quite typical of gazelles. Figure 6.2 shows how closely revenue dynamics follow an exponential law for (a) gazelles and (b) non-gazelles. 'Long-lived gazelles' were identified from the whole original sample of 484 gazelles of the 1999–2003 generation. They are the 74 firms that started growing rapidly together with all the gazelles of this generation, but who managed, in contrast to the rest, to maintain high growth rates up through 2006. The control group was a sample of the same size (74 firms) randomly selected from among the permanent firms for the same period.

The results of a comparison between the two groups are extremely interesting: a virtually perfect approximation of growth dynamics to the exponential function ($R^2 > 0.98$) is demonstrated by 50 per cent of long-lived gazelles, whereas for conventional firms this is only a rare exception (4 per cent of firms). Another important point is that near-exponential growth

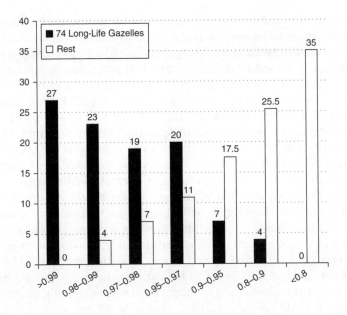

Notes:
a. Entire population of identified gazelles (74 firms) showing an annual revenue growth rate of over 20% (at constant prices) every year during 1999–2006.
b. Random sample of the same size (74 firms) from among the permanent firms in 1999–2006.

Source: Financial University – Expert Database.

Figure 6.2 Quality of exponential approximation of gazelle[a] and non-gazelle[b] revenue dynamics (percentage of firms with given coefficient of determination R^2)

($R^2 > 0.95$) is characteristic of the overwhelming majority (89 per cent) of long-lived gazelles.

What is then the source of this strange ability of many gazelles to grow as if nothing were happening around them, moving year after year – with amazing accuracy, like a train running on schedule – to the next point on a steep exponential curve? Why do the factors that keep disrupting the development of other firms fail to deflect gazelles from their exponential path?

In nature such dynamics are seen in the development of processes with positive feedbacks (self-amplifying processes) in the absence of resource constraints. For example, the population of rabbits that were brought by Europeans to Australia and within a few years spread across the continent grew at precisely an exponential rate. The reason for this is that each doe rabbit produced six to eight young rabbits once a month, each time increasing the total number of rabbits by a certain percentage. And since grass was in abundance, there was nothing else to prevent the rabbits from sustaining this natural reproduction rate from generation to generation.

Can it be that the same growth mechanism operates in an entrepreneurial firm, turning it into an exponentially growing gazelle? By organizing the production of some highly sought-after product a successful entrepreneur removes demand constraints, such that everything the firm produces is snapped up. The firm's growth rate in these conditions depends not on demand but on the firm's ability to increase the supply of its product and, consequently, on the rate of increase in its internal specific assets.

As for the latter, they too often grow exponentially. An entrepreneur capable of training two highly skilled and aggressive executives, each of whom will then mentor two talented deputies, who will then take on two deputies of their own, and so on, is no different from a doe rabbit in terms of process dynamics. From the fact that in 2000 Russian Standard had 221 employees, and in 2006, 36 617, it is clear that the ability to train proper management personnel was the main constraint on growth, because the once tiny firm that rapidly recruited almost 40 000 new employees would have otherwise become unmanageable.

The same method used in training management personnel is sometimes also used to train rank-and-file employees. The chief executive officer (CEO) of U Palycha (the Russian manufacturer of premium handmade *pelmeni* – specialty dumplings) reasoned along similar lines, saying that the growth rate of his gazelle was limited by the ability of his experienced workers to teach newcomers how to make the dumplings.

For gazelles, even financial resources acquire the features of internal specific assets. External investing in fast-growing small to medium-sized enterprises is extremely risky. As a result many gazelles are financed through the total reinvestment of profits. And then everything proceeds as in the case of rabbits: reinvested profits make it possible to expand production, which makes it possible to make more profits, the reinvestment of which once again expands production, and so on.

As our surveys show, such reasoning is not mere theoretical speculation – it is precisely how the top managers of Russian gazelles understand the situation. The constraint on growth that seems most natural for firms in a market economy – lack of demand – was named a significant factor by only 10–14 per cent of gazelles.[2] At the same time, resource constraints – shortage of funds and difficulties in recruiting management and other personnel – are seen by gazelles as the most serious factors, being named by 38–40 per cent, 33–45 per cent, and 38–45 per cent of gazelles respectively.

This pattern does not mean that gazelles are insensitive to the volume of demand. Rather the opposite, as in all likelihood a company can reach the rank of gazelle only after the problem of demand has already been resolved and the barrier of limited demand breached – for a time at least. This idea was expressed in almost the same words by Mikhail Kershtein, CEO of Ramfood, a meat producer: 'We produce as much output – of a quality that suits us and in a variety required by the market – as we can. One gets the impression that if we had the opportunity to double our output within two or three months, the market would swallow this up.'

Analysing the phenomenon of the exponential growth of gazelles allows us to take a fresh look at the influence the mechanism of entrepreneurship has on economic evolution. The overwhelming majority of firms in the economy operate under rigid demand constraints and therefore grow rather slowly. The very fact of a firm's belonging among high-tech enterprises does not automatically make it an exception to this rule. We recollect the problem of the acute shortage of demand that hampered the growth of R&D-intensive firms in Russia (Section 2). The nature of growth changes considerably only with those firms that, thanks to the creation of highly sought-after products, appear capable of removing demand constraints. This type of growth acquires a long-term and steadily faster character and generates considerable structural changes in the economy. In other words the familiar statement that 'Only few gazelles are high-tech firms' can be reworded as 'Only a few high-tech firms manage to become gazelles and make an essential impact on the evolution of the economy'.

We assume that the prevalence of LMT firms among gazelles is related to this. Certainly the high-tech sector creates mostly supply-driven innovations which, by definition, are risky as far as market approval is concerned. After all, market demand for a new product is not supported at first by anything save the enthusiasm of the innovator. By contrast, in the low-tech sector innovation is usually based on monitoring demand; searching for a good that is capable of causing a significant increase in demand is the goal and main motivation of an entrepreneur. Innovation only serves as the means to achieving this goal. It is not surprising that, consequently, the percentage of commercial success is significantly higher, and that, in accordance with this, we observe the most gazelles among LMT firms.

But the strong impact of gazelles on structural changes in the economy is not only a matter of the fast growth of these companies themselves. An important point is connected with network effects, as the appearance of such players in the market generates a wave of deliberate adaptive changes in other companies (Dumnaya, 2009). We have empirically identified in the Russian market the following mechanisms for diffusing favorable changes within industries and in related sectors: (1) imitation, (2) competitive enforcement, and (3) mutual advantage, or synergy.

6.5 CONCLUSIONS AND POLICY IMPLICATIONS

The development of Russian gazelles had a spontaneous character based exclusively on private initiative, without the slightest attempt at support from the government. Lately we have noticed a trend of the government returning to the innovation sphere. For the first time in the history of post-Soviet Russia, the purposes of economic modernization have been formulated, measures to support R&D-intensive firms developed, and national projects in the major fields of scientific and technical development launched. As a result KIE exists in modern Russia on two different and poorly interacting levels.

The first of them is the innovation ecosystem of gazelles. Members of this ecosystem are, as a rule, far from formal R&D activity. The overwhelming majority of gazelles are concentrated in low-tech industries. The innovations they introduce are mostly incremental rather than radical in character. Moreover, very often innovation in gazelles is simply the result of successfully adapting the world's experience to Russian conditions – a mixture of imitation and innovation in the narrow meaning of the word. The even more innovative activity of gazelles is not connected with technological changes at all – it lies in either the marketing or management sphere. Apparently only this type of NIS could develop and survive spontaneously without any state support under conditions of superior foreign competition in an ultra-liberal transition economy.

At the same time, the innovation ecosystem of gazelles is an extremely viable community of firms, actively and positively influencing the evolution of the Russian economy. Modest in size – at least, at the initial stages of development – gazelles appeared capable in just a few years to create new industries and/or to considerably change the image of old industries. The gazelles' typical exponential character of growth leads to innovations spreading through the economy at a high speed after receiving market support. Powerful networking effects have been revealed by which a gazelle can force other firms to innovate or involve them in innovation, or gazelles may mutually support each other's innovations.

The second level is represented by high-tech companies that were restored with the active support of the government. By now in Russia almost all the types of institutions for KIE support found in developed countries have been organized. Yet it may take considerable time before a community of R&D-intensive firms can form around these institutions.

We should not forget that market conditions in the country continue to remain unfavorable for such companies, and that state support only partially makes their operations easier.

Under these conditions, the most reasonable decision would seem to be to expand economic policy to support all knowledge-intensive enterprises, including the already existing innovation ecosystems of gazelles that generate demand for innovation. We would also risk the supposition that this recipe would be useful not just in Russia. It is well known that the R&D expenditures of a few new EU member states are even lower than Russia's obviously insufficient indicators. Yet large numbers of gazelles are also registered in those countries (Mitusch and Schimke, 2011). A policy of supporting LMT high-growth firms and thereby stimulating demand for innovation might in these conditions prove to be at least no less effective than directly forcing R&D activity.

NOTES

1. This chapter is based on research financed within the European Commission's 7th Framework programme, Project AEGIS (No. 225134).
2. A survey of 20 firms in Moscow in November 2008 and of 22 firms in Yekaterinburg in March 2009. It should be borne in mind that the firms' responses refer to the pre-crisis period.

REFERENCES

Birch, David L. (1987), *Job Creation America: How Our Smallest Companies Put the Most People to Work*, New York, USA: The Free Press.

Birch, David L. and James Medoff (1994), 'Gazelles', in Lewis C. Solomon and Alec R. Levenson (eds), *Labor Markets, Employment Policy and Job Creation*, Boulder, CO, USA: Westview Press, pp. 159–68.

Chepurenko, A.Y. and A.A. Yakovlev (2013), 'Theory of Entrepreneurship: The Importance of the Context', *Russian Management Journal*, **11** (2), 51–60 (in Russian).

Davis, S.J., J. Haltiwanger and S. Schuh (1996), 'Small Business and Job Creation: Dissecting the Myth and Reassessing the Facts', *Small Business Economics*, **8** (4), 297–315.

Delmar, F., P. Davidsson and W.B. Gartner (2003), 'Arriving at the High-Growth Firm', *Journal of Business Venturing*, **18** (2), 189–216.

Dumnaya, Natalya N. (2009), *The New Market Economy*, Moscow: Max Press (in Russian).

Henrekson, M. and D. Johansson (2010), 'Gazelles as Job Creators: A Survey and Interpretation of the Evidence', *Small Business Economics*, **35** (2), 227–44.

Hirsch-Kreinsen, H. (2008), '"Low-Tech" Innovations', *Industry and Innovation*, **15** (1), 19–43.

Hirsch-Kreinsen, Hartmut and David Jacobson (eds) (2008), *Innovation in Low-Tech Firms and Industries*, Cheltenham, UK and Northampton, MA, USA: Edward Elgar.

Hölzl, W. and K. Friesenbichler (2010), 'High-Growth Firms, Innovation and the Distance to the Frontier', *Economics Bulletin*, **30** (2), 1016–24.

Kirchhoff, Bruce A. (1994), *Entrepreneurship and Dynamic Capitalism: The Economics of Business Firm Formation and Growth*, Westport, USA: Praeger.

Kirner, E., S. Kinkel and A. Jaeger (2009), 'Innovation Paths and the Innovation Performance of Low-Technology Firms – An Empirical Analysis of German Industry', *Research Policy*, **38** (3), 447–58.

Kirzner, I.M. (1997), 'Entrepreneurial Discovery and the Competitive Market Process: An Austrian Approach', *Journal of Economic Literature*, **35** (1), 71–90.

Malerba, Franco (2010), *Knowledge-Intensive Entrepreneurship and Innovation Systems, Evidence from Europe*, London, UK and New York, USA: Routledge.

Medovnikov, D., I. Imatudinov and S. Rosmirovich (2009), 'To Go through the Pubertal Period', *Expert*, **2** (641) (in Russian).

Mitusch, K. and A. Schimke (2011), 'Gazelles – High-Growth Companies', final report, INNOVA Sectoral Innovation Watch Europe, available at http://ec.europa.eu/enterprise/policies/innovation/files/proinno/gazelles-final-report_en.pdf (accessed 25 July 2013).

NESTA (2011), 'Vital Growth: The Importance of High-Growth Business to the Recovery', available at www.nesta.org.uk/library/documents/Vital_Growth_v19.pdf (accessed 16 June 2013).

OECD (1996), *Science, Technology and Industry Outlook*, Paris: OECD.

OECD (2002), *OECD Frascati Manual: Proposed Standard for Surveys on Research and Experimental Development*, 6th edn, Paris: OECD.

OECD (2005a), *Oslo Manual: Guidelines for Collecting and Interpreting Innovation Data*, 3rd edn, Paris: OECD.

OECD (2005b), *Science, Technology and Industry Scoreboard 2005*, Paris: OECD.

Rigby, J., M. Bleda, K. Morrison and Jong-Seok Kim (2007), 'Mini Study 01 – Are Gazelles Leaping Ahead? Innovation and Rapidly Growing Small Firms', INNO GRIPS, available at http://grips-public.mediactive.fr/knowledge_base/dl/128/orig_doc_file/ (accessed 19 July 2013).

Rosstat (2012), Russian in Figures, Moscow.

Rosstat (2013), Russian in Figures, Moscow.

Russian Standard Bank (2005), 'Annual Report 2005', available at http://www.russianstandardbank.com/upload/iblock/3aa/rs2005_enweb.pdf (accessed 23 January 2014).

Russian Standard Bank (2012), 'Annual Report 2012', available at http://www.russianstandardbank.com/upload/iblock/aef/annual_report_eng_2012.pdf (accessed 23 January 2014).

Schumpeter, Joseph Alois (1912/1951), *The Theory of Economic Development: An Inquiry into Profits, Capital, Credit, Interest, and the Business Cycle*, Cambridge, MA, USA: Harvard University Press.

Yudanov, Andrei (2000), 'Economic Change and the National Question in Twentieth-Century USSR/Russia: The Enterprise Level', in Alice Teichova, Herbert Matis and Jaroslav Pátek (eds), *Economic Change and the National Question in Twentieth-Century Europe*, Cambridge, UK: Cambridge University Press, pp. 404–24.

Yudanov, Andrei (2007a), *The Experience of Competition in Russia: Causes for Success and Failure*, Moscow: KnoRus (in Russian).

Yudanov, A.Y. (2007b), 'Fast Growing Firms and the Evolution of the Russian Economy', *Social Sciences*, **38** (4), 18–35.

Yudanov, A. (2009), '"Russische Gazellen" – Schnell wachsende mittelgroße Unternehmen als neue Träger wirtschaftlicher, Entwicklung in Russland', working paper, available at www.hs-bremen.de/internet/einrichtungen/fakulta-eten/f1/forschung/kmu/01-sme_working_papers_yudanov.pdf (accessed 5 July 2013).

7. The relevance of the 'dynamic capabilities' perspective in low-tech sectors[1]

Aimilia Protogerou, Yannis D. Caloghirou and Glykeria Karagouni

7.1 INTRODUCTION

Dynamic capabilities (DCs) and their role in firm strategy, value creation and competitive advantage have attracted a great deal of attention among scholars in recent years (e.g. Teece et al., 1997; Eisenhardt and Martin, 2000; Winter, 2003; Teece, 2007; Helfat et al., 2007). In their landmark article Teece et al. (1997) argue that dynamic capabilities enable organizations to integrate, build and reconfigure their resources and competencies and, therefore, maintain performance in the face of changing business environments. The notion of DCs was subsequently refined and expanded (e.g. Eisenhardt and Martin, 2000; Zollo and Winter, 2002; Teece, 2007; Helfat et al., 2007, among others) and was also related to the concept of entrepreneurship (e.g. Zahra et al., 2006; Boccardelli and Magnusson, 2006; Teece, 2010), entrepreneurial management (e.g. Augier and Teece, 2009) and knowledge management (e.g. Easterby-Smith and Prieto, 2008). Yet, despite the increasing research interest, there is limited empirical and theoretical work on dynamic capabilities and their role in knowledge-intensive entrepreneurship (KIE) (Protogerou and Karagouni, 2012). Therefore, several questions – related to DCs' conceptualization and role – still remain open.

There is significant variation in the literature regarding the kind of external business environments that are relevant to dynamic capabilities: researchers have not yet reached a consensus on the role and usefulness of DCs in environments of varying degrees of dynamism (Zahra et al., 2006; Barreto, 2010). There are those who clearly suggest that the nature of DCs makes them synonymous with highly dynamic environments (e.g. Teece et al., 1997); those who acknowledge the applicability of the concept not only to rapidly changing environments but also in environments subject to lower rates of change (Zollo and Winter, 2002; Eisenhardt and Martin,

2000; Helfat et al., 2007; Ambrosini et al., 2009); and those who do not include specific environmental characteristics in their line of research/ argument (e.g. Makadok, 2001).

Thus additional research efforts are required, especially on an empirical basis, to shed more light on the relevance of dynamic capabilities under distinct environmental conditions. For example, one might expect the development and use of DCs to vary on average with the rate of change in an industry itself. Therefore it would be interesting to examine the relevance of the dynamic capabilities concept for different industries. However, DCs have been primarily studied in high-technology industries (Zahra et al., 2006; Easterby-Smith et al., 2009), since these contexts are considered turbulent enough to drive the development – and consequently justify the cost – of specific dynamic capabilities (Wang and Ahmed, 2007; Winter, 2003). Despite the fact that an increasing number of scholars see an important role for DCs also in moderately dynamic environments, there is hardly any evidence of dynamic capabilities' role in low-tech industries which, compared to their high-tech counterparts, are normally considered relatively more stable contexts.

This chapter contributes to the literature in reporting an empirical analysis of extensive quantitative and qualitative data on the relationship between dynamic capabilities and firm performance measures in the novel context of young entrepreneurial ventures in low-tech industries. More specifically, our qualitative analysis focuses on knowledge-intensive low-tech cases supporting the recently developed view that KIE can be found in low-tech industries as well (Malerba and McKelvey, 2010; McKelvey and Lassen, 2013). In this way we shed more light on the still open issue of whether dynamic capabilities have a role to play in an environment which by definition is characterized as stable and lacking in any significant amount of innovation. Following von Tunzelmann and Acha (2005: 429), we suggest that *in the modern world there is no low-tech sector*, and empirically we show that the concept of DCs clearly applies to traditional, mature industries. Thus, this chapter advocates that empirical analysis also takes into account other types of environmental conditions than technological dynamism, which in most research on DCs has thus far been the center of attention.

7.2   THEORETICAL BACKGROUND

7.2.1   Are Dynamic Capabilities Relevant to Low-Tech Industries?

DCs reflect 'the capacity of an organization to purposefully and systematically create, extend or modify its resource base' (Helfat et al., 2007: 4).

A firm's resource base includes tangible, intangible and human assets such as labor, capital, technology, knowledge, property rights, and also the structures, routines and processes needed to support its productive activities. 'Creating' a resource includes obtaining new resources through acquisitions and alliances as well as through innovation and entrepreneurial activity. 'Extending' a firm's resource base may be promoting growth in an ongoing business. 'Modifying' a resource base includes any reaction to change, for example, a response to external environment shifts.

Several works (e.g. Teece et al., 1997; Teece, 2007) explicate the meaning of dynamic capabilities and their importance in achieving a competitive advantage in rapidly changing environments. In a dynamic business context the potential value of DCs lies in enabling firms to renew and reconfigure their resources to better fit into shifting environmental conditions. However, frequent use of dynamic capabilities can also be justified in moderately changing environmental contexts (e.g. Eisenhardt and Martin, 2000; Helfat et al., 2007; Helfat and Peteraf, 2009). Although in a relatively stable environment external changes do occur, they are to a large extent predictable and incremental, and the rate of change is lower compared to that experienced by firms operating in more dynamic environmental contexts. However, in spite of the lower level and intensity of changes, there should still be some need to adapt or continuously improve the existing resource base in order for resources to maintain their value. This suggests that DCs not only have a role in rapidly changing environments, but they can also be of value in less dynamic contexts by exploiting existing knowledge to effect incremental change (Protogerou et al., 2012). Additionally, Helfat and Peteraf (2009) claim that not all fast-paced environments are characterized by regular disruptive change, suggesting that some are better characterized by continuous, incremental shifts. In such contexts DCs may be critically important. Furthermore, dynamic capabilities have the potential to advance ongoing adaptation, rendering disruptive change less crucial (O'Reilly and Tushman, 2004).

According to Miller and Friesen (1983), both volatility (rate and amount of change) and unpredictability (uncertainty) can be considered fundamental constituents of environmental dynamism. Business environments can be dynamic in many different ways (Duncan, 1972; Dess and Beard, 1984). For example, changes in the industry structure, the instability of market demand, the intensity of competition or the likelihood of environmental shocks are important dimensions of environmental dynamism.

It is quite evident that to date researchers have not managed to provide a compelling explanation of the role of DCs under conditions of various levels of environmental dynamism, and especially in contexts considered less dynamic, such as the so-called mature or low-tech industries. These industries are usually acknowledged to be less dynamic and agile than high-tech ones. They are characterized by 'remarkable stability' which is due to 'stagnant demand for low-tech products, or . . . declining international competitiveness and import penetration' (Kaloudis et al., 2005: 28). They are also assumed to spend rather insignificant amounts on R&D, resulting in slow-paced changes.[2] However, the new millennium seems to have brought certain changes to such established views. Mature industries no longer enjoy a stable and well-protected environment. Therefore, 'while high-tech sectors may have greater innate capacity to spawn product innovations, LMT industries may be faced with a greater necessity to do so' (von Tunzelmann and Acha, 2005: 415).

In addition, what business environments at all can be characterized as stable nowadays? Rapid change is a condition that currently prevails in a growing number of industries because

> . . . the global economy has undergone drastic changes that have accelerated the rhythm at which firms innovate. The decreased cost of communication and data flow, the reduced barriers to trade, and the liberalization of labour and financial markets in many parts of the world are forcing firms to confront agile and/or low-cost competitors early in the product cycle . . . (Teece, 2010: 694)

Thus, the prevailing views on the 'stagnation' of the low-tech sector have been challenged in recent years. Although not dynamic by definition (Sciascia et al., 2009), low-tech traditional industries are characterized today as subject to environmental hostility and major changes.

Therefore we can assume that dynamic capabilities can be useful even in less turbulent environments and, indeed, play a role in more mature, traditional industries. Under these circumstances DCs do not essentially transform the firm's resource base, but mainly support its adaptive change through incremental improvements. Admittedly, when an environmental context is perfectly stable, the potential of DCs might be limited because there are few occasions to exercise them effectively, especially with the high costs of their development. However, as a literature review reveals, low-tech industries are far more dynamic than usually believed as they have to confront the instability of global markets, the fast pace of intersectoral technological advances and the high probability of environmental shocks – major elements of environmental dynamism. Thus, the need to change a firm's resource base can also occur in the low-tech sector (Teece, 2010).

7.2.2   The Volatile Global Environment of Low-Tech Industries

This section briefly presents some key dimensions of the globally changing business environment in low-tech industries. In particular, the instability caused by globalization and trade liberalization, changing industry structures and regulations, increasing social pressures, transformation of the technology base of mature industries resulting in significant product and process innovations, as well as the changes caused by the 2008 world financial crisis delineate a vulnerable, volatile and rapidly changing environment.

Globalization and trade liberalization have caused interesting new problems and significant challenges for low-tech industries (von Tunzelman and Acha, 2005; Skuras et al., 2011). For example, the textiles and clothing industry is facing fierce market competition,[3] extremely high unpredictability and ambiguity as well as global regulatory changes.[4] The business environment in the wood and furniture industry is also drastically changing as a result of the unprecedented opening up of the furniture trade at global levels and Chinese domination[5] of the global furniture market over the past ten years.

Technology pressure and the need for innovation are gradually becoming more evident in the so-called mature industries (von Tunzelmann and Acha, 2005; Sarkar and Costa, 2008; Karantininis et al., 2010; Skuras et al., 2011). The food industry, typically described as 'mature', 'conservative' and 'slow-growing' (Costa and Jongen, 2006) with a relatively low level of R&D investment, has embraced open innovation as increasingly crucial for sustainability (Sarkar and Costa, 2008). In the textiles industry, 'smart' materials in the form of responsive and adaptive fibers and fabrics combined with electronically active devices and ICT have been increasingly welcomed by the leisure industry and interactive consumers, and even more so by the healthcare industry (Farrer and Finn, 2011). Novel composite materials to cope with the natural wood shortage, development of 'smart', 'eco-friendly' furniture, and a real revolution in product technologies to suit novel design trends are all changing the dynamics of the 'ever slow' wood and furniture sector (Likar, 2008).

Furthermore, low-tech industries are forced to innovate in complex environments and changes in these industry structures are more rapid than usually thought. Bröring et al. (2006) uses the term 'industry convergence' to emphasize the 'blurring' of boundaries among industries and the rather 'symbiotic relationship between sectors' (Robertson and Patel, 2007). Novel knowledge coming from advanced fields of science creates lucrative markets for radically innovative products (such as functional foods, microfibers, engineered wood and smart textiles and furniture). Innovation in low-tech industries is characterized by a complex structure of the knowledge base in which technological innovations and patents constitute only the visible and perhaps smaller part of total innovations (Skuras et al., 2011). Within this complex interplay, velocity, in the form of new opportunities (Eisenhardt, 1989) and challenging disturbances, is evident. Advances in interdisciplinary and inter-sectoral knowledge bases combine to change the nature of both demand and supply and, coupled with an ever-increasing level of competitiveness, cause ongoing environmental changes which can be very rapid. However, even incremental changes can be highly ambiguous and difficult to understand, which is due to the combinations of intra- and inter-sectoral dimensions of market, technology and other contextual factors.

Regulatory (e.g. new types of environmental regulations) and *social changes* impose further strong pressures on low-tech industries (Dixon et al., 2010; von Tunzelmann and Acha, 2005). Low-tech industries have to deal with intense pressure from action groups, communities, governments, shareholders and consumers to produce safer and more environmentally friendly items (Gereffi et al., 2001; de Bakker and Nijhoff, 2002). For instance, the food sector is driven by and continuously responds to consumer demands such as adherence to safety standards (in terms of microbiology and toxicology), health and well-being (nutritional benefits, health-enhancing properties), higher quality, convenience, good taste and price (Fryer and Versteeg, 2008; Bruhn, 2008).

Finally, it is worth mentioning that during periods of economic recession the environment can be considered highly volatile (Jansen et al., 2006). For example, environmental instability in the 2008 global financial crisis led to a drastic economic downturn. Although firms differ in how they experience crises (some suffer considerably while others manage to avoid the worst effects), it is quite evident that they have to cope with a highly unstable environment regardless of their respective industrial sector.

Though environmental dynamism is usually interpreted as technological change or environmental volatility in general (e.g. Teece et al., 1997; Ambrosini et al., 2009), our literature review indicates that instability in the market environment of low-tech industries can come in many forms. Therefore low-tech traditional industries are far more volatile and turbulent than commonly thought and DCs can have a significant role to play in such environments. However, there is limited empirical research on a definite role for dynamic capabilities in low-tech firms, either in their start-up phase or later.

7.2.3 Dynamic Capabilities in Low-Tech Firms

Only lately has research effort been put into relating the concept of DCs to the LMT sectors. As a consequence empirical studies on dynamic capabilities in these sectors are still rather limited and thus the potential of the DCs approach remains largely unexplored.

Helfat (1997) was perhaps one of the first scholars to study a medium-tech industry in her research and confirm R&D as a dynamic capability in the U.S. petroleum industry. Since then a stream of empirical research has been slowly emerging to capture the impact of DCs on LMT sectors. These research efforts, both qualitative and quantitative, address issues such as the relationship between dynamic capabilities and firm performance, the role of DCs in achieving competitive advantage and their impact on innovative performance and change capability (Abro et al., 2011; Salvato, 2003; Borch and Madsen, 2007; Telussa et al., 2006). In addition, some of these studies explain how DCs are actually developed and manifested in low- and medium-tech industries (Jones et al., 2013; Chirico, 2007), mostly in cases of internationalization (Evers, 2011; Kuuluvainen, 2011; Quentier, 2011). Finally, Makkonen et al. (2013), using both quantitative and qualitative data, investigate how low-tech firms cope with the drastic effects of the global financial crisis from the perspective of dynamic capabilities.

7.3   METHODS

7.3.1   Empirical Strategy

The empirical reporting unfolds in two stages. The first stage focuses on the extensive AEGIS survey conducted in 2011 in different industries, and tests for the impact of specific types of DCs on diverse measures of firm performance on the full sample of low-tech firms in ten European countries. The second stage analyses in more depth key variables of interest in the Greek context using extensive case studies in three low-tech industries, namely food and beverage, textiles and clothing and wood and furniture.

7.3.2   Quantitative Survey

The quantitative analysis data originate from the AEGIS project survey. This survey targeted three broad sectoral groups – high-tech manufacturing, low-tech manufacturing and knowledge-intensive business services.[6] A total of 1479 low-tech firms operating in different low-tech manufacturing

Table 7.1   Sample industrial distribution

Industrial classification	NACE Rev. 2	Number of firms	% of firms
Food, beverages and tobacco	10,11	294	19.9
Textiles and clothing	13,14,15	203	13.7
Paper and printing	17,18	472	31.9
Wood and furniture	16,31	237	16.0
Non-ferrous metals	24	35	2.4
Fabricated metal products	25	238	16.1
Total		1479	100

Source: AEGIS Survey, data processing by LIEE/NTUA.

industries responded to the survey in telephone interviews with one of the firm founders (see Table 7.1). The firms are in ten European countries, namely the UK, Germany, France, Italy, Sweden, Denmark, Greece, Portugal, Croatia and the Czech Republic.

The low-tech sample firms are independent, young entities founded between 2001 and 2007 with an average age of 7.2 years (min: 4; max: 10 years). Thus, all companies have been in operation for at least 4 years and therefore it can be assumed that they have managed to exceed the critical 3-year survival threshold.

7.3.3   Quantitative Variables

The variables used to capture *dynamic capabilities* were: market- and technology-sensing capability, new product-development capability, networking capability and the capability of participating in technology collaborations. Each of these was measured with specific questionnaire items. Firm founders were asked to indicate on a five-point Likert-type scale the extent to which the particular capabilities have been developed in their firms.

Sensing capability (market- and technology-sensing)
In Teece's (2007) terminology, sensing capabilities denote the firm's skills in noticing and monitoring changes in operating environments, identifying new market and technological opportunities, probing markets and listening to customers.

Market-sensing involves understanding and responding to market intelligence (Pavlou and El Sawy, 2011) by observing, counteracting and/or capturing related opportunities. More specifically, customer feedback and processes of market-shift recognition are used to identify new market segments and changing customer needs. However, sensing entails also processes of learning and understanding technology developments in the business environment. An organization that has a high level of technology-sensing capability will constantly look for information about potential technological opportunities and threats (Srinivasan et al., 2002) and respond to technological changes in its environment.

In our research market-sensing was captured by employing items reflecting adaptation to best practices, response to competitive moves, customer feedback, recognition of shifts in markets, consideration of the consequences of changing market demand and the capturing of new opportunities. Technology-sensing was measured by three items, namely the existence of formal R&D and technical departments and the frequent exchange of practical experience among employees.

New product development capability
New product development (NPD) is considered a key source of competitive advantage: as a strategic function of the organization, it constitutes a major requirement for success (Teece, 2007).

NPD has been closely associated with dynamic capabilities (e.g. Eisenhardt and Martin, 2000). In industries populated by low-tech enterprises the rapid development of new products can be a key factor in success. In this context demand differentiation and competitive pressure force firms to reflect on their established practices, identify new market segments and stimulate customer demand through introducing new or upgraded products (von Tunzelmann and Acha, 2005).

NPD was measured by three items, namely: the capability to offer novel products, to adapt products to the specific needs of different customers and market niches, and to actively promote and market the developed products/services.

Networking capability
Networking refers to the formation of mutually beneficial personal or business relationships in order to expand and accelerate the acquisition of useful resources and skills. These resources include the exchange of information and knowledge as well as the discovery and control of opportunities, and the term is also extended to various types of financial and institutional support.

Networks have been found important for firms to create competitive advantages (Dahl and Pedersen, 2004; Littunen, 2000). Common goals may be shared by network members regarding markets, market shifts and customer needs, and the establishment of best practice techniques in advertising and promotion. Incentives for participating in networks can also be of a more strictly economic nature such as financial assistance in the form of loans or fund seeking.

To operationalize the different underlying dimensions of networking capability we first used items related to market processes such as collecting information about competitors, accessing distribution channels, exploring export opportunities, advertising and promotion. To capture the technology side of networking capability we employed variables assessing networks' impact on the development of new products/services, the management of production and operations, as well as on easy access to skilled personnel. Finally, to grasp the economic and more generic value of networking, we used variables relating to networks' help in obtaining business loans, attracting funds or getting legal support.

Participation in technology-collaborative agreements
Firms develop technology collaborations of various types depending on the expected benefits: to share the costs of R&D development, introduce new products on global markets, minimize costs, develop sales or gain access to rare or expensive resources.

R&D and technical cooperation agreements in particular have become a strategically important part of business decision-making in many industries in recent years in both high- and low-tech sectors. They include any agreed-upon cooperative R&D or technology arrangements between firms, such as joint ventures, technology partnerships and informal networking arrangements.

The various types of collaboration appear to play a special role when new firms try to develop competitive advantages. Collaboration is important for startups to gain the knowledge necessary to develop or acquire the capabilities needed for NPD, R&D, innovation, design, manufacturing, or even technical services (Haeussler et al., 2012; Stam et al., 2007), as well as higher rates of growth (Stearns, 1996).

In the present research, firms' collaborative activities were operationalized by five variables: participation in strategic alliances, agreements regarding R&D, technical cooperation, licensing and contracting out research.

All multi-item scales pertaining to dynamic capabilities were tested by Confirmatory Factors Analysis (CFA) in order to confirm that particular items relate to a specific dynamic capabilities construct. Therefore five different DCs constructs or composite variables were produced. All of these composite variables were constructed as averages of multi-item Likert-type scales, on which higher numbers pointed to a 'higher quantity' of what was measured. (The Appendix to this chapter includes all relevant CFA details. As shown there, all multi-item scales representing DCs are reasonably valid and reliable.)

Performance measures

We gauged firms' performance by three performance measures, namely the percentage of sales obtained in international markets during the last three years, employment growth in the past three years and innovative firm performance. Internationalization exposes young firms to multiple and diverse exogenous stimuli (e.g. competitive conditions) and endogenous stimuli (e.g. resource demand) (Sapienza et al., 2006). It reflects the degree of young low-tech firms' success in pursuing opportunities beyond domestic markets.

Firms generally find unprofitable growth difficult to sustain over time. Therefore growth in firm size provides an alternative basis for assessing patterns of firm performance over time. Here, growth is measured by the variations in the number of employees. It is widely agreed that measuring employee number growth is especially appropriate for new ventures, in which the number of employees often grows before any sales occur (Colombo et al., 2010). In addition, human resources are among the most important assets the new low-tech firm has.

Finally, we measured innovative performance in terms of the radicalness of product innovation in the last three years as an ordinal variable taking the values of: 0 (= no innovation); 1 (= new-to-firm product innovation); 2 (= new-to-market product innovation); and 3 (= new-to-world product innovation).

As the *control variable* we used firm size in terms of the number of full-time employees.

7.3.4   Qualitative Case Studies

A multiple case study enriches and improves our understanding of the relevance of dynamic capabilities in the low-tech sector on the level of the individual firm. The case studies were conducted in three low-tech industries: food and beverages (F&B), textiles and clothing (T&C) and wood and furniture (W&F).

All three industries occupy a prominent position in the European and Greek manufacturing sector. They have also undergone important changes and significant restructuring since almost the mid-1990s. However, as described in the following paragraphs, each sector has followed a different evolutionary path, having important implications for their response to recently changing environmental conditions.

The Greek economy was one of the fastest growing in the Eurozone from 1996 to 2007. However, the repercussions of the 2008 global financial crisis were unavoidably felt also in Greece. Since late 2009 the country has been submerged in a financial crisis unparalleled in its modern history.

Within this context a mixture of threats and opportunities has determined the course and evolution of the three industries selected for our qualitative study.[7]

The food and beverage industry is one of the most dynamic industries of the Greek economy and, most importantly, it appears to be responding satisfactorily to the remarkable development of the sector at the global level. Although the Greek F&B industry showed almost no propensity to innovate till the mid-1990s, with the dawn of the new millennium a small but constantly increasing number of new firms has been gaining a global presence by offering novel products and targeting new market niches. These firms have been taking advantage of rapid technological advances such as the 'biotechnology revolution' and novel packaging technologies to develop new products and 'eco-friendly' production methods.

On the other hand, the Greek textiles and clothing industry has been facing a severe decline since the mid-1990s, which is due to the fierce competition from Asian countries, dramatically changing global market structures and global regulatory changes (e.g. the World Trade Organization Agreement on Textiles and Clothing on the structural removal of quotas in 1993). Thus, it operates within a hostile environment (in contrast to the F&B sector), pressed by both low-wage competitors and value-adding global producers. Moreover, the sector appears not to be reacting satisfactorily to the changes imposed by new types of suppliers (new industries and sciences like biotechnology and nanotechnology) and customers (e.g. healthcare, the automobile industry), rapidly changing customer preferences, the speed of product changes (e.g. the 'fast fashion' concept) and technology-related pressures.

The Greek wood and furniture sector stands somewhere midway between the above-mentioned industries. In general it is highly fragmented and labor intensive with many firms operating in a 'craft' production mode to cover domestic demand, while exports are rather insignificant. As change has been rather slow up to the end of the 2000s, Greek W&F firms were not able to foresee the oncoming multilevel crisis. After 2008 the sector was dramatically hit by the crisis; it had already become vulnerable by its decreasing production capacity and the increasing imports of trendy products (from Italy and Spain) or cheaper products (from Turkey, China and India). In addition, Greek W&F firms do not appear to be responding effectively to the changing conditions of the global environment which have spurred both product and process innovations such as 'eco-design' or 'intelligent' furniture. In this respect they can be characterized as followers of these trends, mainly reacting by restructuring production methods on the basis of advanced computer-integrated manufacturing systems.

Firm selection criteria

The firms selected for the case-study work were new companies established in 2001–07 which at the same time were reckoned among the most innovative companies in their market or product field after the definition of knowledge-intensive entrepreneurial ventures provided by Malerba and McKelvey (2010).

The data gathering took place in face-to-face, in-depth interviews with key personnel using a semi-structured questionnaire. Additional sources of information were also used to complement the interview data such as plant visits, company reports, awards and company websites. The case studies were carried out in Greece during the 2010–11 period. Eight firms in total are presented in this study: three in the F&B and three in the W&F sectors, while the T&C industry is represented by two cases – a new firm and a corporate case. Despite its long historical industrial tradition the T&C sector has been in a deep recession ever since the mid-nineties. Therefore there are almost no new and at the same time innovative firms registered in the sector after 2000. On the other hand it is worthwhile to explore how large Greek firms have reacted to the rapidly changing T&C environment which has turned from being highly stable and protected to extremely negative, vulnerable and ambiguous.

7.4 RESULTS

7.4.1 The Impact of Dynamic Capabilities on Performance

The first stage of the empirical analysis using survey data focuses on testing the relationship between DCs and performance. The linear regression results presented in Table 7.2 suggest that, in general, dynamic capabilities appear to have a positive and statistically significant impact on the different performance measures.

More specifically, Table 7.2 shows that networking activities, technology-collaboration agreements and technology-sensing capability are positively related to the firms' presence in international markets. The findings suggest that the low-tech firm's capability to exploit network ties and technology-collaboration agreements to access and develop critical resources are key factors in internationalization. Given the liability of newness and the highly competitive international markets it seems essential for young low-tech firms to mobilize networks and strategic collaborations to overcome resource and knowledge deficiencies and achieve international presence and growth. Technology-sensing also appears to have a statistically significant positive impact on international sales. New international

Table 7.2   The impact of DCs on low-tech firm performance

Independent variables	Dependent variable: % of sales in international markets (N=1465)	Dependent variable: average growth in employment (N=1320)	Dependent variable: innovative performance (N=1465)
(Constant)	1.027 ns	1.137**	−0.520**
	(3.720)	(0.200)	(0.148)
Market-sensing	0.472 ns	0.030 ns	0.064*
	(0.719)	(0.043)	(0.029)
Technology-sensing	2.043**	0.016 ns	0.135**
	(0.674)	(0.037)	(0.027)
New product development	−1.403 ns	0.018 ns	0.211**
	(0.851)	(0.046)	(0.034)
Networking	1.741*	0.133**	0.023 ns
	(0.839)	(0.044)	(0.033)
Participation in technology collaborations	2.479**	0.121*	0.134**
	(0.915)	(0.049)	(0.036)
Firm size	0.158**	0.007**	0.001ns
	(0.032)	(0.002)	(0.001)
R	0.212	0.198	0.323
R squared (adjusted)	0.041	0.035	0.100

Notes: Standard errors in parentheses, * $p < 0.05$, **$p < 0.01$, ns: not significant.

Source: AEGIS Survey, data processing by LIEE/NTUA.

ventures usually position themselves through product differentiation and the development of unique, knowledge-intensive offerings facilitated by technological innovations. Thus, technology-sensing and adaptation (i.e. the capability to absorb and integrate new technological knowledge and information) is vital to create value-adding activities and thus be able to target and deliver to global (niche) markets.

The growth performance of young low-tech firms is found to be positively related to networking and technology-collaboration capabilities. This suggests that the leverage and mobilization resulting from various network ties and technology collaborations helps young low-tech firms acquire market knowledge, know-how, technological knowledge, finance and other resources that they do not possess but which are essential to their survival and growth.

Moreover, DCs have a positive and significant effect on the innovative performance of young low-tech firms. Market- and technology-sensing capabilities help them effectively look for new opportunities on both market and technology fronts and thus may play a catalytic role in innovative performance. Furthermore, participation in technology collaborations lets low-tech firms absorb new knowledge from external sources that are essential to identifying new product and process development opportunities. Product-development capability relates significantly to innovative performance, as both the potential for developing higher-quality products and new products counterbalance the inevitable maturation of low-tech industries. In this respect companies can alter their products and services to suit shifting demands from simple requirements to differentiated products of increasing value and quality.

7.4.2   Case Analyses

Table 7.3 presents general information on the eight case firms indicating that they are either small, or very small, new entrepreneurial ventures – except for T&C2, which is a well-established firm.

Market-sensing capability
The F&B cases with strong market-sensing capability (F&B1, F&B2) observe markets at a global level using information collection and filtering processes such as regular market research. They have also developed a fast-response mechanism to customer feedback and changing regulations or trends which in turn translate into new or improved products. Promotion methods and best practices are also significant for creating novel competitive advantages. F&B3 has much less market-sensing capability, mainly in its weaker response to customer feedback and monitoring of 'bio-' and 'eco-friendly' trends. This weakness may be primarily attributed to the firm's dominant orientation to the domestic market.

An international player, T&C2 develops and constantly upgrades its internal mechanisms and processes of scanning for international trends while at the same time participating in networks that create global trends. T&C2 has also developed a strong benchmarking mechanism in order to adapt to best practices. Customer feedback, world fashion and demand-change monitoring seem to constitute the only market-sensing process for T&C1. Thus, our findings further confirm the assumption that market-sensing processes are more common and well organized among established companies (Hirsch-Kreinsen and Schwinge, 2011).

A common feature of the three W&F firms is their focus on the domestic market, which appears to affect their DCs development as well. All three cases have introduced processes of customer-feedback selection

Table 7.3 Description of case data

	F&B1	F&B2	F&B3	T&C1	T&C2	W&F1	W&F2	W&F3
Foundation year	2002	2006	2003	2005	2000 (restructuring)	2007	2003	2001
Employees in establishment and in 2010	18 & 30	18 & 35	3 & 9	9	60 & 230	4 & 10	8 & 11	8 & 6
Product family	Organic gluten-free wheat flour and 'bio-functional' foods	Cheese snacks	Organic and quasi-pharmaceutical chocolate	Innovative dying treatments	Jeans, T-shirts	Veneer stitching, marquetry inlays	Glue-laminated products, decorative parts	Lightweight honeycomb furniture
Percentage of sales in national/inter-national markets	90/10	0/100	97/3	100/0	45/55	90/10	100/0	100/0
Patents	Yes	Yes	No	No	No	Yes	No	No
Average annual sales growth rate since establishment and up to 2011 %	41.2	62.50	39.7	0	48	40	31	1.80
Max and min sales increase %	182 −3	162 13	184 3.20	9 1.40	57 0.20	74 56	67 12	39 20
Sales decrease during the crisis period %	2009: -9.0 2010: -9.1	0	2009: -1.3	2009:-16.9 2010:-3.1	2008: -5.8 2009: -9.0 2010: -6.6 2011: -1.1	2010: -15	0	2008: -58.0 2010: -0.6

and elaboration, while they appear to acquire market knowledge though multiple external sources such as technological institutes, sectoral experts, journals and trade shows. W&F1 and W&F2 have developed processes for regular meetings with designers, suppliers and architects to identify market shifts and adapt to best practices. W&F1 also has a benchmarking mechanism for monitoring competitors. But market-sensing is very weak at W&F3, as the firm appears unable to translate feedback or respond to challenges and exploit market opportunities.

NPD and technology-sensing
F&B1 and F&B2 have had formal R&D departments since their establishment. All three companies are operating in niche markets[8] and invest heavily in NPD to maintain the competitive advantage of being market leaders. They have introduced a significant number of new or upgraded products since their establishment. F&B1 and F&B2 patent their new products and develop advanced marketing and promotion activities. NPD is, however, particularly weak at F&B3.

In the T&C sector, the established T&C2 firm has a well-developed technical and design department with a team able to translate the collected information into new products. T&C2 has processes for industry innovation monitoring and benchmarking in production management, sales networks and automation. NPD is further supported by strong marketing, branding and promotion activities. T&C1 is strong in design activity, offering novel products adapted to specific needs, but it appears rather weak in marketing and promotion activities.

None of the three W&F firms have formal technical or R&D departments; however, they all engage in design activities aiming at product differentiation within Greece. Their NPD efforts involve suppliers, and they focus on experimenting with innovative materials produced elsewhere and alternative production processes following mainly trial-and-error methods. W&F2 has joined EU-funded research clusters exploring opportunities for innovative waste and by-product exploitation, while W&F1 has developed benchmarking and competitor-monitoring processes. W&F3 does not have any formal processes of technology-sensing, depending on informal sources including internet, sectoral journals, and personal contacts.

Networking and participation in collaborations
F&B1 and F&B2 complement in-house R&D by cooperating with universities, research institutes and other firms in diverse areas such as biotechnology and medicine, transcending national or sectoral borders. They further cooperate with machine manufacturers, packaging companies and suppliers in order to manage production issues. F&B3 has developed

formal and informal collaborations with universities (plant and food technology) and organic food stores and drugstores to acquire complementary distribution channels. Yet advertising, promotion and export-oriented networking activities are rather underdeveloped.

'Networking is everything' reported the CEO at T&C2. The company invests heavily in networking to learn about and enter desired markets. It also uses networking for NPD, technology upgrading and new processes. By contrast T&C1 lacks the relevant capabilities; however, it has developed close and long-lasting relations with suppliers and customers; these and international fashion shows are their main knowledge sources.

Networking and collaborations do not seem to be very popular among W&F firms. This can be attributed to their rather limited social capital, their introversion and lack of trust in bigger companies. W&F1 and W&F2 have established long-lasting relations with machine and raw-material suppliers for NPD, production and process-advancing purposes. Yet W&F1 is the only one to have had licensing agreements and technical cooperation on a regular basis till now. All three companies appear rather weak in any kind of networking capability in market processes. All efforts of W&F3 to form any type of collaboration have ended in failure.

Table 7.4 presents a summary of our findings on DCs development in each case-study firm.

It is worth mentioning that the firms with strong or moderate DCs have presented better-than-average sales growth rates and smaller decreases in sales during the crisis compared to those firms with weak DCs. This might be an indication that strong and moderate DCs may be beneficial to firms in situations of environmental shock such as the severe Greek financial crisis. Moreover, cases with strong capabilities are the only ones with significant exports and show the greatest employee growth (see Tables 7.3 and 7.4).

Table 7.4   DCs development per case-study firm

Dynamic capabilities	F&B1	F&B2	F&B3	T&C1	T&C2	W&F1	W&F2	W&F3
Market-sensing	Strong	Strong	Moderate	Moderate	Strong	Strong	Moderate	Weak
Technology-sensing	Strong	Strong	Moderate	Moderate	Strong	Strong	Moderate	Moderate
New product development	Strong	Strong	Strong	Weak	Strong	Strong	Strong	Weak
Networking & collaborations	Strong	Strong	Moderate	Weak	Strong	Strong	Moderate	Weak

7.5   CONCLUDING REMARKS

Our study using rich quantitative and qualitative data explores the question of whether young entrepreneurial ventures in low-tech industries develop dynamic capabilities and how such capabilities may benefit these firms' performance.

Extensive survey data reveal that dynamic capabilities have a positive impact on diverse performance measures, indicating that they can indeed play a significant role in low-tech industries. Networking and technology-collaboration agreements appear to be key capabilities explaining the growth, innovative performance and international presence of young firms. In addition, sensing capabilities are important for understanding and responding to changing global conditions and thus may affect young low-tech firms' growth and innovative outcomes.

The case analyses show that DCs are present in knowledge-intensive low-tech firms; however, their development appears to be sector dependent. The F&B cases develop and exercise DCs to respond to technological and scientific advances, changing market structures and intense global competition. The T&C cases build DCs to face fierce market competition in an unpredictable and highly ambiguous environment, while W&F firms seem to develop DCs in an effort mainly to differentiate themselves at least within national borders, catch up with globalization and confront crises. In all cases DCs are closely related to the identification of new knowledge – created either outside the boundaries of the industries under study or developed by the recombination of practical knowledge. Furthermore, dynamic capabilities are deeply impacted by the individual firm's development path and choices.

The case findings also suggest that DCs are related to innovative performance. All firms with strong DCs introduce important process and product novelties through time, while firms with moderate DCs launch mainly incremental innovations. The radicalness of the innovations achieved is, again, sector-specific, for example, F&B cases with strong DCs introduce radical innovations at the global level and demonstrate an increasing R&D intensity. Case-study evidence also indicates that strong and moderate dynamic capabilities seem to be related to R&D intensity, export orientation and high performance even during periods of economic crisis. Furthermore, it appears that case firms in collaboration with various network partners use the knowledge resulting from their market- and technology-sensing activities for the development of new products. Thus, DCs maintain and strengthen these firms' adaptations to their changing environment, not only with regard to their current business practices but also in terms of their survival and successful operation in the future.

Finally, an implication emerging from this study would be that managers should draw up a 'dynamic capabilities portfolio' of their firm to help them assess their actual and potential DCs use in relation to their capacity for adding value to the business. This process could further the development of new knowledge and capabilities in relevant areas and facilitate the renewal of existing resources as a means of responding effectively to the changing conditions in low-tech industries. In addition, policy-makers should consider that KIE is a major mechanism for translating knowledge into innovation (and consequently growth) even in low-tech industries, and thus better understand the role of knowledge creation and capability development in LMT sectors as a way to foster their competitiveness and strengthen their role in highly competitive international markets. A central precondition for this is the facilitation and promotion of networking activities of all kinds between LMT firms and global knowledge sources such as research-intensive knowledge and technology suppliers, low-medium-tech firms, R&D-intensive organizations and/or leading customers/users (Hirsch-Kreinsen, 2013).

NOTES

1. The empirical part of this chapter is based on the AEGIS project survey data and case-study work.
2. Yet, they still account for perhaps 97 per cent of output in modern developed economies, contributing more than 32 per cent of global manufacturing exports (Mendonça, 2009).
3. China nearly doubled its exports and increased its market share from 18 per cent to 30.7 per cent between 2004 and 2010 (UNECE/FAO, 2011).
4. The textile and clothing production transfer to countries of Eastern Europe and later Asia, the liberalization following the abolition of import quotas of the WTO Agreement on Textiles and Clothing in 1993, etc. (e.g. Skuras et al., 2011; Goedhuys et al., 2008).
5. China's furniture exports have risen from $3 billion in 1999 and $7 billion in 2003 to almost $30 billion in 2008. In 2005 it exported for $13.8 billion, surpassing Italy, until then the largest supplier on the global furniture market (UNECE/FAO, 2011).
6. A total of 4004 firms participated in the survey with an average response rate of 31.2 per cent across countries.
7. Information on the selected Greek sectors was based on interviews with sectoral experts, national and EU reports and other internet sources.
8. In the areas of 'bio-functional' and medical foods, health-and-wellness foods and quasi-pharmaceutical products.

REFERENCES

Abro, Q.M.M., N.A. Memon and P.I.A.S. Arshdi (2011), 'Dynamic Capabilities and Firm Performance: A Case of Two SMEs in Pakistan', working paper, available at http://publications.muet.edu.pk/research_papers/pdf/pdf137.pdf (accessed 4 July 2013).

Ambrosini V., C. Bowman and N. Collier (2009), 'Dynamic Capabilities: An Exploration of How Firms Renew their Resource Base', *British Journal of Management*, **20** (1), 9–24.

Augier, M. and Teece, D.J. (2009), 'Dynamic Capabilities and the Role of Managers in Business Strategy and Economic Performance', *Organization Science*, **20** (2), 410–21.

Barreto, I. (2010), 'Dynamic Capabilities: A Review of Past Research and an Agenda for the Future', *Journal of Management*, **36** (1), 256–80.

Boccardelli, P. and M.G. Magnusson (2006), 'Dynamic Capabilities in Early-Phase Entrepreneurship', *Knowledge and Process Management*, **13** (3), 162–74.

Borch, O. and E. Madsen (2007), 'Dynamic Capabilities Facilitating Innovative Strategies in SMEs', *International Journal of Technoentrepreneurship*, **1** (1), 109–25.

Bröring, S., L.M. Cloutier and J. Leker (2006), 'The Front End of Innovation in an Era of Industry Convergence – The Case of Nutraceuticals and Functional Foods', *R&D Management Journal*, **36** (5), 487–98.

Bruhn, Christine M. (2008), 'Consumer Food Safety Concerns: Acceptance of New Technologies that Enhance Food Safety', in John R. Whitaker, Norman F. Haard, Charles F. Shoemaker and R. Paul Singh (eds), *Food for Health in the Pacific Rim: 3rd International Conference of Food Science and Technology*, Trumbull, USA: Food & Nutrition Press, pp. 476–81.

Chirico, F. (2007), 'The Value Creation Process in Family Firms: A Dynamic Capabilities Approach', *Electronic Journal of Family Business Studies*, **1** (2), 137–67.

Colombo, M.G., E. Piva, A. Quas and C. Rossi-Lamastra, (2010), 'Dynamic Capabilities during the Global Crisis: Evidence from Italian New Technology Based Firms', available at http://papers.ssrn.com/sol3/papers.cfm?abstract_id=1722507 (accessed 8 May 2013).

Costa, A.I.A. and W.M.F. Jongen (2006), 'New Insights into Consumer-led Food Product Development', *Trends in Food Science and Technology*, **17** (8), 457–65.

Dahl, M.S. and C.O.R. Pedersen (2004), 'Knowledge Flows through Information Contracts in Industrial Districts: Myth or Reality?', *Research Policy*, **33** (10), 1673–86.

De Bakker, F. and A. Nijhof (2002), 'Responsible Chain Management: A Capability Assessment Framework', *Business Strategy and the Environment*, **11** (1), 63–75.

Dess, G.G. and D.W. Beard (1984), 'Dimensions of Organizational Task Environments', *Administrative Science Quarterly*, **29** (1), 52–73.

Dixon, S.E.A., K.E. Meyer and M. Day (2010), 'Stages of Organizational Transformation in Transition Economies: A Dynamic Capabilities Approach', *Journal of Management Studies*, **47** (3), 416–36.

Duncan, R.B. (1972), 'Characteristics of Organizational Environments and Perceived Environmental Uncertainties', *Administrative Science Quarterly*, **17** (3), 313–27.

Easterby-Smith, M. and I.M. Prieto (2008), 'Dynamic Capabilities and Knowledge Management: An Integrative Role for Learning?', *British Journal of Management*, **19** (13), 235–49.

Easterby-Smith, M., M.A. Lyles and M. Peteraf (2009), 'Dynamic Capabilities: Current Debates and Future Directions', *British Journal of Management*, **20** (s1), S1–S8.

Eisenhardt, K.M. (1989), 'Making Fast Strategic Decisions in High-Velocity Environments', *Academy of Management Journal*, **32** (3), 543–76.

Eisenhardt, K.M. and J.A. Martin (2000), 'Dynamic Capabilities: What Are They?', *Strategic Management Journal*, **21** (10–11), 1105–21.

Evers, N. (2011), 'International New Ventures in Low-Tech Sectors – a Dynamic Capabilities Perspective', *Journal of Small Business & Enterprise Development*, **18** (3), 502–28.

Farrer, J. and A.L. Finn (2011), 'Sustainable Fashion Textiles Design: Value Adding through Technological Enhancement', paper presented at the Fabricating the Body: Textiles and Human Health in Historical Perspective Conference, University of Exeter, 6–7 April 2011, available at http://eprints.qut.edu.au/40983/3/Pasold_farrer_finn_eprints.pdf (accessed 8 May 2013).

Fryer, P.J. and C. Versteeg (2008), 'Processing Technology Innovation in the Food Industry', *Innovation: Management, Policy & Practice*, **10** (1), 74–90.

Gereffi, G., J. Humphrey, R. Kaplinsky and T.J. Sturgeon (2001), 'Introduction: Globalisation, Value Chains and Development', *IDS Bulletin*, **32** (3), 1–8.

Goedhuys, M., N. Janz, P. Mohnen and J. Mairesse (2008), 'Micro Evidence on Innovation and Development (MEIDE): An Introduction', *European Journal of Development Research*, **20** (1), 167–71.

Haeussler, C., L. Jiang, J. Thursby and M. Thursby (2012), 'Strategic Alliances and Product Development in High Technology New Firms: The Moderating Effect of Technological Capabilities', *Journal of Business Venturing*, **27** (2), 217–33.

Helfat, C.E. (1997), 'Know-How and Asset Complementarity and Dynamic Capability Accumulation: The Case of R&D', *Strategic Management Journal*, **18** (5), 339–60.

Helfat, C.E., S. Finkelstein, W. Mitchell, M.A. Peteraf, H. Singh, D.J. Teece and S.G. Winter (eds) (2007), *Dynamic Capabilities: Understanding Strategic Change in Organizations*, Malden, MA, USA: Blackwell Publishing.

Helfat C.E. and M.A. Peteraf (2009), 'Understanding Dynamic Capabilities: Progress along a Development Path', *Strategic Organization*, **7** (1), 91–102.

Hirsch-Kreinsen, H. and I. Schwinge (2011), 'Knowledge-Intensive Entrepreneurship and Innovativeness in Traditional Industries: Conceptual Framework and Empirical Findings', Deliverable 1.3.1 AEGIS Project, available at www.aegis-fp7.eu/index.php?option=com_docman&task=doc_download&gid=64&Itemid=12 (accessed 6 June 2013).

Hirsch-Kreinsen, H. (2013), '"Low-Tech" Research Revisited', paper presented at the 35th DRUID Conference, Barcelona, 17–19 June 2013.

Jansen, J.J.P., F.A.J. Van Den Bosch and H.W. Volberda (2006), 'Exploratory Innovation, Exploitative Innovation, and Performance: Effects of Organizational Antecedents and Environmental Moderators', *Management Science*, **52** (11), 1661–74.

Jones, O., A. Ghobadian, N. O'Regan and V. Antcliff (2013), 'Dynamic Capabilities in a Sixth-Generation Family Firm: Entrepreneurship and the Bibby Line', *Business History*, **55** (6), 1–32.

Kaloudis, Aris, Tore Sandven and Keith Smith (2005), 'Structural Change, Growth and Innovation: The Roles of Medium and Low Tech Industries, 1980–2000', in Gerd Bender, David Jacobson and Paul L. Robertson (eds), *Non-Research-*

Intensive Industries in the Knowledge Economy, published in *Perspectives on Economic, Political and Social Integration*, **XI** (1–2), special issue, 49–74.

Karantininis, K., J. Sauer and W.H. Furtan (2010), 'Innovation and Integration in the Agri-Food Industry', *Food Policy*, **35** (2), 112–20.

Kuuluvainen, A. (2011), 'Dynamic Capabilities in the International Growth of Small and Medium-Sized Firms', Publications of Turku School of Economics: Series A-4: 2011/Turun kauppakorkeakoulun julkaisuja, A-4:2011.

Likar, B. (2008), 'The Influence of Innovation, Technological and Research Processes on the Performance of Slovenia's Woodworking Industry', *Wood Research*, **53** (4), 115–20.

Littunen, H. (2000), 'Networks and Local Environmental Characteristics in the Survival of New Firms', *Small Business Economics*, **15** (1), 59–71.

Makadok, R. (2001), 'Toward a Synthesis of the Resource-Based and Dynamic-Capability Views of Rent Creation', *Strategic Management Journal*, **22** (5), 387–401.

Makkonen, H., M. Pohjola, R. Olkkonen and A. Koponen (2013), 'Dynamic Capabilities and Firm Performance in a Financial Crisis', *Journal of Business Research* (in press).

Malerba, F. and M. McKelvey (2010), 'Conceptualizing Knowledge-Intensive Entrepreneurship: Concepts and Models', paper presented at the DIME/AEGIS Conference, Athens, Greece, 7–10 October 2010.

McKelvey, Maureen and Astrid Heidemann Lassen (2013), *Managing Knowledge Intensive Entrepreneurship*, Cheltenham, UK and Northampton, MA, USA: Edward Elgar.

Mendonça, S. (2009), 'Brave Old World: Accounting for "High-Tech" Knowledge in "Low-Tech" Industries', *Research Policy*, **38** (3), 470–82.

Miller, D. and P.H. Friesen (1983), 'Strategy-Making and Environment: The Third Link', *Strategic Management Journal*, **4** (3), 221–35.

O'Reilly, C.A. and M.L. Tushman (2004), 'The Ambidextrous Organization', *Harvard Business Review*, **82** (4), 74–83.

Pavlou P. and O.A. El Sawy (2011), 'Understanding the Elusive Black Box of Dynamic Capabilities', *Decision Sciences*, **42** (1), 239–73.

Protogerou, A., Y. Caloghirou and S. Lioukas (2012), 'Dynamic Capabilities and Their Indirect Effect on Performance', *Industrial and Corporate Change*, **21** (3), 615–47.

Protogerou, A. and G. Karagouni (2012), 'Identifying Dynamic Capabilities in Knowledge-Intensive New Entrepreneurial Ventures Actors Sectoral Groups and Countries', Deliverable 1.8.2 AEGIS Project, available at www.wfdt.teilar.gr/papers/AEGIS_Deliverable_1.8.2.pdf (accessed 6 May 2013).

Quentier, J.-M. (2011), 'International New Ventures in the Commodity Sector: A Dynamic Capabilities Perspective', IABD 23rd Annual Conference, New Orleans, Louisiana, USA, 7–9 April 2011.

Robertson, P. and P.R. Patel (2007), 'New Wine in Old Bottles: Technological Diffusion in Developed Economies', *Research Policy*, **36** (5), 708–21.

Salvato, C. (2003), 'The Role of Micro-Strategies in the Engineering of Firm Evolution', *Journal of Management Studies*, **40** (1), 83–108.

Sapienza, H.J., E. Autio, G. George and S.A. Zahra (2006), 'A Capability Perspective on the Effects of Early Internationalization on Firm Survival and Growth', *Academy of Management Review*, **31** (4), 914–33.

Sarkar, S. and A.I.A. Costa (2008), 'Dynamics of Open Innovation in the Food Industry', *Trends in Food Science & Technology*, **19** (11), 574–80.

Sciascia, Salvatore, Fernando G. Alberti and Carlo Salvato (2009), 'Firm-Level Entrepreneurial Contents for Strategic Renewal: A Knowledge-Based Perspective', in Tom G. Lumpkin and Jerome A. Katz (eds), *Entrepreneurial Strategic Content: Advances in Entrepreneurship, Firm Emergence and Growth*, vol. XI, Bingley, UK: Emerald Group Publishing, pp. 41–75.

Skuras D., K. Tsekouras and E. Dimara (2011), 'Deciphering the Effects of Agglomeration Economies on Firms' Productive Efficiency', working paper, available at www-sre.wu.ac.at/ersa/ersaconfs/ersa11/e110830aFinal00696.pdf (accessed 10 May 2013).

Srinivasan, R., G.L. Lilien and A. Rangaswamy (2002), 'The Role of Technological Opportunism in Radical Technology Adoption: An Application to e-Business', *Journal of Marketing*, **66** (3), 47–60.

Stam, E., P. Gibcus, J. Telussa and E. Garnsey (2007), 'Employment Growth of New Firms', Scales Research Report, available at www.entrepreneurship-sme.eu/pdf-ez/H200716.pdf (accessed 14 May 2013).

Stearns, S. (1996), 'Collaborative Exams as Learning Tools', *College Teaching*, **44** (3), 111–12.

Teece, D.J., G. Pisano and A. Shuen (1997), 'Dynamic Capabilities and Strategic Management', *Strategic Management Journal*, **18** (7), 509–33.

Teece, D.J. (2007), 'Explicating Dynamic Capabilities: The Nature and Microfoundations of (Sustainable) Enterprise Performance', *Strategic Management Journal*, **28** (13), 1319–50.

Teece, D.J. (2010), 'Business Model, Business Strategy and Innovation', *Long Range Planning*, **43** (2–3), 172–94.

Telussa, J., E. Stam and P. Gibcus (2006), 'Entrepreneurship, Dynamic Capabilities and New Firm Growth', SCALES Working Paper, available at www.entrepreneurship-sme.eu/pdf-ez/H200623.pdf (accessed 19 June 2013).

UNECE and FAO (2011), 'Forest Products Annual Market Review 2010–2011', Geneva Timber and Forest Working Paper, available at www.unece.org/fileadmin/DAM/publications/timber/FPAMR_2010–2011_HQ.pdf (accessed 16 May 2013).

Von Tunzelmann, Nick and Virginia Acha (2005), 'Innovation in "Low-Tech" Industries', in Jan Fagerberg, David C. Mowery and Richard R. Nelson (eds), *The Oxford Handbook of Innovation*, New York, USA: Oxford University Press, pp. 407–32.

Wang, C.L. and P.K. Ahmed (2007), 'Dynamic Capabilities: A Review and Research Agenda', *The International Journal of Management Reviews*, **9** (1), 31–51.

Winter, S.G. (2003), 'Understanding Dynamic Capabilities', *Strategic Management Journal*, **24** (10), 991–5.

Zahra, S.A., H.J. Sapienza and P. Davidsson (2006), 'Entrepreneurship and Dynamic Capabilities: A Review, Model and Research Agenda', *Journal of Management Studies*, **43** (4), 918–55.

Zollo, M. and S.G. Winter (2002), 'Deliberate Learning and the Evolution of Dynamic Capabilities', *Organization Science*, **13** (3), 339–51.

APPENDIX

Table A7.1   CFA analysis results for sensing capability

Sensing capability	Construct indicators	Standardized first-order loadings
Market-sensing	Our firm actively observes and adopts the best practices in our sector	0.650[a]
	Our firm responds rapidly to competitive moves	0.707*
	We change our practices based on customer feedback	0.676*
	Our firm regularly considers the consequences of changing market demand in terms of new products and services	0.750*
	Our firm is quick to recognize shifts in our market (e.g. competition, regulation, demography)	0.779*
	We quickly understand new opportunities to better serve our customers	0.770*
Technology-sensing	Employees share practical experiences on a frequent basis	0.524[a]
	There is a formal R&D department in our firm	0.640*
	There is a formal engineering and technical studies department in our firm	0.719*
Goodness-of-fit statistics		
	χ^2(d.f.)	920.378(35) p=0.00
	CFI	0.911
	RMSEA	0.79

Notes:
a.   Loadings are fixed to 1 for identification purposes.
*   All factor loadings are significant at p < 0.05 level.

Source: AEGIS Survey, data processing by LIEE/NTUA.

Table A7.2   CFA analysis results

Firm capability	Construct indicators	Standardized first-order loadings
New product-development capability	Capability to offer novel products/services	0.712[a]
	Capacity to adapt the products/services to the specific needs of different customers/ market niches	0.484*
	Marketing and promotion activities	0.407*
R&D and alliance-related capabilities	R&D activities	0.761[a]
	Networking with scientific research organizations (universities, institutes, etc.)	0.621*
	Goodness-of-fit statistics	
	χ^2(d.f.)	178.30(8)
		p = 0.00
	CFI	0.942
	RMSEA	0.73

Notes:
a.   Loadings are fixed to 1 for identification purposes.
*   All factor loadings are significant at p<0.05 level.

Source: AEGIS Survey, data processing by LIEE/NTUA.

Table A7.3   CFA analysis results: networking capability

Construct indicators	Standardized first-order loadings
Selecting suppliers	0.592[a]
Recruiting skilled labor	0.565*
Collecting information about competitors	0.580*
Accessing distribution channels	0.612*
Assistance in obtaining business loans/attracting funds	0.596*
Advertising and promotion	0.588*
Developing new products/services	0.621*
Managing production and operations	0.677*
Assistance in arranging taxation or other legal issues	0.559*
Exploring export opportunities	0.559*
Goodness-of-fit statistics	
χ^2(d.f.)	920.378(38)
CFI	0.919
RMSEA	0.79

Notes:
a.   Loadings are fixed to 1 for identification purposes.
*   All factor loadings are significant at p <0.05 level.

Source: AEGIS Survey, data processing by LIEE/NTUA.

Table A7.4   CFA analysis results: participation in collaborations

Construct indicators	Standardized first-order loadings
Strategic alliance	0.548[a]
R&D agreement	0.743*
Technical cooperation agreement	0.702*
Licensing agreement	0.523*
Research contract-out	0.549*
Goodness-of-fit statistics	
χ^2(d.f.)	160.688(5)
	p=0.00
CFI	0.963
RMSEA	0.88

Notes:
a.   Loadings are fixed to 1 for identification purposes.
*   All factor loadings are significant at p < 0.05 level.

Source: AEGIS Survey, data processing by LIEE/NTUA.

Table A7.5   Reliability analysis for CFA constructs

Constructs	Cronbach's Alpha
Market-sensing	0.857
Technology-sensing	0.617
New product development capability	0.611
Networking capability	0.845
Participation in technological collaborations	0.742

Note: All capabilities constructs can be considered reliable on Cronbach's Alpha indicator (>0.6).

Source: AEGIS Survey, data processing by LIEE/NTUA.

8. Readjusting the perspective on LMT firms in product supply chains in light of knowledge-intensive activity[1]

Isabel Schwinge

8.1 INTRODUCTION

The main objective of this chapter is to readjust the prevalent perspective on low- and medium-low-tech (LMT) firms in product supply chains in the debate on innovation and knowledge intensity. With regard to sources of innovation, the prevalent view of LMT firms is dominated by the science and technology perspective that classifies them as supplier-dominated firms with weak internal innovation capabilities (e.g. Heidenreich, 2009). In contrast to this, industrial innovation studies describe more differentiated innovation activities of LMT firms (Hirsch-Kreinsen, 2008). Robertson et al. (2009) criticize the fact that the contribution of LMT customers is often not grasped statistically. Other studies show that some LMT firms increase their competitiveness by moving up the product supply chain (Bender, 2006). Through interaction with customers and suppliers they create new products, increase their product capabilities or open up new markets, and can also play an important role in high-tech products (ibid.), which has already been stressed by von Tunzelmann and Acha (2005) and Robertson and Patel (2005).

There are, besides, indications – with respect to significant environmental changes like intensive international price competition, liberalization of international trade, and rising energy and material costs as innovation drivers – leading to the conclusion that incremental innovations along mature technological paths are no longer sufficient for LMT manufacturing firms (see also Protogerou et al. in Chapter 7 in this volume). For these reasons, increased knowledge-intensive activity can probably also be expected from LMT firms. Knowledge-intensive activities are thereby understood as those going beyond what is provided by a certain share of

R&D expenses and staff. The creation of new knowledge deviating from the widespread incremental, routinized innovation activities and existing problem-solving methods of the respective sectoral knowledge base requires instead knowledge-intensive activity from LMT firms (Schwinge and Hirsch-Kreinsen, 2012).

Readjusting the dominant perspective on LMT enterprises in product supply chains means to take into account internal activities as well as interactions with suppliers and customers (Section 2). Empirical material is analysed by using the interaction model of the Industrial Marketing and Purchasing Group (IMP), modified for the dimension of 'distributed knowledge bases' as the framework of analysis (Section 3). Two explanatory arrangements for LMT firms in the supply chain are presented based on two qualitative case studies from the AEGIS project (Schwinge and Hirsch-Kreinsen, 2012) (Section 4). These initial empirical insights help us derive some first hypotheses about the sources of knowledge and conditions for extending knowledge bases for further directed research and generalizations in this field (Section 5).

8.2   LMT FIRMS IN PRODUCT SUPPLY CHAINS

LMT firms can be understood as low- or non-research-intensive companies predominantly in manufacturing industries such as the food, wood and furniture, pulp and paper industries, and the manufacture of basic metal or rubber and plastic products (Hirsch-Kreinsen et al., 2008). They are integrated into various product supply chains ranging from low- to high-tech products. Therefore they can be in different positions in the supply chain – as suppliers as well as purchasers, and as end-producers for consumer or industrial markets.

A literature review reveals a prevalent view of LMT firms that is rather one-sided. In this view LMT firms, in contrast to high-tech firms, are supposed to conduct mainly process innovations (Kirner et al., 2009; Heidenreich, 2009). Heidenreich (2009: 483) argues that the optimization of product processing is more important for LMT firms than are product innovations because the former mainly focus on unit costs, and for that reason process technology is of substantial importance to LMT companies. Their innovativeness is held to rely mainly on the acquisition of machinery and equipment, software and the competence of external technology suppliers causes their weak internal innovation (ibid.). Besides, LMT companies are thought to be less cooperative towards innovation and have less recourse to non-R&D sources of knowledge such as patents and training, and so on (ibid.). Their most important cooperation partners and sources of knowledge are, on this view, suppliers (Heidenreich, 2008: 241).

Against this background, LMT companies are widely termed 'supplier-dominated firms' following Pavitt's taxonomy of sectoral innovation modes (Heidenreich, 2008, 2009; Robertson et al., 2003). Upon a closer look at Pavitt's taxonomy (1984), it appears that he does not classify firms in the low-tech sector such as food and metal processing as 'supplier-dominated', but as 'scale-intensive firms'. Because Pavitt's classification mainly addresses technological characteristics, he classifies financial and commercial services, for instance, also as 'supplier-dominated', though these industries and firms are usually considered knowledge-intensive. As von Tunzelmann and Acha (2005: 480) state, 'LMT industries resist easy classification, precisely because many of them are not very distinctive or singular in technological terms'. In consequence, the category 'supplier-dominated firm' seems insufficient for an analysis of innovation activities of LMT firms in product supply chains, as innovation is not only defined by technology (Godîn, 2008; see also Havas in Chapter 9 in this volume).

Smith (2005) alerts us to the challenges of innovation studies in general. Likewise Arundel et al. (2008) point to the shortcomings of innovation surveys. As Heidenreich (2008: 221) notes:

> 'Learning and innovation can take place without research and development (R&D), for example through acquisition of tacit and practical knowledge, and through formal and informal diffusion between firms' (Jacobson and Heanue, 2005: 315). Technological upgrades, better designs or customer-specific applications or, on a more general level, learning-by-interacting and practical, experience-based, often implicit knowledge is considered to be an essential source of innovation especially for low- and medium-technology industries.

Additionally, Robertson et al. (2009) stress the widely underestimated importance of LMT firms' knowledge input to suppliers when they purchase their machines and equipment. The contributions of LMT firms in formal alliances with their suppliers or customers to improve products and processes are very hard to grasp in statistics (ibid.: 441 et seq.). In any case – leaving aside the prevalent view of LMT firms as supplier-dominated – neither of these facts means that technological innovation is excluded or that LMT firms are not creating technological innovations at all.

As an alternative to the supplier-dominated perspective, low-tech innovation studies (Hirsch-Kreinsen, 2008; Hirsch-Kreinsen et al., 2008) provide a more differentiated view of the innovation activity and position of LMT firms in product supply chains. Taking a broad range of low-tech industries into consideration, Hirsch-Kreinsen (2008: 25 et seq.) identifies innovation-process specialists and customer-oriented LMT firms, among others. LMT enterprises pursuing the strategy of process specialization are classed as industrial subsectors with products mostly manufactured on a relatively high level of automation like textiles, paper or metal manufacturing (ibid.). Instead of the term 'supplier-dominated firm', the 'process specialists' described by Hirsch-Kreinsen are comparable to Pavitt's (1984) category of 'scale-intensive firms', among which food and metal manufacturing firms have also been placed. 'In these categories, innovative firms produce relatively high proportion of their own process technology, to which they devote a relatively high proportion of their own innovative resources; they have a high level of vertical technological diversification into equipment related to their own process technology' (ibid.: 359). LMT firms applying a 'customer-oriented strategy' are characterized by innovation activities directed not only towards securing and improving the sales market situation through incremental innovations in product design or functional and technical upgrading, they are also directed towards taking advantage of market niches by meeting special customer requirements as well as opening up new, anticipated market segments (Hirsch-Kreinsen, 2008: 26). Such knowledge-intensive innovation activity of LMT firms enables (high- and medium-high-tech) customers to reduce the weight of their products or apply new components with better or even new features (e.g. new textile materials in the automotive industry).

Given that the markets of LMT sectors – compared to those of high-tech industries – are generally mature, slow-growing and characterized by overcapacity and high levels of price competition (Robertson et al., 2009: 441), there is an increasing need for LMT firms to align their innovation strategies towards opening up new market niches that create new demand and secure growth. In line with this it is assumed that the existing mature sectoral and firm-specific knowledge bases need to be extended, which requires increasing knowledge-intensive activities from LMT firms.

For that reason we analyse in the following the position of LMT firms within product supply chains from the industrial innovation perspective on LMT sectors. This implies that innovations are not created in a linear innovation process proceeding from high-tech suppliers to low-tech customers, but in a recursive interaction process. Additionally, increasing knowledge intensity is not limited to investments in R&D and the creation of new technologies, but depends much more on the referential framework of innovation. Innovations in terms of new processes or products that have thus far not been applied by firms in low-tech industries or introduced on markets qualify as knowledge-intensive activities because they increase the knowledge base at the firm and sectoral level (Hirsch-Kreinsen and Schwinge, 2011). In other words, the existing knowledge in the firm and the shared knowledge at the sectoral knowledge base are not sufficient for setting up the innovation – instead, new knowledge needs to be created, and this is considered a knowledge-intensive process.

8.3   READJUSTING THE PRODUCT SUPPLY CHAIN PERSPECTIVE

The economic and political debate can give the impression that new knowledge for innovation can only be created by science or by firms doing R&D, because the indicators for this activity can be measured more easily (Som, 2012: 109).

The significance of interorganizational and inter-sectoral relations for the creation of innovation, on the other hand, has already been stressed by several authors (Kline and Rosenberg, 1986; Dyer and Singh, 1998; Robertson and Smith, 2008). But research on supply chains has been conducted mainly in complex product supply chains (e.g. automotives) and mostly from the perspective of original equipment manufacturers (OEMs) and/or their relations to big system suppliers, which does not necessarily cover the perspective of LMT companies.

The realignment of the perspective on LMT firms not only implies a closer look at their relationships to suppliers or their internal innovation activities, it also requires consideration of the demand side. Von Tunzelmann and Acha (2005) emphasize that demand is of particular importance for LMT industries and that market opportunities can be as important as technological ones. 'The availability of advanced technologies may be an important factor for innovation strategies in LMT firms through dictating the scope for such new products, and even then may not result in products that customers find attractive, as has been the case for genetically modified (GM) foodstuffs in some countries' (ibid.: 415). The importance of the customer or demand side to LMT firms' operations is statistically underscored by data from the Community Innovation Survey (CIS) (2002–04) as illustrated in Heidenreich (2009). The indicator 'highly important sources of information for innovation' shows that clients or customers (24.1 per cent) are almost as important as suppliers of equipment, materials, and so on. (24.9 per cent) for innovative LMT firms (Heidenreich, 2009: 489). Indeed, innovation activity and cooperation undertaken by innovative LMT firms is less common with customers and clients (11.3 per cent) than with suppliers (14.3 per cent) (the figures for high-tech firms are respectively 37 per cent and 55 per cent). But this could also indicate in-house innovation activity of innovative LMT companies, or significant informal or involuntary knowledge sourcing activity (besides formal cooperation) in developing innovations.

The following is an account from the LMT firms' perspective – conceptually realigned to consider also the demand side, and taking into account especially the interaction and knowledge flows between them and their customers and suppliers. These conceptual considerations are complemented and illustrated by case-study data collected within work package 1.3 of the AEGIS project (Hirsch-Kreinsen and Schwinge, 2011). Also for that reason, the widely known (Fischer, 2006) basic model of interaction between customers and suppliers of the International Marketing and Purchasing Group (IMP) is especially modified here for the dimension of sectoral knowledge bases. This interaction approach (Turnbull and Valla, 1986) was initially developed as an explanatory framework for understanding the internal dynamics of industrial markets. It emphasizes the active participation of the industrial buyer, as referred to by Robertson et al. (2009), and the transactions that occur through an interactive process between individuals within functional departments and hierarchical levels at both supplier and customer firms (Turnbull and Valla, 1986). Moreover, the framework takes into consideration both short-term exchanges and long-lasting relations in buyer–supplier interactions. This is important for a deeper understanding of flows of knowledge and their creation, since knowledge transfer occurs not only in long-term cooperative relationships, but can also diffuse or give incentives to new knowledge creation unconsciously and involuntarily in short-term market relationships (ibid.). As shown above, Heidenreich's (2009) evaluated CIS data points in that direction. Besides this, the concept allows an examination of the dependencies of power in customer–supplier relationships and the influence of technology on the interaction between a supplier's product technology and the customer's manufacturing technology. Furthermore, the influence of the macro-environment in terms of market size, structure and dynamism, as well as of social systems, can be considered in this approach (see Figure 8.1).

The interaction model of Turnbull and Valla (1986) was actually designed for analysing marketing and purchasing strategies in industrial markets. However, for the purpose of analysing LMT firms in product supply chains and their increasing knowledge intensity, the model has been realigned towards the concept of distributed knowledge bases (Robertson and Smith, 2008) as shown in Figure 8.1. Here distributed knowledge bases have been particularly stressed in the innovation activities of LMT firms (ibid.):

> Older technologies do not just die away when new ones emerge. Instead, they join up with one another as inputs into the existing or new products. What is more, new technologies are not just sourced out of supplier sectors:

cutting-edge knowledge about them is more distributed across industries than usually acknowledged. (Mendonça, 2009: 480)

Accordingly, Smith (2003) considers knowledge as basically distributed among different agents and knowledge bases. Together with Robertson (2008: 99 et seq.) he describes the production-relevant knowledge content of an industry through the different levels of accessibility of knowledge bases. They distinguish between *firm-specific, sector- or product field-specific* and *widely applicable knowledge bases*. The *firm-specific* knowledge base is often described as highly localized and specific knowledge of the firm's product, connected to process technologies for its production, which varies with its complexity. This specific knowledge is the basis for competing with other firms in the sector (ibid.). The *sector-specific or product field-specific* knowledge base refers to particular shared knowledge at the industry or product-field level, and concerns 'technical functions, performance characteristics, use of materials and so on of products' (Robertson and Smith, 2008: 100). This knowledge is in general available to all firms producing in this industry or product field. Besides the firm- and sector-specific level there exists also the *widely applicable* knowledge base. Robertson and Smith locate on this level also the general scientific knowledge base which itself can be further differentiated and of varying significance for industrial production (ibid.).

The new combinations of distributed knowledge from different knowledge bases create heterogeneity and innovation in mature industries. Moreover, the new knowledge that is created by adjusting and aligning already existing knowledge describes knowledge-intensive activity because it results in increased knowledge intensity at the level of the LMT firm-specific knowledge base, and additionally affects the knowledge base of the sector or product field.

Furthermore, at the sectoral- as well as the firm-specific level, one can find interfaces with other sectoral- and firm-specific knowledge bases, particularly along cross-sectoral product supply chains. As Robertson and Smith (2008: 100) further point out, 'the knowledge base does not exist in a vacuum. It is developed, maintained and disseminated by institutions of various kinds, and it requires resources'. Figure 8.1 shows the *macro-environment* of interaction as market structure and dynamics, as well as the *atmosphere of the relationship* in terms of power-dependence and expectations, as institutional aspects.

Along product supply chains there are several inter-sectoral and interorganizational interfaces structuring *knowledge flows* and the different *knowledge bases*. Thus LMT suppliers are expected to know to a certain extent the product field of their customer for whom they are manufacturing

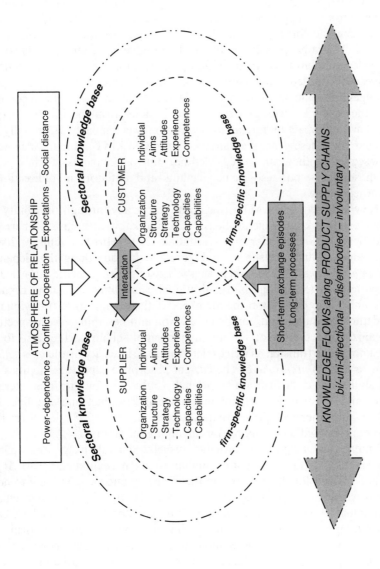

Macro-Environment of Interaction

MARKET SIZE, STRUCTURE AND DYNAMISM – SOCIAL SYSTEM – DEGREE OF INTERNATIONALIZATION

ATMOSPHERE OF RELATIONSHIP
Power-dependence – Conflict – Cooperation – Expectations – Social distance

Sectoral knowledge base

CUSTOMER

Organization   Individual
- Structure   - Aims
- Strategy   - Attitudes
- Technology   - Experience
- Capacities   - Competences
- Capabilities

firm-specific knowledge base

Interaction

SUPPLIER

Organization   Individual
- Structure   - Aims
- Strategy   - Attitudes
- Technology   - Experience
- Capacities   - Competences
- Capabilities

firm-specific knowledge base

Sectoral knowledge base

Short-term exchange episodes
Long-term processes

KNOWLEDGE FLOWS along PRODUCT SUPPLY CHAINS
bi/-uni-directional – dis/embodied – in/voluntary

Source: Based on the interaction model of IMP Group (Turnbull and Valla, 1986).

Figure 8.1   Analytical framework for knowledge-intensive activity in supply chains

components or supplying technologies. On the other hand, in spite of increasing division of labor and outsourcing strategies, LMT customers are also supposed to have a certain amount of knowledge about the products and components they are sourcing (constituting an interface between the two firm-specific knowledge bases). As is widely known from intersected product supply chains, changes in one link – if only slight changes in the demands of users – usually have an impact on the rest of the chain as well. The same is likely to hold for knowledge bases and the increasing knowledge intensity of firms within product supply chains. Accordingly, increased knowledge intensity at a firm can be caused by dynamics and changes upstream or downstream in the supply chain. Vice versa, a company's increasing knowledge activities that broaden firm-specific knowledge can have an impact on interactions with supply chain partners. Initially we assume that these general assumptions apply to LMT companies as well. Consequently, they can be regarded not only as recipients of knowledge from suppliers, but also as participants and initiators in bidirectional knowledge flow.

New knowledge in LMT firms occurs especially through the ability to relate external knowledge to the firm-specific knowledge base (Robertson and Smith, 2008; Bender and Laestadius, 2005; Hirsch-Kreinsen, 2008; Mendonça, 2009). As shown in Figure 8.1, for one thing this depends on *organizational factors* such as the existing firm-specific knowledge base (applied technologies, organizational capabilities, etc.), and capacities which also depend on the members of the organization (individuals) and their attitudes and competences. For another thing, the respective organizational factors of the interacting supply chain partner also form the knowledge transfer, as well as determine the intensity of the *interaction process* and its *atmosphere*. The current absorptive capacities, abilities or capabilities of each firm are additionally influenced by previous interactions and 'its historic participation in specific product markets, lines of R&D, and other technical activities' (He et al., 2006: 248) that form the expectation, conflict and cooperation among the actors.

Enterprises acquire knowledge usually cumulatively and path-dependently in fields that are familiar to them (Faulkner, 1994). It is rather difficult for them to extend their existing knowledge base into new fields which implicate knowledge-intensive activity (ibid.). In particular, technological paradigms of the surrounding sectoral knowledge base can 'have a "powerful exclusion effect", thus limiting the ability of firms to "see" knowledge (including technological options) that is available outside' (ibid.: 441 et seq.). Nevertheless, external sources seem to be of particular importance for moving into new fields. Accordingly, the integration and position of LMT enterprises into product supply chains, as familiar and contingent dynamic fields, can be of particular relevance to their knowledge-intensive activities.

From the above-outlined state of the art and analytical framework, increased knowledge-intensive activity in LMT enterprises can be assumed to result from environmental changes in the form of increasing competition and, above all, technological upgrading in low-cost countries and emerging economies (see also Protogerou et al. in Chapter 7 in this volume). Incremental, 'step-by-step strategies' (Hirsch-Kreinsen, 2008) to improve processes or quality strategies are no longer considered sufficient to secure business and growth today. The same can be said to be the case for applying cutting-edge technology. As the example of genetically modified foods (von Tunzelmann and Acha, 2005: 415) illustrates, innovation cannot be reduced to only R&D and process technologies – the demand side has to be considered too. In this context we assume that LMT firms expand their knowledge base not only through interactions with suppliers but with customers as well. The preliminary qualitative research suggests that knowledge flows in two directions – out of as well as into LMT companies. Next, the readjusted perspective on LMT firms in product supply chains will be illustrated by empirical insights from case studies.

8.4 INSIGHTS FROM CASE STUDIES

To judge from the existing empirical work in this field, it is evident that research on innovation activities of low-tech firms has thus far been limited (Robertson et al., 2009) – with the exception of some initial qualitative analyses (e.g. Bender, 2006; Bender and Laestadius, 2005). Statistical analyses mainly measure quantities at the sectoral level and are not necessarily appropriate for investigating increased knowledge intensity at the firm level. According to Eurostat, which defines knowledge-intensive industries as those with more than a 33 per cent share of tertiary-educated persons in the total sectoral employment (Eurostat, EU Labour Force Survey data), the indicator 'human resources in science and technology-occupation' shows that low-tech industries are still far from becoming knowledge-intensive industries. As mentioned initially, knowledge-intensive activities are defined as going beyond the common indicators of quantitative analysis. Knowledge-intensive activities should not be reduced to only a certain share of R&D expenditures or R&D staff employed. The constituent characteristic of knowledge-intensive activity as outlined in this chapter is the extension of the firm-specific knowledge base and existing product field (sectoral knowledge base) by deviating from established practices and creating new, problem-solving knowledge (Hirsch-Kreinsen and Schwinge,

2011). Therefore even one person – who may not even need an academic degree – can already be sufficient. Though statistically insignificant, a low number of LMT enterprises are carrying out such activities, but these cases can nevertheless have a considerable economic impact on competitors, customers and suppliers.

The empirical insights refer to qualitative case studies of knowledge-intensive entrepreneurship (KIE) in low-tech industries collected in 2009 and 2010 for the AEGIS project (Schwinge and Hirsch-Kreinsen, 2012). The data from the explorative case studies illustrate knowledge-intensive innovation activities in LMT companies that took place between 2000 and 2006. From this sample, two cases of LMT firms were selected to be contrasted with the dominant view of LMT firms as 'supplier-dominated firms'. In one case, an LMT company is in the position as customer; in the second case, another LMT company is considered in the position of supplier. As in the outlined analytical framework (Figure 8.1), the increasing knowledge intensity of LMT enterprises is described by their innovative capabilities and the knowledge which flows in the interaction process with their partners across different knowledge bases. The empirical findings are not generalizable, but do illustrate the complexity and broad range of industrial innovation processes in a more comprehensive way than does the currently dominant view of LMT firms.

8.4.1   The Case of DanCream[2] – in the Position of the Customer Organization

The first case[3] could be termed supplier-driven, since the idea for the innovation that led to knowledge-intensive activities and extended the knowledge base of the firm DanCream and its product field, came from a supplying company. But different to the 'supplier-dominated firm' in the sense of Pavitt or Heidenreich, the new technological knowledge was created internally by DanCream. The supplier of the small dairy firm was also located in the low-tech food sector. The interaction between the supplier and customer firm can be described as a win-win constellation.

The *knowledge-intensive activity* in this case was realized in the form of a product innovation new to the market. In 2003 DanCream introduced, as a first mover, energy-dense ice cream for people whose nutritional needs are not sufficiently covered by their diet, or who have lost their appetite for food. Thus, existing knowledge from the product field of ice cream and the field of nutrition science was combined into new, problem-solving knowledge. The product contains a high level of protein and carbohydrate which helps the body to regenerate itself. Though the inventor at DanCream had more than 30 years' experience in the food industry and knew how to make fatty ice cream, the bigger problem was to increase the percentage of protein. Skimmed milk powder was not enough to increase the level of protein, as – by itself – it does not contain much protein. When the inventor finally found a suitable protein powder to work with, he started mixing things together in a process of trial and error and learning by doing. He did not use any books to find the right recipe. In theory what he did was impossible, for in principle you can put a maximum of 35 to 37 per cent protein as dry material into ice cream. However, in his final recipe he used as much as 50 per cent. The elaboration process took about one year as he made samples at the firm laboratory and sent them to a hospital for testing. The results were not immediately scientifically documented, but dietary consultants there conducted an initial project to test the ice cream's effect. The conclusion was that the ice cream delivered an increased amount of energy and protein beneficial to people with reduced appetite.

This *LMT firm* has been manufacturing dairy products since 1888. The family business sells butter, cheese and ice cream directly to consumer markets like supermarkets, restaurants and catering firms, and to customers at their retail outlet. In the course of developing the new ice cream, hospitals and elderly homes have been opened up as a new customer market. The main suppliers are raw material suppliers of milk, sugar, fruit purée and other ingredients, as well as production equipment suppliers. The company has been producing ice cream and ice cream cakes for 20 years and has proven its competence by winning several prizes and awards. For that reason it can be classified as a process specialist. In all, 15 employees work at DanCream. There are no staff with academic degrees – the majority are skilled workers including dairymen, dairy technicians, and confectioners. The small firm size allows DanCream to have an organizational culture of experiment and creative flow. Supporting this culture is a laboratory with machines that can make ice cream in smaller volumes. If a customer wants a new type of ice cream, samples are made in small amounts. When the experiments are completed and the product is finalized, they begin mass production. It sometimes happens that an employee comes in at the evening with an idea and then different things are tried out in the laboratory – sometimes even in the middle of the night. In fact, development projects are not planned or organized in a specific way, and yet this culture enables the employees to come up with new ideas and initiate development projects.

The *inventor* of the company's new ice cream is the owner. He was trained in another dairy company and gained his knowledge of producing ice cream in Iceland. He also collected work experience in the UK and Pakistan. Before he entered his father's business he worked as a manager at another dairy firm. Besides this *work experience* and his *competences*, he has an *attitude* towards innovation that can be described as an interest in trying out new things and an openness towards new ideas regardless of their source. When developing new products he uses the resources from his network of nutrition, advertising, and packaging experts or students, drawing upon their special competencies. One other employee involved in the development process of finding the right mixture and taste for the product innovation was a cook who had worked for DanCream for 17 years. It is always these two alone who develop new products, because both 'have the taste'. The firm was capable of financing the knowledge-intensive innovation activity on its own. The development cost was about 200 000 euros, invested in new machines and spent on staff, an external consultancy for nutrition calculation, and ingredients. In the firm's estimate, on average 5 per cent of sales is spent annually on innovation activities (including personnel and related costs).

The *trigger* for this knowledge-intensive activity was a Swedish food company supplying fruit purées among other things. A dietician from the supplier firm contacted the small dairy firm and suggested making energy-dense ice cream for patients and 'small-portion-eating' people. The dietician worked for the special-foods department that supplied mashed vegetables and fruit to hospitals and nursing homes and had been looking for a manufacturer of high-fat ice cream. The contact emerged via a hospice that was supplied by both companies. According to the dietician, 65 per cent of people in nursing homes in Denmark are undernourished and could benefit from such a product. For the inventor from DanCream it was an incentive to develop functional products for such a customer group. The *supplier organization* is part of a big group with 6000 employees at different locations. In Denmark 25 people work for this supplier firm that produces frozen food products for the retail and food-service market (restaurants, canteens and cafés). Fruit purée products are one of eight product groups (e.g. fish, meat, vegetables, bread, sauces, etc.) sold on the food market. The firm is known for its quality products. People in the health sector know the brand well and recognize it as high quality. The supplier suggested developing the energy-dense ice cream in the company's fruit purée flavors. Though their purée is rather expensive, DanCream agreed. In return, it was advised on nutrition by the supplier dietician and introduced to potential customers. After the product development, the supplying company's traveling consultants also promoted the new energy-dense ice cream to hospitals by giving out samples during hospital visits and at trade fairs without actually selling it at that time.

It was a win-win *relation* for both parties. The more they promoted the product, the more ice cream had to be produced, and the more fruit purée DanCream had to order from the supplier. Altogether the relation between the supplier and LMT customer can be described as cooperative with episodes of exchange and interaction, though they had not known each other before. The big frozen food supply firm was not economically dependent on the purchases of the small dairy firm. But on the other hand, it lacked the required knowledge, or perhaps the interest, in order to exploit this idea on its own.

Regarding the *sources of knowledge*, we can assess in this case the existing sector- and firm-specific process knowledge involved in ice cream production, and the *disembodied* knowledge, especially that of the LMT firm's owner and one employee. They developed new knowledge regarding how to raise the proportion of protein in the ice cream, knowledge which had not existed in the knowledge base of the product field before. The external knowledge came from the sectoral knowledge base of nutrition and dietary science, especially from the field of nutrition for elderly people and underweight patients. But also doctors and nursing staff provided user knowledge. Practical knowledge came from users (elderly or underweight patients) who described problems in the field of application. The dietician also contributed market knowledge about the nutritional situation of undernourished people in the domestic care market.

Disembodied *knowledge flow* through components or machines did not play a role in this case since the product innovation could be elaborated with existing processing technologies. Most of the necessary knowledge was unidirectionally sourced by the LMT company, which reconfigured and assembled new knowledge. The newly created knowledge was kept secret and not communicated to the supplier. DanCream decided not to apply for a patent because after ten years the recipe would be accessible to everyone. The knowledge sourcing was not always voluntary or in formal cooperation. Once for instance, while the inventor was looking for the right proteins to solve the problem of increasing the protein, he talked to one of his suppliers from whom he used to buy additives for sugar-free ice cream. This supplier also had protein powder, but this powder was too expensive. The inventor, discovering that this supplier's powder was made from whey protein, located cheaper whey protein powder supplied as a standard product. This could be seen as involuntary knowledge diffusion without a formal cooperation or business relation.

One *impact* of this knowledge-intensive activity is that the resulting product innovation contributed 10 per cent of DanCream's total turnover in 2009. The LMT firm developed a new market segment in the health sector, where it is still the market leader. Moreover, the new product also motivated the company to enter foreign markets in a more proactive manner than before. In the past the company had only reacted to customer inquiries rather than actively marketing and promoting its products. In the meantime different product variants have been developed, including a special omega-3 ice cream for heart disease patients.

Although knowledge-intensive activity at DanCream started in 2001, the proportion of skilled workers, compared to that of semi- or unskilled workers, decreased from 2000 to 2009 by 20 per cent. No significant proportion of academics, or greater proportion of skilled staff – indicators of increased knowledge intensity – can be observed to have an effect on this case. When the company entered this market in 2003 it had no competitor supplying energy-dense ice cream. Since 2009 there has been one competitor producing and selling a similar – but organic – energy-dense ice cream to the same target customers in Denmark. DanCream expects more competitors in the future. However, the company is not concerned about the situation because sales of this product have been increasing steadily even after the competing product was introduced. Furthermore, they see potential markets in neighboring countries like Germany, Sweden and Norway, since there are still no similar products in these countries and the product concept is so simple and universal that it probably can be easily sold in other countries. But at the same time this could also be seen as a problem for this small-sized company since it has not enough resources to enter multiple export markets, and because the concept can be easily copied without patent protection. Decision-makers at DanCream decided against the patent because the health effects of the product had not yet been scientifically proven. Once the products' effects were proven it would become a medicinal product, which might imply complications not wanted by the firm (such as the requirement of pharmaceutical approval or prescription).

8.4.2   The Case of E-Thread[4] – in the Position of the Supplier Organization

In this case the initiative for the market innovation came from the LMT supplier, fictively named E-Thread, with support from a small high-tech service provider (fictively named InnoServ) during implementation. E-Thread is a producer of elastic yarn in the German textile industry. The market introduction of the strategically technology-driven innovation required continuing knowledge-intensive activity from E-Thread, as potential customers declined to design new product applications using the innovative yarn. Therefore the yarn producer took on the development of the first product prototypes and the first production series downstream in the textile supply chain.

Knowledge-intensive activity here refers to the development and introduction of a new electrically conductive elastic thread unique in its construction and features in the emerging industrial field of variable electronics. Other existing metal-yarn combinations, for example in the field of fencing clothing, do not provide sufficient flexibility, conductivity or processability. In the course of E-Thread's knowledge-intensive activities, existing sectoral and firm-specific knowledge in elastic thread production was newly combined with existing electronics knowledge. The innovative thread was invented in 2002–03 in cooperation with researchers from InnoServ. Thereafter, different applications were developed in several collaborative research projects with potential customers for the textile, as well as biomedical, automotive industry and research institutes.

The *LMT firm* is a limited company, founded as a family business in 1953. It mainly manufactures elastic thread for compression stockings in continuous process production and single or low-volume production for products with customer-specific variations. E-Thread is generally positioned between fiber-producing suppliers and buyer manufacturers of compression stockings as well as woven-product and fabric producers. The LMT firm employed 74 full-time and nine part-time employees in 2009. The staff are mostly skilled but none have academic degrees. The labor turnover rate is low. Before the knowledge-intensive activities began, innovation activities had been instead incremental and routine, for example concerned with minor customized changes in the flexibility or design of threads. The firm-specific knowledge base in thread spinning and design for elastic fabrics had been built up for more than 50 years. In the course of a change of owner at the beginning of the nineties the firm became part of a shareholder group, whereupon considerable investments in location and cutting-edge equipment were made. Related to this, the main shareholder had expectations of significant innovation activities on the part of E-Thread. Against the environmental background of a serious contraction of this industry and the ending product life cycle of the main product (compression stockings), the managing director decided to look for a completely new innovative business field. The only condition was that it should be producible with the newly acquired machines and equipment.

The managing director can be identified as the *main driver* and promoter of the knowledge-intensive activities at E-Thread. He is a skilled export merchant who began working in distribution for E-Thread in 1979 and in 1993 was made managing director. His *motivation* for opening up a new field was to make the location and workforce sustainable. To do that he turned to innovation management literature and lectures. He contacted InnoServ, a small high-tech service provider of scientists for technical innovation projects at small and medium-sized firms. During the development process, E-Thread's substitute head of development was additionally involved as the technical promoter at E-Thread, since the head of the department could not be won over to the venture. As the human and

2

financial resources were limited, E-Thread had to rely on external sources and technical knowledge from the high-tech partner and government R&D funding.

The *sources of knowledge* were the internal, firm-specific knowledge base of E-Thread, but also other – external – sources from other sectoral knowledge bases, particularly, the thread design and processing knowledge, and the knowledge of the electro-technical and aerospace engineers later recruited by E-Thread. External sources were also physical and basic electrical and electro-technical knowledge of the high-tech partner InnoServ, who also provided E-Thread with patent and feasibility analyses and established contacts with the first development partners and potential buyers. Furthermore, industrial processing partners provided application knowledge in clothing, batteries, heating systems and automotives in cooperative research projects. One collaboration with a customer from the heat-blanket industry enabled access to the existing sectoral knowledge regarding technical standards and product requirements in the field.

In relation to the different interacting partners, different qualities of *knowledge flows* can also be observed in this case. In general there is a limited permeability of knowledge along the textile supply chain. Often a specialized textile enterprise possesses knowledge no more far reaching than that needed to deal with the direct business partner. During the three-year relation with the high-tech firm, a *bidirectional* knowledge flow was established, embodied in development documents created by the externally hired researchers, in the patent process, as well as the disembodied knowledge of the partners and employees involved. Before engineers were hired at E-Thread, the perceptions gained and learning processes begun in interactions with InnoServ had been slow and limited. According to them the textile firm's employees hardly understood the requirements of the applications and so were incapable of creating new useful knowledge in their field. The patent played a decisive role for the LMT firm, as the design of the innovative thread might be easily recreated by anyone with procedural expertise in spinning yarns. The knowledge might diffuse involuntarily this way, but – if patented – cannot be used commercially by competitors.

For the emergence of the innovation, no specific *relation* with a single customer of E-Thread was identified as relevant. There had been several interactions already in the development phase of four applications in cooperative projects. The character of exchanges ranged from short-term business relations to episodes of collaboration in which *conflicts* also appeared. For instance, E-Thread tried to win over a sportswear manufacturer to the idea of introducing a heatable jacket to the market. The LMT firm developed a prototype but had only talked to developers of that firm. When issues regarding the serial production appeared, the potential buyer's management retreated from the project with the argument that heatable jackets would not fit into the sports image of the firm. Further marketing activities showed that potential buyers had very different perceptions and demanded customized products. Clothing manufacturers, for instance, had different expectations and requirements regarding the electrical supply to and integration of the conductive threads in a heatable vest. And each time before selling anything to a customer the LMT firm had to prove a functioning prototype developed to the specific demand, and with still no guarantee of an order. Additionally, potential buyers often asked for exclusivity. When E-Thread asked in return for a certain guaranteed number of ordered goods, buyers were often only willing to order low numbers. Hence a customer-orientated strategy was hard to implement for the LMT firm as a mass producer who was used to thinking in terms of economy of scale. At the same time, the thread producer had no option but to order large amounts of custom-made components for the heatable vests from an electrical supplier.

In the field of car seat heating there was a similar situation. But now E-Thread consulted first with an expert from the automotive industry. It turned out that the supplying firms in the middle of the (automotive) chain were less attracted by the efforts in favor of the new application – instead it was the end-producers (OEMs) who needed to be convinced. In the usual *power-dependence* relation along the automobile supply chain, the original equipment manufacturers (OEMs) can exert pressure on suppliers from the middle part of the chain, such as a supplier of seat heating. These suppliers are usually busy with day-to-day operations and may be occupied with their own firm- or field-specific innovation projects. But these fields of innovation themselves are mostly restricted to established technological regimes and primarily oriented toward end-producer demand – and tend not to consider innovative ideas of suppliers from other business fields (downstream in the supply chain). Hence by the strategy of targeting powerful buyers at the end of the supply chain (OEMs), E-Thread skipped the marketing activities directed at the subsequent processing firms in the product supply chain. Once the OEMs' interest is awakened and a potential demand is articulated, in-between suppliers in the supply chain are also willing to develop products based on such new materials.

The *macro-environment* and *atmosphere* in clothing and home textile markets can be described in general as very cautious and risk averse. Investments in new technologies and innovation costs are passed along the supply chain because no one is willing to reduce their own profit margin. In the end the new consumer product is often too expensive to put on the market. Because of the high level of division in business, most textile specialists have hardly an idea of the value processes upstream in the product supply chain, except maybe for those of their direct customers. The power-dependence proceeds upstream towards the end-producer. Thus the position of the LMT firm at the beginning of the product supply chain in this case is the most constraining.

The knowledge-intensive activities had an enormous *impact* on the LMT firm above all. E-Thread has become a pioneer in radiation blocking technology, thin textile heating and data transfer material. For implementing the innovative product, highly skilled staff experienced in electro-technical engineering and aerospace were hired. Moreover, a new business unit was established with a unit manager as a relational promoter for interactions with customers and research partners from development projects. The firm-specific knowledge base was extended into product applications upstream in product supply chains during the development of prototypes like heatable coats and jackets. Furthermore, it created knowledge in electrical textile interfaces and the integration of electronic devices into textile systems. The managing director and business unit manager state that the innovation culture of the firm has changed, their way of thinking having become more systematic and focused on R&D activity. On average E-Thread spent annually 3 per cent of its turnover on R&D and 5 per cent on the implementation for the innovation. Through cooperative research projects they expanded their circle of customers in new markets and their network for incorporating external knowledge. Even though only a small amount of the material has been sold and customers are still working on product certification, E-Thread has received considerable publicity and an image upgrade vis-à-vis their regular main customer and new potential buyers.

During the innovation process the business *strategy* also changed over that time. This shows the company's initial insecurity and a certain lack of knowledge and experience in sales strategy and new sales markets for such far-reaching innovations. Initially focused on the clothing and home textile markets, the first feedback from potential buyers in cooperative research projects made it clear that it required much more than 'just' a developed prototype. Its offers had to be more advanced and show marketable value. Then E-Thread decided to become itself the driver of innovation, repositioning itself as a system supplier for innovative thread applications in new product supply chains such as 'wearable electronics'. It created a heatable vest as its own consumer product in order to gain experience of putting a finished product directly on the clothing market. This was set up by production order and network building so that only the thread was produced internally. Yet the basic strategy was to continue to be a yarn producer while opening up new business fields, and not to become an end-producer of consumer products. When the hoped-for success in marketing clothing prototypes was not realized, the management and marketing strategy was shifted to other customer industries, for example seat heating for vehicles and heating blankets. Because market diffusion is so long lasting, the business unit was finally downsized again. Most of the staff returned to the core business, and the engineer from the aerospace industry left the firm.

8.5   CONCLUSION

Both of the case studies presented here contrast quite well with the picture of LMT firms as 'supplier-dominated firms' regarding innovation activities. Suppliers of machines and equipment as well as process innovations had no significant role in the knowledge-intensive innovation activities in these cases. Instead, product innovations were developed together with suppliers and/or customers, or in collaborative efforts combining newly existing knowledge from other sectoral knowledge bases.

Both LMT firms showed internal innovation capabilities that they developed further in the course of knowledge-intensive activities. Moreover, their increased knowledge intensity was revealed in terms of recruiting and patenting activities. However, this did not necessarily result in a highly skilled workforce in either case. During their knowledge-intensive activities the firms' investments in innovation and R&D were often above the average for the low-tech sector. But this does not necessarily mean that these investments will remain constant at this higher level, as is commonly thought to be the case for knowledge-intensive firms (Starbuck, 1992). In conclusion, the internal capabilities and initiative of the LMT firms were the essential prerequisite for the knowledge-intensive activities. In other words, the firm-specific knowledge base is a determining factor.

The *knowledge-intensive activities* described in both cases go beyond creative activities such as 'bricolage' or 'effectuation', when firms recombine means at hand, sometimes without really defining beforehand the end result (Pacheco et al., 2010: 1003). Instead, existing components of these LMT firms' heartland were reused and unconventionally combined with components from other sectoral knowledge bases, for instance from elderly care and electronics. These knowledge-intensive activities may be better described by the term 'exaptation' (ibid.). This refers to the reuse of existing (often inactive) features or devices in a new, useful context for new markets, such as in electronic textiles. Moreover, exaptation is explicitly distinguished from reactive adaptation through creative ex-ante initiative (ibid.). The two cases demonstrate in this way Mendonça's argument that established technologies 'do not just die away' (2009: 480) but are newly combined with distributed knowledge. Moreover, these LMT companies succeeded in overcoming the path-dependence of their familiar business and technological fields, as described by Faulkner (1994). They extended their firm-specific knowledge base into new areas such as functional foods and electronic textiles using different *knowledge sources* from distributed knowledge bases across firms and industries.

While the case of the inventor of energy-dense ice cream illustrates the strong internal innovation capabilities of a small LMT customer firm – notwithstanding the common statistical indicator of knowledge-intensive firms (a 30 per cent highly skilled workforce) – the case of the traditional thread producer illustrates how the limited ability of firms to sense external knowledge can be overcome. Without the external perspective of the on-site researchers, the LMT supplier firm would have probably not been able to see the potential of integrating conductive wires into their existing design of elastic yarn, because staff were used to thinking along the path of incremental customized innovation for product optimization. In this respect, disembodied *knowledge flow* in particular played a significant role, more so than did knowledge embodied in machines and equipment.

Another insight from the two cases concerns the *position* of the LMT firm in the product supply chain and the related situation of *power-dependence* and the atmosphere of the relationships. The LMT customer firm (DanCream) had no major difficulties introducing the new ice cream directly on the consumer market. It was additionally supported by the big supplier company, so that the relation can be considered complementarily cooperative. By contrast, the LMT supplier firm (E-Thread) was confronted with a rather hostile innovation environment and conflicting relations with potential buyers. It faced considerably reluctant and risk-averse customers, especially on the low-tech textile and clothing market. For it turned out that, for a manufacturer of material from the beginning of the textile product supply chain, practices and expectations regarding profit margins and innovation costs upstream in the supply chain make it quite hard to implement innovation. The *technology* as well as the investment and innovation *strategies* of potential customers in the textile and clothing industry seem to differ seriously from those of the knowledge-intensive LMT firm (E-Thread). Above all, LTM firms in this position are most likely to lack the power and convincing marketing capabilities necessary to overcome this barrier. In the case of the automotive supply chain this problem could be overcome by skipping the marketing activities intended to convince the next processor in the supply chain, in favor of winning over right away the powerful end-producer. This way firms in the middle of the supply chain, who resisted the implementation of the innovative material in new products, changed their mind. Though the power structures of product supply chains can differ from sector to sector, the position of the LMT firm can be assumed to be a constitutive determining factor in their success or even earlier in their motivation of knowledge-intensive activity.[5]

This barrier, and the huge efforts required, make it difficult to expect a general trend of such knowledge-intensive activities at LMT firms. It can be assumed, rather, that such activities will occur in a minority of cases. The majority of LMT enterprises seem to progress haltingly, preferring to follow successful examples of first movers. But, particularly for this pioneering function and effects, these few cases of knowledge-intensive activity are of economic significance.

All in all, research on product supply chains is fast becoming a very complex task. The first empirical findings reveal that it is worthwhile to better understand innovation activities and knowledge-intensive activity at LMT firms. The two explanatory cases are just a small sample from further collected cases contradicting the prevalent view of supplier-dominated LMT firms (Schwinge and Hirsch-Kreinsen, 2012). They promise further insights into the different interaction arrangements of knowledge-intensive activities in product supply chains. Hence, the first step is to realign the analytical perspective on LMT firms, as in this chapter, in order to show that LMT firms are not only recipients of externally created knowledge or supplier-dominated firms. They can also be the drivers and initiators of innovation and carry out knowledge-intensive activities. The next step now is to gather more representative data on this topic – focusing thereby on specific industries, perspectives or positions of LMT firms as customers or suppliers – and to attempt to validate the hypotheses that:

- in the course of knowledge-intensive activities LMT firms reposition themselves in the product supply chains of new niche markets; and
- the success of these knowledge-intensive activities is determined by the initial position of the LMT firm and the relations of power-dependence along product supply chains.

NOTES

1. This chapter draws on the Deliverable 1.3.2 'Repositioning of low- and medium-low-tech firms in product supply chains and their increasing knowledge intensity' of the AEGIS project (Schwinge and Hirsch-Kreinsen, 2012).
2. DanCream is a fictional name for the company profiled in this case study.
3. We thank Eun Kyung Park and Christian Østergaard from Aalborg University, Denmark, for collecting this case study.
4. E-Thread is a fictional name for the company profiled in this case study.
5. For the interplay of an LMT firm's institutional environment and its institutionalization of knowledge-intensive innovation, see Schwinge (PhD dissertation, forthcoming).

REFERENCES

Arundel, A., C. Bordoy and M. Kanerva (2008), 'Neglected Innovators: How Do Innovative Firms that Do Not Perform R&D Innovate? Results of an Analysis of the Innobarometer 2007', INNO-Metrics Thematic Paper, available at http://arno.unimaas.nl/show.cgi?fid=15406 (accessed 21 June 2013).

Bender, Gerd and Staffan Laestadius (2005), 'Non-Science Based Innovativeness: On Capabilities Relevant to Generate Profitable Novelty', in Gerd Bender, David Jacobson and Paul L. Robertson (eds), *Non-Research-Intensive Industries in the Knowledge Economy*, published in *Perspectives on Economic, Political and Social Integration*, **XI** (1–2), special issue, 123–70.

Bender, G. (2006), 'Peculiarities and Relevance of Non-Research-Intensive Industries in the Knowledge-Based Economy', final report of the project PILOT, Policy and Innovation in Low-Tech, available at http://citeseerx.ist.psu.edu/viewdoc/download?rep=rep1&type=pdf&doi=10.1.1.134.743 (accessed 23 May 2013).

Dyer, J.H. and H. Singh (1998), 'The Relational View: Cooperative Strategy and Sources of Interorganizational Competitive Advantage', *Academy of Management Review*, **23** (4), 660–79.

Eurostat, 'EU Labour Force Survey', available at http://epp.eurostat.ec.europa.eu/portal/page/portal/employment_unemployment_lfs/data/database (accessed 21 December 2013).

Faulkner, W. (1994), 'Conceptualizing Knowledge Used in Innovation: A Second Look at the Science–Technology Distinction and Industrial Innovation', *Science, Technology & Human Values*, **19** (4), 425–58.

Fischer, Bettina (2006), *Vertikale Innovationsnetzwerke: Eine theoretische und empirische Analyse*, Dissertation, Universität Mainz, Wiesbaden: Deutscher Universitätsverlag.

Godîn, Benoit (2008), 'The Moral Economy of Technology Indicators', in Hartmut Hirsch-Kreinsen and David Jacobson (eds), *Innovation in Low-Tech Firms and Industries*, Cheltenham, UK and Northampton, MA, USA: Edward Elgar, pp. 64–84.

He, Q., A. Ghobadian, D. Gallear and A. Sohal (2006), 'Knowledge Transfer between Supply Chain Partners: A Conceptual Model', *International Journal of Process Management and Benchmarking*, **1** (3), 231–62.

Heidenreich, Martin (2008), 'Low-Tech Industries between Traded and Untraded Interdependencies: A Dynamic Concept of Industrial Complementarities', in Hartmut Hirsch-Kreinsen and David Jacobson (eds), *Innovation in Low-Tech Firms and Industries*, Cheltenham, UK and Northampton, MA, USA: Edward Elgar, pp. 221–44.

Heidenreich, M. (2009), 'Innovation Patterns and Location of European Low- and Medium-Technology Industries', *Research Policy*, **38** (3), 483–94.

Hirsch-Kreinsen, H. (2008), '"Low-Tech" Innovations', *Industry and Innovation*, **15** (1), 19–43.

Hirsch-Kreinsen, Hartmut, Katrin Hahn and David Jacobson (2008), 'The Low-Tech Issue', in Hartmut Hirsch-Kreinsen and David Jacobson (eds), *Innovation in Low-Tech Firms and Industries*, Cheltenham, UK and Northampton, MA, USA: Edward Elgar, pp. 3–22.

Hirsch-Kreinsen, H. and I. Schwinge (2011), 'Knowledge-Intensive Entrepreneurship and Innovativeness in Traditional Industries: Conceptual Framework and Empirical Findings', Deliverable 1.3.1 AEGIS Project, available at www.aegis-fp7.eu/index.php?option=com_docman&task=doc_download&gid=64&Itemid=12 (accessed 6 June 2013).

Jacobson, David and Kevin Heanue (2005), 'Implications of Low-Tech Research for Policy', in Hartmut Hirsch-Kreinsen, David Jacobson and Staffan Laestadius (eds), *Low-Tech Innovation in the Knowledge Economy*, Frankfurt am Main, Germany: Lang, pp. 315–31.

Kirner, E., S. Kinkel and A. Jaeger (2009), 'Innovation Paths and the Innovation Performance of Low-Technology Firms – An Empirical Analysis of German Industry', *Research Policy*, **38** (3), 447–58.

Kline, Stephen J. and Nathan Rosenberg (1986), 'An Overview of Innovation', in Ralph Landau and Nathan Rosenberg (eds), *The Positive Sum Strategy: Harnessing Technology for Economic Growth*, Washington, DC, USA: National Academy Press, pp. 275–305.

Mendonça, S. (2009), 'Brave Old World: Accounting for "High-Tech" Knowledge in "Low-Tech" Industries', *Research Policy*, **38** (3), 470–82.

Pacheco, D.F., J.G. York, T.J. Dean and S.D. Sarasvathy (2010), 'The Coevolution of Institutional Entrepreneurship: A Tale of Two Theories', *Journal of Management*, **36** (4), 974–1010.

Pavitt, K. (1984), 'Sectoral Patterns of Technical Change: Towards a Taxonomy and Theory', *Research Policy*, **13** (6), 343–73.

Robertson, P., E. Pol and P. Caroll (2003), 'Receptive Capacity of Established Industries as a Limiting Factor in the Economy's Rate of Innovation', *Industry and Innovation*, **10** (4), 457–74.

Robertson, Paul L. and Primal R. Patel (2005), 'New Wine in Old Bottles: Technological Diffusion in Developed Economies', in Gerd Bender, David Jacobsen and Paul L. Robertson (eds), *Non-Research-Intensive Industries in the Knowledge Economy*, published in *Perspectives on Economic, Political and Social Integration*, **XI** (1–2), special issue, 271–304.

Robertson, Paul L. and Keith Smith (2008), 'Distributed Knowledge Bases in Low- and Medium-Technology Industries', in Hartmut Hirsch-Kreinsen and David Jacobson (eds), *Innovation in Low-Tech Firms and Industries*, Cheltenham, UK and Northampton, MA, USA: Edward Elgar, pp. 93–117.

Robertson, P., K. Smith and N. von Tunzelmann (2009), 'Introduction: Innovation in Low- and Medium-Technology Industries', *Research Policy*, **38** (3), 441–6.

Schwinge, Isabel (forthcoming), *The Paradox of Knowledge-Intensive Entrepreneurship in the Low-Tech Sector*, PhD dissertation, TU Dortmund University.

Schwinge, I. and H. Hirsch-Kreinsen (2012), 'Repositioning of Low- and Medium-Low-Tech Firms in Product Supply Chains and Their Increasing Knowledge Intensity', Deliverable 1.3.2 AEGIS Project, available at www.aegis-fp7.eu/index.php?option=com_docman&task=doc_download&gid=65&Itemid=12 (accessed 6 June 2013).

Smith, K. (2003), 'What is the Knowledge Economy? Knowledge-Intensive Industries and Distributed Knowledge Bases', paper presented at the PILOT Workshop on Concepts, Theory, Taxonomies and Data, Royal Institute of Technology, Stockholm, 26–27 September 2003, available at www.intech.unu.edu/publications/discussion-papers/2002-6.pdf (accessed 21 October 2013).

Smith, Keith (2005), 'Measuring Innovation', in Jan Fagerberg, David Mowery and

Richard R. Nelson (eds), *The Oxford Handbook of Innovation*, Oxford, UK and New York, USA: Oxford University Press, pp. 148–77.

Som, Oliver (2012), *Innovation without R&D – Heterogeneous Innovation Patterns of Non-R&D-Performing Firms in the German Manufacturing Industry*, Wiesbaden, Germany: Springer Gabler.

Starbuck, W.H. (1992), 'Learning by Knowledge-Intensive Firms', *Journal of Management Studies*, **29** (6), 713–40.

Turnbull, Peter W. and Jean Paul Valla (1986), 'The Interaction Approach to Marketing Strategy – An Introduction', in Peter W. Turnbull and Jean Paul Valla (eds), *Strategies for International Industrial Marketing: The Management of Customer Relationships in European Industrial Markets*, London, UK: Croom Helm, pp. 1–10.

Von Tunzelmann, Nick and Virginia Acha (2005) 'Innovation in "Low-Tech" Industries', in Jan Fagerberg, David C. Mowery and Richard R. Nelson (eds), *The Oxford Handbook of Innovation*, Oxford, UK and New York, USA: Oxford University Press, pp. 407–32.

PART III

Policy issues

9. Trapped by the high-tech myth: the need and chances for a new policy rationale

Attila Havas

9.1 INTRODUCTION

Evidence-based policy has become a buzzword in most policy domains, including science, technology and innovation (STI) policies. Research efforts have indeed provided a significant amount of evidence: insights as to the nature and dynamics of knowledge creation, diffusion, and exploitation processes, lending theoretical justification for policy interventions. These results have influenced policy documents of major supranational organizations, too, such as the EU, the OECD and various UN organizations. Policy-making processes – in a broader sense: policy governance subsystems – themselves, together with the impacts of various STI policy tools have also become subjects of thorough analyses.

Evidence cannot be turned into an 'optimal' set of policy measures in an 'objective', 'scientific' way as it needs to be interpreted in the context of given policy issues and then translated into actions. Moreover, different schools of thought offer contrasting policy advice, and perhaps more importantly, various actors also influence the policy-setting processes, pursuing their own interests and values. Thus, in spite of major research results, policy-making is still more of an art than an easy-to-handle 'technology', that is, a set of proven methods prescribed in handbooks with engineering precision – and STI policies are no exception.

It is no surprise, therefore, that the world of STI policy-making is characterized by major puzzles. One of these is the apparent contradiction between the perceived 'European paradox' and the still dominant view of the importance of 'high-tech' research and 'high-tech' industries. The first claims that the European Union achieves excellent research results, but is ineffective in exploiting those. The policy response should thus be to put more emphasis on fostering knowledge exploitation. Yet, various EU documents and the policy practice discernible from the composition of important monitoring tools still 'push' for a science-push model of innovation.

This chapter aims to analyse whether it is beneficial to focus on supporting high-tech research and promoting structural changes in favor of the high-tech sector, or, whether a different policy rationale, one promoting knowledge-intensive activities across the whole economy, would be more appropriate to enhance competitiveness and improve quality of life.* It is structured as follows: first, economics paradigms are compared briefly along their fundamental assumptions and underlying notions concerning innovation, as well as the major policy implications of these paradigms, contrasted with the policy rationales advanced by the EU and the OECD. The latter issue is analysed in more detail by reviewing the choice and use of indicators in the Innovation Union Scoreboard (EC, 2013a), and in a 2013 league table compiled by the EC Directorate-General for Research and Innovation (EC, 2013b). The concluding section highlights the potential drawbacks of the persistent high-tech myth, considers possible reasons for its perseverance and discusses policy implications of the systemic view of innovation.

9.2   ECONOMICS OF INNOVATION, POLICY IMPLICATIONS AND MODELS OF INNOVATION

The role of innovation in economic development is analysed by various schools of economics in diametrically different ways.[1] The underlying assumptions and key notions of these paradigms lead to diverse policy implications.

9.2.1   Innovation in Various Schools of Thought in Economics

Innovation had been a major theme in classical economics. Then neoclassical (general equilibrium) economics essentially abandoned research questions concerned with dynamics, and instead focused on static comparative analyses and optimization. Technological changes were treated as exogenous to the economic system. Given compelling empirical findings and new theoretical insights on firm behavior and the operation of markets, various industries of mainstream economics[2] have relaxed the most unrealistic assumptions of neoclassical economics; especially perfect information, deterministic environments, perfect competition, and constant or diminishing returns. Yet, 'this literature has not addressed institutional issues, it has a very narrow concept of uncertainty, it has no adequate theory of the creation of technological knowledge and technological interdependence amongst firms, and it has no real analysis of the role of government' (Smith, 2000: 75).

The quintessential axiom of mainstream economics[3] is that rational agents seek to maximize their profits. Evolutionary economics of innovation, in contrast, stresses that *uncertainty* is inherent in innovation, and thus profit maximization is impossible on theoretical grounds. Whereas mainstream economics is concerned with the availability of *information*, innovation studies show that the success of firms depends on their accumulated *knowledge* – both codified and tacit – and *skills*, as well as *learning capabilities*. Information can be purchased, and hence can be accommodated in mainstream economics as a special good. Yet, knowledge – and *a fortiori*, the types of knowledge required for innovation – cannot be bought and used instantaneously. A learning process cannot be spared if one is to acquire knowledge and skills, and it is not only time-consuming, but the costs of *trial and error* need to be incurred as well. Thus, the uncertain, cumulative and path-dependent nature of innovation is reinforced. Cumulativeness, path-dependence and learning lead to *heterogeneity* both at micro and meso levels (Castellacci, 2008a; Dosi, 1988; Dosi et al., 1988; Fagerberg et al., 2005; Hall and Rosenberg, 2010; Malerba, 2002; Pavitt, 1984; Peneder, 2010).

Innovators are not lonely champions of new ideas. While talented individuals might develop radically new, brilliant scientific or technological concepts, successful innovations require different types and forms and knowledge, rarely possessed by a single organization. A close collaboration among firms, universities, public and private research organizations and specialized service-providers is, therefore, a prerequisite of major innovations. In other words, 'open innovation' is not a new phenomenon at all (Mowery, 2009; von Hippel, 1988). Innovation cooperation can take various forms from informal communications through highly sophisticated R&D contracts to alliances and joint ventures (Freeman 1991, 1994, 1995; Lundvall and Borrás, 1999; OECD, 2001; Smith, 2000, 2002; Tidd et al., 1997).

9.2.2   Policy Rationales Derived from Theories

As already stressed, different policy rationales can be drawn from competing schools of economic thought. Policy advice derived from mainstream economics is primarily concerned with *market failures*: unpredictability of knowledge outputs from inputs, inappropriability of full economic benefits of private investment in knowledge creation, and indivisibility in knowledge production lead to 'suboptimal' level of business R&D efforts. Policy interventions, therefore, are justified if they aim at (1) creating incentives to boost private R&D expenditures by ways of subsidies and protection of intellectual property rights, or (2) funding for public R&D activities.

Evolutionary economics of innovation investigates the role of knowledge creation and exploitation in economic processes. This school considers various types and forms of knowledge, including practical or experience-based knowledge acquired through learning by doing, using and interacting. As these are *all* relevant for innovation, scientific knowledge is far from being the only type of knowledge required for a successful introduction of new products or processes, let alone non-technological innovations. As to the sources of knowledge, not only the results of in-house R&D activities, but those of other R&D projects are also widely utilized during the innovation process: extramural projects conducted in the same or other industries, at public or private research establishments, home or abroad. More importantly, there are a number of other sources of knowledge, also essential for innovations, such as design, scaling-up, testing, tooling-up, troubleshooting and other engineering activities, ideas from suppliers and users, inventors' ideas and practical experiments (Hirsch-Kreinsen et al., 2005; Klevorick et al., 1995; Lundvall, 1992; Lundvall and Borrás, 1999; von Hippel, 1988). Innovative firms also utilize knowledge embodied in advanced materials, other inputs, equipment and software. All rounds of the Community Innovation Survey clearly and consistently show that firms regard a wide variety of sources of information as highly important to innovation.[4]

The evolutionary account of innovation leads to sobering lessons concerning the very nature of policy-making, too: in a world of uncertainty, policy cannot bring about *the* optimum either. Furthermore, given the importance of variety, selection and uncertainty, the potentially successful policies are *adaptive* ones, that is, they rely on, and learn from, feedback from the selection process, which in turn leads to further variation (Metcalfe and Georghiou, 1998). In other words, policy formation is increasingly becoming a learning process (Lundvall and Borrás, 1999). Thus, policy evaluation and assessment practices are of crucial importance (Dodgson et al., 2011; Edler et al., 2012; Gök and Edler, 2012; OECD, 1998, 2006a). Technology foresight can also contribute to design appropriate policies: more 'robust' policies can be devised when (1) multiple futures are considered, and (2) participants of foresight processes, given their diverse backgrounds, bring wide-ranging accumulated knowledge, experience, aspirations and ideas into policy dialogues.

In sum, evolutionary economics of innovation posits that firms' performance is largely determined by their abilities to exploit various types of knowledge, generated by both R&D and non-R&D activities. Knowledge generation and exploitation takes place in, and is fostered by, various forms of internal and external interactions. The quality and frequency of the latter are largely determined by the institutions – the 'rules of the game' – and other properties of a given innovation system, in which these interactions take place. STI policies, therefore, should aim at strengthening the respective innovation system and improving its performance by tackling *systemic failures* hampering the generation, diffusion and utilization of any type of knowledge required for successful innovation[5] (Edquist, 2011; Foray, 2009; Dodgson et al., 2011; Freeman, 1994; Lundvall and Borrás, 1999; OECD, 1998; Smith, 2000). From a different angle, deliberate, coordinated policy efforts are needed to promote knowledge-intensive activities in all sectors.

9.2.3   Models of Innovation

The first models of innovation had been devised by natural scientists and practitioners before economists showed a serious interest in these issues.[6] The idea that basic research is the main source of innovation was already proposed in the beginning of the 20th century, gradually leading to what is known today as the science-push model of innovation, forcefully advocated by Bush (1945). By the second half of the 1960s the so-called market-pull model contested that reasoning, portraying demand as the driving force of innovation. Then both became the variants of the linear model of innovation when Kline and Rosenberg suggested the chain-linked model, stressing the non-linear property of innovation processes, the variety of sources of information, as well as the importance of various feedback loops. This latter one has also been extended into the networked model of innovation, more recently called the multi-channel interactive learning model (Caraça et al., 2009).

  In sum, the science-push model of innovation had become widely accepted before the market failure policy rationale was first expressed in the late 1950s, but the latter has certainly lent scientific support to the former by focusing policy-makers' attention to R&D as *the* decisive element of innovation processes.[7]

9.3   INDICATORS: NEUTRAL MEASUREMENT TOOLS OR HERALDS OF POLICY CONCEPTS?

Significant progress has been achieved in measuring R&D and innovation activities since the 1960s (Grupp, 1998; Grupp and Schubert, 2010; Smith, 2005) with the intention to provide comparable data sets as a solid basis for assessing R&D and innovation performance and thereby guiding policy-makers in devising appropriate policies.[8] Although there are widely used guidelines to collect data on R&D and innovation – the Frascati and Oslo Manuals (OECD, 2002 and 2005a, respectively) – it is not straightforward to find the most appropriate way to assess R&D and innovation performance. To start with, R&D is such a complex, multifaceted process that it cannot be sufficiently characterized by two or three indicators, and that applies to innovation *a fortiori*. Hence, there is always a need to select a certain set of indicators to depict innovation processes, and especially to analyse and assess innovation performance. The choice of indicators is, therefore, an important decision reflecting the mindset of those decision-makers who have chosen them. These figures are 'subjective' in that respect, but as they are expressed in numbers, most people perceive indicators as being 'objective' by definition.

An equally difficult task is to devise so-called composite indicators to compress information into a single figure in order to compile eye-catching scoreboards. A major source of complication is choosing an appropriate weight to be assigned to each component. By conducting sensitivity analyses of the 2005 European Innovation Scoreboard (EIS), Grupp and Schubert (2010: 72) have shown how unstable the rank configuration is when the weights are changed. Besides assigning weights, there are three widely used ranking methods, namely: unweighted averages, Benefit of the Doubt (BoD) and principal component analysis. Comparing these three methods, the authors conclude: '. . . even using accepted approaches like BoD or factor analysis may result in drastically changing rankings' (ibid.: 74). Hence, they propose using multidimensional representations, for example spider charts, to reflect the multidimensional character of innovation processes and performance. That would enable analysts and policy-makers to identify strengths and weaknesses, that is, more precise targets for policy actions (ibid.: 77).

Other researchers also emphasize the need for a sufficiently detailed characterization of innovation processes. For example, a family of five indicators – R&D, design, technological, skill, and innovation intensities – offers a more diversified picture on innovativeness than the Summary Innovation Index of the EIS (Laestadius et al., 2005). Using Norwegian data they demonstrate that the suggested method can capture variety in knowledge formation and innovativeness both within and between sectors. It thus supports a more accurate understanding of creativity and innovativeness inside and across various sectors, directs policy-makers' attention to this diversity (suppressed by the OECD classification of sectors), and thus can better serve policy needs.

9.3.1 The European Innovation Scoreboard

As already stressed, firms exploit various types of knowledge for their innovation activities. Testing this general observation by using the Danish DISKO survey data, Jensen et al. (2007) introduced an elementary distinction between two modes of innovation: (1) one based on the production and use of codified scientific and technical knowledge, and (2) another relying on informal processes of learning and experience-based know-how (called DUI: Doing, Using and Interacting). They have noted that none of the 22 indicators that had been used to compile the EIS 2004 captured the DUI mode of innovation, which is not an accident:

> There now exist internationally harmonised data on R&D, patenting, the development of S&T human resources, ICT expenditures and innovation expenditures more generally, whereas at present there are no harmonised data that could be used to construct measures of learning by doing and using. We would contend, though, that these limitations of the data reflect the same bias at a deeper level. . . . The lack of DUI measures reflects political priorities and decision-making rather than any inevitable state of affairs (ibid.: 685).

The EIS's indicators have been revised several times since its first edition in 2000, and the scoreboard was renamed the Innovation Union Scoreboard in 2011. Its 2013 edition is based on 25 indicators, grouped by eight innovation dimensions (EC, 2013a). A rudimentary classification exercise reveals a strong bias towards R&D-based innovations: 10 indicators are *only* relevant for, and a further four *mainly* capture, R&D-based innovations, a mere five focus on non-R&D-based innovations, while six could be relevant for both types of innovations (Table 9.1). Given that (1) the IUS is used by the European Commission to monitor progress, and (2) its likely impact on national policy-makers, this bias towards R&D-based innovation is a source of major concern.

The current composition of IUS indicators can be seen either as a half-full or a half-empty glass. Compared to the EIS 2004 – as assessed by Jensen et al. (2007) – it is an improvement. Considering the economic weight of LMT sectors and the fact that the bulk of innovation in these sectors is not based on intramural R&D efforts (Sandven et al., 2005; von Tunzelmann and Acha, 2005), a much more significant improvement is still needed to better reflect innovation processes by the IUS, and thus underpin effective and sound policies.

Table 9.1   The 2013 Innovation Union Scoreboard indicators

	Relevance for R&D-based innovation	Relevance for non-R&D-based innovation
Human resources		
New doctoral graduates (ISCED 6) per 1000 population aged 25–34	X	
Percentage population aged 30–34 having completed tertiary education	b	b
Percentage youth aged 20–24 having attained at least upper secondary level education		X
Open, excellent and attractive research systems		
International scientific co-publications per million population	X	
Scientific publications among the top 10% most cited publications worldwide as % of total scientific publications of the country	X	
Non-EU doctoral students as a % of all doctoral students	X	
Finance and support		
R&D expenditure in the public sector as % of GDP	X	
Venture capital investment as % of GDP	x	
Firm investments		
R&D expenditure in the business sector as % of GDP	X	
Non-R&D innovation expenditures as % of turnover		X
Linkages & entrepreneurship		
SMEs innovating in-house as % of SMEs	b	b
Innovative SMEs collaborating with others as % of SMEs	b	b
Public-private co-publications per million population	X	
Intellectual assets		
PCT patents applications per billion GDP (in PPS€)	X	
PCT patent applications in societal challenges per billion GDP (in PPS€) (environment-related technologies; health)	X	
Community trademarks per billion GDP (in PPS€)		X

Table 9.1   (continued)

	Relevance for R&D-based innovation	Relevance for non-R&D-based innovation
Community designs per billion GDP (in PPS€)		X
Innovators		
SMEs introducing product or process innovations as % of SMEs	b	b
SMEs introducing marketing or organizational innovations as % of SMEs		X
High-growth innovative firms	b	b
Economic effects		
Employment in knowledge-intensive activities (manufacturing and services) as % of total employment	x	
Contribution of medium- and high-tech product exports to the trade balance	x	
Knowledge-intensive services exports as % total service exports	x	
Sales of new to market and new to firm innovations as % of turnover	b	b
License and patent revenues from abroad as % of GDP	X	

Notes:
X: only relevant; x: mainly relevant; b: relevant for both types.
ISCED 6: "The indicator is a measure of the supply of new second-stage tertiary graduates in all fields of training. For most countries ISCED 6 captures PhD graduates only, with the exception of Finland, Portugal and Sweden where also non-PhD degrees leading to an award of an advanced research qualification are included." (EC, 2013a: 67) ISCED stands for International Standard Classification of Education; see www.uis.unesco.org/Education/Pages/international-standard-classification-of-education.aspx. Please note that ISCED 2011 revised the classification of the education levels. ISCED 6 as used in the 2013 Innovation Union Scoreboard is based on ISCED 1997.
PCT: "The Patent Cooperation Treaty (PCT) assists applicants in seeking patent protection internationally for their inventions, helps patent offices with their patent granting decisions, and facilitates public access to a wealth of technical information relating to those inventions. By filing one international patent application under the PCT, applicants can simultaneously seek protection for an invention in 148 countries throughout the world" (www.wipo.int/pct/en/).
PPS€: Euro expressed at purchasing power parity; calculation is based on the Purchasing Power Standard.

9.3.2 A New League Table: Research and Innovation Performance of EU Member States and Associated Countries

The EC Directorate-General for Research and Innovation is publishing country profiles aimed at 'providing policy-makers and stakeholders with concise, holistic and comparative overviews of research and innovation (R&I) in individual countries' (EC, 2013b: 2). The 2011 report identified nine groups of countries, and then Hungary – together with the Czech Republic, Italy, Slovakia and Slovenia – belonged to group 8, characterized by '*medium-low knowledge capacity* with an important industry base' (EC, 2011: 436). A new feature in the 2013 edition is a synthesis table with some striking figures: Ireland has the highest level of knowledge-intensity, and Hungary is ranked ninth, ahead of Germany, Austria and the EU average, for example, and just behind Denmark and Finland (Table 9.2).

The 'knowledge-intensity of the economy' is defined as follows (ibid.: 321–2):

Eight compositional structural change indicators have been identified and organized into five dimensions:

- The R&D dimension measures the size of business R&D (as a per cent of GDP) and the size of the R&D services sector in the economy . . .;
- The skills dimension measures changing skills and occupation in terms of the share of persons employed in knowledge intensive activities;
- The sectoral specialization dimension captures the relative share of knowledge intensive activities;
- The international specialization dimension captures the share of knowledge economy through technological (patents) and export specialization (revealed technological and competitive advantage);
- The internationalization dimension refers to the changing international competitiveness of a country in terms of attracting and diffusing foreign direct investment (inward and outward foreign direct investments).

. . . The five pillars have also been aggregated to a single composite indicator of structural change . . .

Knowledge is understood again in a narrow sense: only higher education and R&D activities are supposed to create it and thus all other types of knowledge are disregarded. The name of this indicator is, therefore, misleading. The inclusion of high-tech exports and foreign direct investment in this composite indicator explains the unexpectedly high ranking of Ireland and Hungary: in both countries high-tech goods account for an extremely large share in exports (Table 9.3) and high-tech industries are dominated by foreign-owned firms.

Table 9.2 Overview of research and innovation performance in selected EU countries

	R&D intensity (2011)	Excellence in S&T (2010)	Index of economic impact of innovation (2010–11)	Knowledge-intensity of economy (2010)	HT & MT contribution to trade balance (2011)
Ireland	1.72	38.11	0.690	65.43	2.57
Sweden	3.37	77.20	0.652	64.60	2.02
United Kingdom	1.77	56.08	0.621	59.24	3.13
Belgium	2.04	59.92	0.599	58.88	2.37
France	2.25	48.24	0.628	57.01	4.65
Netherlands	2.04	78.86	0.565	56.22	1.68
Denmark	3.09	77.65	0.713	54.95	−2.77
Finland	3.78	62.91	0.698	52.17	1.69
Hungary	1.21	31.88	0.527	50.23	5.84
European Union	2.03	47.86	0.612	48.75	4.20
Estonia	2.38	25.85	0.450	46.48	−2.70
Slovenia	2.47	27.47	0.521	45.90	6.05
Germany	2.84	62.78	0.813	44.94	8.54
Austria	2.75	50.46	0.556	42.40	3.18
Portugal	1.50	26.45	0.387	41.04	−1.20
Czech Republic	1.84	29.90	0.497	39.58	3.82
Spain	1.33	36.63	0.530	36.76	3.05
Italy	1.25	43.12	0.556	35.43	4.96
Lithuania	0.92	13.92	0.223	35.28	−1.27
Latvia	0.70	11.49	0.248	34.38	−5.42
Greece	0.60	35.27	0.345	32.53	−5.69
Poland	0.77	20.47	0.313	31.78	0.88
Slovakia	0.68	17.73	0.479	31.64	4.35
Romania	0.48	17.84	0.384	28.35	0.38

Notes:
Countries are ranked by the knowledge-intensity indicator.
S&T: Science and technology.
HT & MT: High-tech and medium-tech products.

Source: EC (2013b: 5).

Table 9.3   *Share of high-tech goods in industrial exports, EU countries, 2001–09 (%)*

	2001	2005	2006	2007	2008	2009
Ireland	58.0	52.1	48.9	46.6	48.9	52.2
Hungary	28.3	31.7	30.8	29.9	30.6	35.5
Netherlands	29.6	30.1	28.7	27.4	25.2	29.1
United Kingdom	35.8	27.7	27.4	26.1	25.1	n.a.
France	25.2	22.8	23.7	22.5	23.0	n.a.
Finland	24.3	25.3	21.9	20.0	19.7	17.1
Slovak Republic	6.0	11.3	14.4	16.9	19.4	n.a.
Sweden	23.1	21.3	21.4	18.9	18.6	21.9
Czech Republic	11.8	15.0	16.8	17.5	17.9	18.8
Belgium	14.4	17.8	16.8	17.7	17.4	22.0
Germany	20.3	19.7	19.5	17.7	17.2	19.5
Denmark	19.6	20.1	18.1	17.3	15.6	17.9
Slovenia	10.8	10.7	11.5	11.6	13.0	15.0
Austria	15.4	13.3	12.9	12.8	12.4	14.0
Greece	8.7	12.9	11.5	10.7	11.8	14.8
Spain	10.2	11.1	10.6	10.3	10.1	11.3
Poland	6.5	6.3	7.4	8.1	9.8	n.a.
Italy	11.8	10.7	10.1	9.3	9.1	10.8
Estonia	25.5	21.5	16.4	9.5	8.9	8.0
Luxembourg	15.7	10.1	10.0	8.6	6.8	10.4
Portugal	11.3	11.5	11.4	n.a.	n.a.	n.a.

Note: n.a.: data are not available.

Source: Author's calculation based on data from Structural Analysis (STAN) Databases, OECD.Stat (http://stats.oecd.org/#, extracted on 9 September 2013).

These 'twinned' characteristics warrant further remarks from the point of view of knowledge-intensity. The bulk of exported high-tech goods are developed outside Ireland or Hungary;[9] the main activity of most foreign subsidiaries is the assembly of high-tech goods by semi-skilled workers, and thus the local knowledge content is rather low. These features cannot be reflected in this indicator, and thus it does not necessarily express knowledge-intensity in the case of countries with similar structural characteristics. Hence, it may only be used 'with a pinch of salt' to compare countries' performance or devise policy measures.

In more detail, two major policy lessons can be drawn from this. First, policies aimed at promoting innovation and hence competitiveness should consider the actual activities of firms, rather than relying on the OECD classification of sectors. Four levels of analysis should be distinguished:

activities, products, firms and sectors. Firms belonging to the same statistical sector might possess quite different innovation, production, management and marketing capabilities. Furthermore, they are unlikely to
produce identical goods, in terms of, for example, skills and investment
required, quality or market and profit opportunities. Finally, they perform
different activities, especially in regard to their knowledge-intensity. These
dissimilarities are likely to be even more pronounced when we consider
sectors, firms, products and activities across different countries. In short,
policies that neglect the intra-sectoral diversity of firms cannot be effective.

Second, various types of foreign direct investment activities have
different longer-term impacts on economic development. Globalization
either poses threats to, or offers opportunities for, economic development, depending on the capabilities and investment promotion policies
of the host country. To use an elementary dichotomy of foreign direct
investment, one type can be called *foot-loose*, that is, characterized by low
local knowledge content, and thus offer low-pay jobs. These companies
are ready to leave at any time for cheaper locations.[10] The other types of
investors, in contrast, are *anchored* into a national system of production
and innovation: they conduct knowledge-intensive activities, create higher-
pay jobs, build close contacts with domestic R&D units and universities
and develop a strong local supplier base.[11] In brief, coordinated, mindful
investment promotion, STI, human resource and regional development
policies are required to embed foreign investors. In this way, skills can be
upgraded, local suppliers' innovation capabilities can be improved to boost
their competitiveness and intense, mutually beneficial business-academia
collaboration can be nurtured. Otherwise most of the investment 'sweet-
eners' are wasted if foreign firms only use a given region or country as a
cheap, temporary production site.

9.4   DISCUSSION AND CONCLUSIONS

9.4.1   A Persistent Devotion to High-Tech and its Pitfalls

Several observers claim that the systems view on innovation has become
widespread in academic and policy-making circles, both in national
and supranational organizations. As for the latter, they are notably the
European Commission and the OECD (Sharif, 2006; Dodgson et al.,
2011). By discussing the indicators selected for the European Innovation
Scoreboard (more recently: Innovation Union Scoreboard), as well as the
use of these and related indicators in a 2013 league table of innovation performance of EU countries, this chapter has shown that the high-tech myth

prevails. Glancing through various EU and OECD reports also confirms that the systems view has not become a systematically applied paradigm in policy circles[12] – in spite of a rich set of policy-relevant research insights. The 'push for science-push' is further reinforced by the images of scientists and/or their sophisticated equipment consistently used on the cover pages of various EU and OECD reports.[13]

The high-tech myth is so powerful that even those researchers who base their work on thorough analysis of facts are taken by surprise when the facts are at odds with the obsession with high-tech. A telling example is Peneder's excellent study on the 'Austrian paradox':

> On the one hand, macroeconomic indicators on productivity, growth, employ-ment and foreign direct investment indicate that overall performance is stable and highly competitive. On the other hand, an international comparison of industrial structures reveals a severe gap in the most technologically advanced industries of manufacturing, suggesting that Austria is having prob-lems establishing a foothold in the dynamic markets of the future (1999: 239).

In contrast, evolutionary economics of innovation claims that any firm – in either LMT or HT industries – can become competitive in 'the dynamic markets of the future' if it is successful in combining its own, firm-specific innovative capabilities with 'extramural' knowledge available in distributed knowledge bases. In other words, Austrian policy-makers need not be concerned with the observed 'paradox' as long as they help Austrian firms sustain their learning capabilities, and maintain thereby their innovative-ness. That would lead to good economic performance – regardless of the share of LMT industries in the economy.

The science-push model neglects the importance of distributed knowledge bases – regional, sectoral and national innovation systems and clusters – in creating, diffusing and exploiting various non-R&D types of knowledge (Dodgson and Rothwell, 1994; Freeman, 1991, 1994; Lundvall and Borrás, 1999; Malerba, 2002; Nelson, 1993; OECD, 2001; Smith, 2002; Tidd et al., 1997), and hence it can easily misguide policy: in a 'hard-core' translation it implies that public money should be primarily spent on promoting research efforts in a handful of fashionable S&T domains, and on boosting high-tech industries. A recent EC document is also pushing – or only hoping? – for structural changes, along similar lines, although this is not explicitly articu-lated in that way: 'Furthermore, in dynamic fields such as ICT-based busi-nesses and in emerging sectors Europe needs more high-growth firms. This calls for an innovation-driven structural change, but Europe is at present missing out on the more radical innovations which drive and lead such structural change' (EC, 2013c: 5). In line with the science-push model, other modes of technological innovation are not mentioned in this document.

The EC documents are rather consistent in that respect over time: the so-called Barcelona target, namely achieving a 3 per cent GERD/GDP[14] ratio in the EU – first set in March 2002, and then relaunched in 2010 as part of the Europe 2020 strategy – is also driven by this rationale: R&D efforts need to be stepped up, because significantly larger inputs would thereby be transformed into useful outputs. In other words, research insights are translated into policy actions in a disappointing way in the Lisbon Agenda: '. . . the focus remains on . . . mobilizing investment for research and development, translating science into technology, and attempting to create a population of new technology-based firms' (Steinmuller, 2009: 29).

The policy rationale derived from mainstream economics, namely the market failure argument, in essence is 'informed' by the science-push model, but in turn it also provides strong scientific support to this type of policy-making, given its roots in rigorous, quantitative analyses. Three comments are in order. First, even when accepting the market failure rationale as a relevant one, '. . . it does not give any secure guide to how to identify areas of market failure, or the appropriate levels of public support which might follow from it' (Smith, 2000: 85). Second, a policy action tackling a market failure would, in most cases, lead to another market failure. Patents, for example, distort prices to the detriment of customers, and may also result either in over- or under-investment in R&D, neither of which is 'socially optimal' (Bach and Matt, 2005). Third, the innovation systems approach has shown that the mainstream economics paradigm offers an inappropriate framework to fully understand innovation processes involving a fundamental element of uncertainty and characterized by cumulativeness and path-dependence. The market failure rationale thus rests on a theory that does not offer a sound, indisputable understanding of those processes that are to be influenced by policies justified by this very rationale. Spending public money guided by an inappropriate – or at best incomplete – policy rationale is, therefore, highly questionable.

In sum, policies driven by the science-push model – or its close 'relative', the market failure argument derived from mainstream economics – disregard non-R&D types of knowledge, which are of huge significance for innovation processes in the LMT sectors of manufacturing and services. Given the substantial economic weight of these sectors in producing value added and creating employment, this policy ignorance is likely to lead to massive opportunity costs, for example, in the form of lost improvements in productivity, 'unborn' new products and services, and thus 'unopened' new markets and 'undelivered' new jobs.

Scoreboards and league tables compiled following the science-push logic, and published by supranational organizations, can easily lead to 'lock-in' situations. National policy-makers – and politicians, in particular – are likely to pay much more attention to their country's position on a scoreboard than to nuanced assessments or policy recommendations in lengthy documents, and hence this inapt logic is 'diffused' and strengthened at the national level, too, preventing policy learning and the devising of appropriate policies.

9.4.2   Possible Reasons for the Observed Persistence

Even without analysing the complex issue of paradigm shifts in STI policy thinking and practice in a systematic and detailed way, it is worth considering some possible reasons why the science-push model is so popular and powerful. Although this chapter has not analysed STI policy rationales at a national level, the ensuing discussion would include that level, too.

To start with a *simple* reason, the science-push model is based on a fairly *simple*, straightforward reasoning.[15] Moreover, it was compellingly explained and popularized many decades ago by Bush (1945), given the unprecedented achievements of major R&D efforts during World War II.[16] Impressive scientific results have been reported in the press ever since then, reiterating the relevance and usefulness of science in the mind of politicians and citizens at large.

The simplicity of policy-making following the science-push model can be important in further respects, too. To rephrase Laestadius et al. (2005), who talk about the advantages of one-dimensional indicators in general, the so-called Barcelona target

> . . . has obvious pedagogical advantages: people remember [it], they react on [it] and (at least believe that) they can identify the meaning of [it]. . . . As regards community creation it may be argued that a simple one-dimensional indicator . . . can be identified as a focal point for orchestrated political action: we can all unite on transforming Europe to a high-tech knowledge-based economy.

The networked model of innovation and other concepts of the evolutionary economics of innovation are, in contrast, not only complex, but can also be 'vague' for policy-makers. Indeed, the systems of innovation approach can easily be interpreted sarcastically: if everything depends on everything else, there is no clear policy guidance.

International politics in the form of the so-called Triadic competition between Europe, Japan and the US also played a role in strengthening the obsession with the science-push model already in the 1960s (Hirsch-Kreinsen et al., 2005), and it still features in recent EU documents: 'Overall, the EU remains specialised in medium-high R&D-intensity sectors which account for half of European companies' R&D investment. By contrast, more than two-thirds of US companies' R&D investment is clustered in high R&D-intensity sectors (such as health and ICT)' (EC, 2013c: 7). This adamant obsession with the EU–US comparison is all the more puzzling when one takes into account some fundamental differences: the EU is not a federal structure, and despite the Single Market principle it is much more fragmented in many respects than the US, with severe consequences for, for example, capital flows and labor mobility – and hence for the diffusion and exploitation of knowledge – as well as for the feasibility of large, mission-oriented R&D projects and EU-wide policy actions, including public procurement with regard to new products or solutions.

Sociological factors are also likely to play an important role. Top STI policy-makers, as well as the majority of middle-ranking staff, tend to be former scientists or engineers, and thus naturally with a strong inclination towards the Bush-model (Bush, 1945). Civil servants at finance ministries, who prepare decisions on the budget lines earmarked for public funding for R&D and innovation activities, are usually trained in mainstream economics, and thus they are not advancing the policy rationale of the evolutionary economics of innovation, either (Dodgson et al., 2011; Lundvall and Borrás, 1999). Prestigious scientists have also become influential in setting STI policies, and their influence is strengthened by their formal positions, too (as chief scientists, advisors to politicians, presidents of learned societies, members of advisory boards, etc.).[17] Finally, the quest for evidence-based policies has significantly increased the intellectual standing and influence of formal modeling among policy-makers (Caracostas, 2007: 479). It should be stressed in light of this that (a) the complexity of innovation systems cannot be translated into econometric models,[18] and (b) in new (endogenous) growth models a main variable is R&D – and not knowledge in its broad sense, even if R&D and knowledge are used as synonyms in many papers.

9.4.3 Policy Implications of the Systemic View of Innovation

A fundamental element of the pragmatic critique of the innovation systems approach certainly holds: policy implications derived from evolutionary theorizing are demanding in terms of both analytical efforts needed to underpin policies and policy design capabilities. The market failure rationale is an abstract concept; its policy implications are supposed to apply to any market in any country, and at any time – but as already stressed, exactly for being abstract, it cannot provide appropriate guidance for policy design. The systemic failures argument, in contrast, cannot offer 'one-size-fits-all' recipes. Instead, it stresses that it is an empirical task to identify what type of failure(s) is (are) blocking innovation processes in what part of the system in order to guide the design of appropriate policies.[19] Besides thorough analyses, it is likely to demand extensive dialogue with stakeholders, too. This is not a trivial task, and the possibility of summarizing widely applicable, easy-to-digest and thus appealing policy 'prescriptions' in one or two paragraphs is excluded on theoretical grounds.

The systemic approach implies, too, that several policies affect innovation processes and performance – and perhaps even more strongly than STI policies. Hence, the task of designing effective and efficient policies to promote innovation is even more complex as policy goals and tools need to be orchestrated across several policy domains, including macroeconomic, education, investment promotion, regional development, and labor market policies, as well as health, environment and social policies aimed at tackling societal challenges.

In an interesting 'cross-tabulation' of innovation research themes and policy perspectives, den Hertog et al. (2002) identified 'black boxes', that is, themes not covered by research and also unknown (unidentified) by policy-makers. Given the importance of non-STI policies affecting innovation policies, it would be useful to add a black box at a 'meta level', too: that is, the impacts of non-STI policies – or even more broadly, that of the framework conditions – on innovation processes and performance.

It is also worth revisiting two issues previously addressed in this chapter from a new angle. The first one is the design and use of scoreboards or league tables for assessing countries' performance. A straightforward implication of the systemic view is that, given the diversity among innovation systems (in this case: among national innovation systems), one should be very careful when trying to draw policy lessons from the 'rank' of a country as 'measured' by a composite indicator. A scoreboard can only be constructed by using the same set of indicators across all countries, and by applying an identical method to calculate the composite index. Yet, analysts and policy-makers need to realize that poor performance as signaled by certain indicators, and leading to a low ranking on the scoreboard, does not automatically identify the area(s) necessitating the most urgent policy actions. For example, in the case of several indicators measuring performance in 'high-tech', for a country at a lower level of economic development it might be more relevant to focus scarce public resources on improving the conditions for knowledge dissemination and exploitation, rather than spending money on creating scientific knowledge. This is a gross oversimplification, of course, that is, far from any policy recommendation at the required level of detail. It is only meant to reiterate that it is a demanding task to devise policies based on the innovation systems approach. Moreover, as the Hungarian and Irish cases have shown, a high value of a composite indicator would not necessarily signal good performance: the devil is always in the details.

The second issue is the major differences between mainstream economics and the evolutionary economics of innovation. The choice of an economics paradigm to guide policy evaluation is likely to be decisive: assessing the impacts of the same policy measure by following the neo-classical paradigm leads to certain conclusions on efficacy and efficiency, while doing so within the evolutionary frame yields drastically different ones (Lipsey and Carlaw, 1998). Policy-makers need to consider these differences, too, when making a choice as to which paradigm is to be followed.

Finally, some basic principles for policy-making can be distilled from the systemic view of innovation. Given the characteristics of the innovation process, public policies should be aimed at promoting learning in its widest possible sense: competence building at individual, organizational and inter-organizational levels; in all economic sectors, in all possible ways, considering all types of knowledge, emanating from various sources. Further, as it already occurs in some countries, innovation (and other) policies should promote the introduction of new processes and methods in public services and administration, too. New indicators that better reflect evolutionary processes of learning and innovation would also be needed to support policy-making in this new way. Developing, piloting and then widely collecting these new indicators would be a major, demanding and time-consuming project, necessitating extensive international cooperation.

NOTES

*   Financial support provided for research by AEGIS (EU RTD FP7, grant agreement No. 225134), and GRINCOH (EU RTD FP7, grant agreement No. 290657) is gratefully acknowledged. I am indebted to Gábor Kőrösi, Sandro Mendonça, Balázs Muraközy, Doris Schartinger, Matthias Weber and seminar participants at the Institute of Economics, CERS, HAS for their comments on an earlier version.
1. Space limits only allow an incomplete introduction to the main ideas. For more detailed and nuanced accounts, see e.g. Castellacci (2008b), Dosi (1988), Dosi et al. (1988), Fagerberg et al. (2005), Freeman (1994), Grupp (1998), Hall and Rosenberg (2010), Laestadius et al. (2005), Lazonick (2013), Lundvall and Borrás (1999), Nelson (1995), OECD (1998) and Smith (2000).
2. Mainstream economics is constantly evolving, driven by its own 'internal' dynamics as well as by integrating new notions, research questions and methods from various branches of economics. Its major features cannot, therefore, be precisely defined. For example, while representative agents were a central feature for decades, more recently heterogeneity has become a key issue, e.g. in the new trade theory.
3. The so-called new or endogenous growth theory is not discussed here separately because its major assumptions on knowledge are very similar to those of mainstream economics (Lazonick, 2013; Smith, 2000). Knowledge in new growth models is reduced to codified

scientific knowledge, in sharp contrast to the much richer understanding of knowledge in evolutionary economics of innovation.

4. In contrast, the OECD classification of industries only takes into account expenditures on formal R&D activities, carried out within the boundaries of a given sector. More precisely, the so-called indirect R&D intensity has also been calculated as R&D expenditures embodied in intermediates and capital goods purchased on the domestic market or imported. Yet, it has been concluded that indirect R&D intensities would not influence the classification of sectors (Hatzichronoglou, 1997: 5). In other words, a number of highly successful, innovative firms, exploiting advanced knowledge created externally in distributed knowledge bases (Smith, 2002) and internally by non-R&D processes, are classified as medium-low-tech or low-tech companies, just because their R&D expenditures are below the threshold set by the OECD. Some policy-makers then might easily think that it is not a mistake to neglect these sectors *en bloc*.

5. In an attempt to systematically compare the market and systemic failure policy rationales, Bleda and del Río (2013) introduce the notion of evolutionary market failures, and reinterpret the neoclassical market failures as particular cases of evolutionary market failures, relying on the crucial distinction between knowledge and information.

6. This brief account can only list the most influential models. Balconi et al. (2010), Caraça et al. (2009), Dodgson and Rothwell (1994) and Godin (2006) offer detailed discussions on their emergence, properties and use for analytical and policy-making purposes.

7. For a thorough analysis refuting the high-tech myth, see e.g. Sandven et al. (2005).

8. 'The Innovation Union Scoreboard 2013 gives a comparative assessment of the innovation performance of the EU27 Member States and the relative strengths and weaknesses of their research and innovation systems' (EC, 2013a: 4).

9. Business Expenditures on R&D (BERD) in the 'Manufacture of computer, electronic and optical products (C26)' sector was €152–5m in Ireland, €53–6m in Hungary, while €527m in Austria in 2009–10 (Eurostat, http://appsso.eurostat.ec.europa.eu/nui/show.do?dataset=rd_e_berdindr2&lang=en, accessed 20 December 2013). Austria has been chosen for comparison given her similar size (in terms of population) and lower ranking in Table 9.2 by knowledge-intensity of economy. BERD in pharmaceuticals is not considered here given the sector's small share in Hungarian manufacturing (and high-tech) exports (around 10 per cent of exports by C26).

10. Radosevic (2002) offers a thorough survey of the electronics industry in Central and Eastern European countries, Scotland and Wales. His analysis of plant closures and downsizing is a good illustration of the behavior of *foot-loose* investors.

11. There are different types of firms among the *anchored* ones, too. This simple dichotomy is used here just to highlight some elementary policy implications, not as a basis for sound policy recommendations.

12. A recent OECD policy document equates innovation with R&D at several points: '*Innovation* today is a pervasive phenomenon and involves a wider range of actors than ever before. *Once largely carried out by research and university laboratories in the private and government sectors*, it is now also the domain of civil society, philanthropic organisations and, indeed, individuals' (OECD, 2010: 3, emphasis added by A.H.). The same document has a subsection entitled 'Low-technology sectors innovate', but the bulk of the text is on R&D.

    A current EU document also consistently equates knowledge with R&D: investment in knowledge is understood as changes in R&D intensity, knowledge-intensity of economic sectors is measured by BERD, and 'knowledge upgrade' is defined as increased R&D intensity (EC, 2013b: 7, 9, 10, 11). The same document, just like many other EC documents (e.g. EC, 2013c), speaks of a 'research and innovation system', and thus implicitly suggests that the (public) research system is not a subsystem of the national innovation system, but a separate entity. Research and innovation is used in a very loose way, practically as synonyms: 'There are still considerable differences between Member States in terms of their research and innovation efficiency. For a given amount of public

investment, some countries achieve more excellence than others in science and technology' (ibid.: 9).
13. See, e.g., the OECD's 'STI Scoreboard' and 'STI Outlook' series until 2007 and 2008, respectively, as well as Eurostat's 'Science, technology and innovation in Europe' series in the late 2000s (OECD, 2004, 2005b, 2006b, 2007, 2008; EC, 2008, 2009, 2010).
14. Gross domestic expenditure on R&D/Gross domestic product.
15. 'Despite the fierce criticism they have attracted from the more popular systemic approaches, these linear models paradoxically continue to influence thinking amongst decision-makers and public opinion because they have the virtue of being simple (or of appearing to be so)' – writes Caracostas (2007: 475), drawing on his extensive work experience as a 'policy-shaper' at the EC. Since then, Balconi et al. (2010) have assembled a set of arguments 'in defence of the linear model'.
16. Hirsch-Kreinsen et al. (2005) offer two further historical considerations: the internal organization and management methods of large corporations in the 20th century, as well as the cold war, namely the 'sputnik panic' and the US reply to that.
17. These factors have been at play in Australia, too: 'Despite significant input from innovation researchers on the value of innovation systems thinking, the Summit's outcomes were largely shaped by neoclassical economic orthodoxy and a continued science-push, linear approach advocated by the research sector' (Dodgson et al., 2011: 1150).
18. This critique has been 'anticipated' and answered by Lipsey and Carlaw (1998: 48): 'For obvious reasons, many economists prefer models that provide precise policy recommendations, even in situations in which the models are inapplicable to the world of our existence. Our own view is that, rather than using neoclassical models that give precise answers that do not apply to situations in which technology is evolving endogenously, it is better to face the reality that there is no optimal policy with respect to technological change.'
19. For various taxonomies of systemic failures, see, e.g. Bach and Matt (2005), Malerba (2009) and Smith (2000).

REFERENCES

Bach, Laurent and Mireille Matt (2005), 'From Economic Foundations to S&T Policy Tools: A Comparative Analysis of the Dominant Paradigms', in Patrick Llerena and Mireille Matt (eds), *Innovation Policy in a Knowledge-Based Economy: Theory and Practice*, Heidelberg, Germany: Springer.

Balconi, M., S. Brusoni and L. Orsenigo (2010), 'In Defence of the Linear Model: An Essay', *Research Policy*, **39** (1), 1–13.

Bleda, M. and P. del Río (2013), 'The Market Failure and the Systemic Failure Rationales in Technological Innovation Systems', *Research Policy*, **42** (5), 1039–52.

Bush, V. (1945), 'Science: The Endless Frontier', US Government Printing Office, Washington, DC, USA, available at www.nsf.gov/od/lpa/nsf50/vbush1945.htm (accessed 10 September 2013).

Caraça, J., B.-Å. Lundvall and S. Mendonça (2009), 'The Changing Role of Science in the Innovation Process: From Queen to Cinderella?', *Technological Forecasting and Social Change*, **76** (6), 861–7.

Caracostas, Paraskevas (2007), 'The Policy-Shaper Anxiety at the Innovation Kick: How Far Do Innovation Theories Really Help in the World of Policy', in Franco Malerba and Stefano Brusoni (eds), *Perspectives on Innovation*, Cambridge, UK: Cambridge University Press, pp. 464–89.

Castellacci, F. (2008a), 'Technological Paradigms, Regimes and Trajectories: Manufacturing and Service Industries in a New Taxonomy of Sectoral Patterns of Innovation', *Research Policy*, **37** (6–7), 978–94.

Castellacci, F. (2008b), 'Innovation and the Competitiveness of Industries: Comparing the Mainstream and the Evolutionary Approaches', *Technological Forecasting and Social Change*, **75** (7), 984–1006.

Den Hertog, P., E. Oskam, K. Smith and J. Segers (2002), 'Usual Suspects, Hidden Treasures, Unmet Wants and Black Boxes in Innovation Research', working paper, Utrecht, The Netherlands: Dialogic.

Dodgson, Mark and Roy Rothwell (eds) (1994), *The Handbook of Industrial Innovation*, Aldershot, UK and Brookfield, VT, USA: Edward Elgar.

Dodgson, M., A. Hughes, J. Foster and S. Metcalfe (2011), 'Systems Thinking, Market Failure, and the Development of Innovation Policy: The Case of Australia', *Research Policy*, **40** (9), 1145–56.

Dosi, G. (1988), 'Sources, Procedures and Microeconomic Effects of Innovation', *Journal of Economic Literature*, **24** (4), 1120–71.

Dosi, Giovanni, Christopher Freeman, Richard R. Nelson, Gerald Silverberg and Luc Soete (eds) (1988), *Technical Change and Economic Theory*, London, UK: Pinter.

EC (2008), *Science, Technology and Innovation in Europe*, 2008 edition, Luxembourg: Office for Official Publications of the European Communities.

EC (2009), *Science, Technology and Innovation in Europe*, 2009 edition, Luxembourg: Office for Official Publications of the European Communities.

EC (2010), *Science, Technology and Innovation in Europe*, 2010 edition, Luxembourg: Office for Official Publications of the European Communities.

EC (2011), 'Innovation Union Competitiveness Report: 2011 Edition', doi: 10.2769/72530, available at http://ec.europa.eu/research/innovation-union/pdf/competitiveness-report/2011/iuc2011-full-report.pdf#view=fit&pagemode=none (accessed 6 July 2013).

EC (2013a), 'Innovation Union Scoreboard 2013', available at http://ec.europa.eu/enterprise/policies/innovation/files/ius-2013_en.pdf (accessed 14 June 2013).

EC (2013b), 'Research and Innovation Performance in EU Member States and Associated Countries: Innovation Union Progress at Country Level', doi: 10.2777/82363, available at http://ec.europa.eu/research/innovation-union/pdf/state-of-the-union/2012/innovation_union_progress_at_country_level_2013.pdf (accessed 9 June 2013).

EC (2013c), 'State of the Innovation Union 2012: Accelerating Change', available at http://ec.europa.eu/research/innovation-union/pdf/state-of-the-union/2012/state_of_the_innovation_union_report_2012.pdf (accessed 24 June 2013).

Edler, J., M. Berger, M. Dinges and A. Gök (2012), 'The Practice of Evaluation in Innovation Policy in Europe', *Research Evaluation*, **21** (3), 167–82.

Edquist, C. (2011), 'Design of Innovation Policy through Diagnostic Analysis: Identification of Systemic Problems or (Failures)', *Industrial and Corporate Change*, **20** (6), 1725–53.

Fagerberg, Jan, David Mowery and Richard R. Nelson (eds) (2005), *The Oxford Handbook of Innovation*, Oxford, UK and New York, USA: Oxford University Press.

Foray, Dominique (2009), *The New Economics of Technology Policy*, Cheltenham, UK and Northampton, MA, USA: Edward Elgar.

Freeman, C. (1991), 'Networks of Innovators, a Synthesis of Research Issues', *Research Policy*, **20** (5), 499–514.

Freeman, C. (1994), 'The Economics of Technical Change: A Critical Survey', *Cambridge Journal of Economics*, **18** (5), 463–514.

Freeman, C. (1995), 'The "National System of Innovation" in Historical Perspective', *Cambridge Journal of Economics*, **19** (1), 5–24.

Godin, B. (2006), 'The Linear Model of Innovation: The Historical Construction of an Analytical Framework', *Science, Technology & Human Values*, **31** (6), 639–67.

Gök, A. and J. Edler (2012), 'The Use of Behavioural Additionality Evaluation in Innovation Policy Making', *Research Evaluation*, **21** (4), 306–18.

Grupp, Hariolf (1998), *Foundations of the Economics of Innovation: Theory, Measurement and Practice*, Cheltenham, UK and Lyme, NH, USA: Edward Elgar.

Grupp, H. and T. Schubert (2010), 'Review and New Evidence on Composite Innovation Indicators for Evaluating National Performance', *Research Policy*, **39** (1), 67–78.

Hall, Bronwyn H. and Nathan Rosenberg (eds) (2010), *Economics of Innovation*, Amsterdam: North-Holland.

Hatzichronoglou, T. (1997), 'Revision of the High-Technology Sector and Product Classification', OECD Science, Technology and Industry Working Papers, available at http://dx.doi.org/10.1787/134337307632 (accessed 15 June 2013).

Hirsch-Kreinsen, Hartmut, David Jacobson, Staffan Laestadius and Keith Smith (2005), 'Low and Medium Technology Industries in the Knowledge Economies: The Analytical Issues', in Hartmut Hirsch-Kreinsen, David Jacobson and Staffan Laestadius (eds), *Low Tech Innovation in the Knowledge Economy*, Frankfurt: Peter Lang, pp. 11–29.

Jensen, M.B., B. Johnson, E. Lorenz and B.-Å. Lundvall (2007), 'Forms of Knowledge and Modes of Innovation', *Research Policy*, **36** (5), 680–93.

Klevorick, A.K., R.C. Levin, R.R. Nelson and S.G. Winter (1995), 'On the Sources and Significance of Interindustry Differences in Technical Opportunities', *Research Policy*, **24** (2), 185–205.

Laestadius, S., T.E. Pedersen and T. Sandven (2005), 'Towards a New Understanding of Innovativeness – and of Innovation Based Indicators', *Journal of Mental Changes*, **11** (1–2), 75–121.

Lazonick, William (2013), 'The Theory of Innovative Enterprise: Methodology, Ideology, and Institutions', in Jamee K. Moudud, Cyrus Bina and Patrick L. Mason (eds), *Alternative Theories of Competition: Challenges to the Orthodoxy*, London, UK: Routledge, pp. 127–59.

Lipsey, R.G. and K. Carlaw (1998), 'Technology Policies in Neo-classical and Structuralist–Evolutionary Models', working paper, available at www.oecd-ilibrary.org/docserver/download/9098221e.pdf?expires=1382001490&id=id&accname=guest&checksum=7E13D3EDF8EEFFED1B817CBDBE55578E (accessed 22 May 2013).

Lundvall, Bengt-Åke (1992), *National Systems of Innovation: Towards a Theory of Innovation and Interactive Learning*, London, UK: Pinter.

Lundvall, B.-Å. and S. Borrás (1999), *The Globalising Learning Economy: Implications for Innovation Policy*, Luxembourg: Office for Official Publications of the European Communities.

Malerba, F. (2002), 'Sectoral Systems of Innovation and Production', *Research Policy*, **31** (2), 247–64.

Malerba, Franco (2009), 'Increase Learning, Break Knowledge Lock-ins and Foster Dynamic Complementarities: Evolutionary and System Perspectives on Technology Policy in Industrial Dynamics', in Dominique Foray (ed.), *The New Economics of Technology Policy*, Cheltenham, UK and Northampton, MA, USA: Edward Elgar, pp. 33–45.

Metcalfe, S.J. and L. Georghiou (1998), 'Equilibrium and Evolutionary Foundations of Technology Policy', working paper, available at www.oecd-ilibrary.org/docserver/download/9098221e.pdf?expires=1382001490&id=id&accname=guest&checksum=7E13D3EDF8EEFFED1B817CBDBE55578E (accessed 29 May 2013).

Mowery, D.C. (2009), 'Plus ça change: Industrial R&D in the "Third Industrial Revolution"', *Industrial and Corporate Change*, **18** (1), 1–50.

Nelson, Richard R. (1993), *National Innovation Systems: A Comparative Study*, New York, USA: Oxford University Press.

Nelson, R.R. (1995), 'Recent Revolutionary Theorizing about Economic Change', *Journal of Economic Literature*, **33** (1), 48–90.

OECD (1998), 'New Rationale and Approaches in Technology and Innovation Policy', working paper, available at www.oecd-ilibrary.org/science-and-technology/sti-review_sti_rev-v1998-1-en (accessed 6 May 2013).

OECD (2001), *Innovative Networks: Co-operation in National Innovation Systems*, Paris, France: OECD.

OECD (2002), *Frascati Manual: Proposed Standard Practice for Surveys on Research and Experimental Development*, 6th edition, Paris, France: OECD.

OECD (2004), *OECD Science, Technology and Industry Outlook 2004*, Paris, France: OECD.

OECD (2005a), *Oslo Manual: Guidelines for Collecting and Interpreting Innovation Data*, 3rd edition, Paris, France: OECD.

OECD (2005b), *OECD Science, Technology and Industry Scoreboard 2005*, Paris, France: OECD.

OECD (2006a), *Government R&D Funding and Company Behaviour: Measuring Behavioural Additionality*, Paris, France: OECD.

OECD (2006b), *OECD Science, Technology and Industry Outlook 2006*, Paris, France: OECD.

OECD (2007), *OECD Science, Technology and Industry Scoreboard 2007: Innovation and Performance in the Global Economy*, Paris, France: OECD.

OECD (2008), *OECD Science, Technology and Industry Outlook 2008*, Paris, France: OECD.

OECD (2010), *The OECD Innovation Strategy: Getting a Head Start on Tomorrow*, Paris, France: OECD.

Pavitt, K. (1984), 'Sectoral Patterns of Technical Change: Towards a Taxonomy and Theory', *Research Policy*, **13** (6), 343–73.

Peneder, M. (1999), 'The Austrian Paradox: "Old" Structures but High Performance?', *Austrian Economic Quarterly*, **4** (4), 239–47.

Peneder, M. (2010), 'Technological Regimes and the Variety of Innovation Behaviour: Creating Integrated Taxonomies of Firms and Sectors', *Research Policy*, **39** (3), 323–34.

Radosevic, S. (2002), 'The Electronics Industry in Central and Eastern Europe: An Emerging Production Location in the Alignment of Networks Perspective', working paper, available at http://discovery.ucl.ac.uk/17557/1/17557.pdf (accessed 9 February 2013).

Sandven, Tore, Keith Smith and Aris Kaloudis (2005), 'Structural Change, Growth and Innovation: The Roles of Medium and Low-Tech Industries, 1980–2000', in Hartmut Hirsch-Kreinsen, David Jacobson and Staffan Laestadius (eds), *Low Tech Innovation in the Knowledge Economy*, Frankfurt, Germany: Peter Lang, pp. 31–59.

Sharif, N. (2006), 'Emergence and Development of the National Innovation Systems Concept', *Research Policy*, **35** (5), 745–66.

Smith, K. (2000), 'Innovation as a Systemic Phenomenon: Rethinking the Role of Policy', *Enterprise & Innovation Management Studies*, **1** (1), 73–102.

Smith, K. (2002), 'What is the "Knowledge Economy"? Knowledge Intensity and Distributed Knowledge Bases', Discussion Paper, United Nations University Maastricht, available at www.intech.unu.edu/publications/discussion-papers/2002–6.pdf (accessed 4 June 2013).

Smith, Keith (2005), 'Measuring Innovation', in Jan Fagerberg, David Mowery and Richard R. Nelson (eds), *The Oxford Handbook of Innovation*, Oxford, UK and New York, USA: Oxford University Press, pp. 148–77.

Steinmuller, Edward W. (2009), 'Technology Policy: The Roles of Industrial Analysis and Innovation Studies', in Dominique Foray (ed.), *The New Economics of Technology Policy*, Cheltenham, UK and Northampton, MA, USA: Edward Elgar, pp. 17–32.

Tidd, Joe, John Bessant and Keith Pavitt (1997), *Managing Innovation: Integrating Technological, Market and Organizational Change*, Chichester, UK: John Wiley & Sons.

Von Hippel, Eric (1988), *The Sources of Innovation*, New York, USA: Oxford University Press.

Von Tunzelmann, Nick and Virginia Acha (2005), 'Innovation in "Low-Tech" Industries' in Jan Fagerberg, David C. Mowery and Richard R. Nelson (eds), *The Oxford Handbook of Innovation*, New York, USA: Oxford University Press, pp. 407–32.

10. Policy measures for the promotion of knowledge-intensive entrepreneurship in low-tech industries

Hartmut Hirsch-Kreinsen and Isabel Schwinge

10.1 INTRODUCTION

The recent discussion in innovation research on 'knowledge-intensive entrepreneurship' (KIE) has paid little attention to firms in low- and medium-low-technology industries (LMT). This holds true especially for the debate on policy conclusions and policy recommendations for the promotion of KIE in LMT industries. The strong emphasis on start-ups in new economic industries focuses the policy-oriented discussion rather on policy measures and recommendations to foster KIE processes in high-tech and R&D-intensive industries (e.g. Malerba and Vonortas, 2010). Without doubt, this KIE debate adds important aspects to the traditional policies that promote entrepreneurship, such as the creation of conditions favorable to the entry of new firms, financial support and venture capital, and the support of later stages of firms' growth after successful transformation (ibid.: 299). However, it does not deal with the specific conditions, determining factors and mechanisms of KIE processes in LMT industries, and therefore the question of appropriate policy measures and recommendations remains unanswered. In other words, dealing with KIE in LMT industries also presents a chance to readjust policy strategies to the benefit of these neglected industries.

Empirical findings show impressively clear indicators for successful KIE activities in LMT industries and for how KIE contributes to the innovativeness of these industries (see the various chapters in this volume). This chapter considers these findings and examines how policy can promote such activities. It aims at an extended perspective on innovation policy and a better understanding of the options policy-makers should have in order to promote KIE in LMT sectors. To achieve this, Section 2 of this chapter summarizes the key drivers of KIE in LMT sectors. Section 3 presents the findings of the empirical analysis of KIE activities in LMT sectors and current policies, on the basis of which initial policy recommendations for promoting KIE in LMT sectors are presented in Section 4. Finally, Section 5 concludes with remarks on the chances for success of policy measures promoting KIE in LMT industries.

10.2   KEY DRIVERS OF KIE IN LMT SECTORS

As to the opportunities and key drivers of KIE processes in LMT industries, the basic consideration is the distinct technological and institutional path-dependency of those industries, which imposes strong constraints on KIE processes (see the introductory chapter in this volume). Unlike the high-tech sector with their prevailing technological contingencies, the technologies of the LMT sector are familiar and established. Processes and products are not only highly routine and standardized, but also advanced. The same holds for the knowledge base, which includes mostly codified, transferable and well-known elements, such as design methods, engineering routines, or know-how about markets and customer preferences. Technological norms, methods and leitmotifs as well as occupations and skills, having existed for many generations, are therefore well developed. Furthermore, the strong competition in prices and costs forces LMT companies to focus continuously on optimizing processes and technology rather than pursuing risky innovation activities.

It can be argued that, paradoxically, this condition of fixed path-dependency can stimulate new ideas and attempts to overcome it, whereby a new path can be created (Deutschmann, 2008). The majority of actors involved may view new ideas and inventions as a dead end, but a minority of entrepreneurial actors may see them as opportunities with great potential for economic success. It may also be argued that competitive pressure forces managers to change their role by adopting an increasingly reflective approach towards established practices and look for breakthrough innovations. This reflective approach may be triggered by a situation of formerly increasing returns ceasing to increase or even decreasing. This may be caused, for example, by conditions of continuously intensifying market competition and growing pressure from low-cost competitors in low-wage countries.

Generally, the intensive competitive pressure in LMT industries forces actors not only to adopt managerial strategies of cost cutting and optimizing existing routines, but may also compel them to adopt a reflective stance towards the established practices in order to overcome their often stagnant situation. Especially because of the high persistence and stability of LMT industries, entrepreneurial activities and a successful deviation from established practices and technology paths promise sustainable competitive advantages and high profitability. And indeed, detailed empirical analysis reveals several factors determining the success of KIE processes in LMT industries. The following main drivers can be identified (see Hirsch-Kreinsen in Chapter 3 in this volume):

- First, *globally available knowledge* provides important opportunities for KIE. New knowledge bases and technologies supplementing the existing resources of the LMT sector include, in particular, scientifically generated knowledge as well as new combinations of practical knowledge. This stock of global knowledge derives from various non-LMT industries as well as the scientific and research activities of formerly unassociated industries. Another important prerequisite for KIE in LMT sectors is knowledge of new markets (at home or abroad) and the emergence of new customer demands. Until now these markets have not existed. They have now been detected – or rather created – by KIE companies in LMT sectors. Very often these market segments have a distinct niche character but may have potential for further development, providing the opportunity for LMT firms to abandon established commodity production with its limited prospects. These trans-sectoral opportunities can be regarded as a necessary condition for KIE in LMT sectors.
- The second prerequisite for KIE in LMT sectors is the ability of companies and entrepreneurs to identify opportunities and to integrate and use new knowledge, because company-specific knowledge and innovation capabilities are often a strong determining factor in path-dependency. Usually management are unable to identify new entrepreneurial opportunities because established organizational routines and strong competitive pressure force them to follow continuous cost-cutting strategies. To be able to identify new opportunities and pursue KIE processes it is crucial that players engender a certain *alertness* and broad-mindedness.
- Third, the specific challenge for LMT firms is therefore to balance their strong orientation to established practices with a reflective stance towards these practices. To do this, a bundle of *capabilities* is required and these depend on the knowledge stock of both the firm and entrepreneurs, the skill sets of staff and, in the case of established companies, organizational routines. Very often the experience of individual entrepreneurs in their industry is a crucial factor in their success, and among these competences, 'transformative capabilities'

are of the utmost importance as they constitute the *sine qua non* for access to the whole stock of trans-sectoral knowledge and to the respective players. 'Transformative capabilities' means an enduring ability to transform generally available knowledge into company-specific knowledge. This core competence of LMT industries involves transferring generally available knowledge to the innovation processes pursued by individual LMT firms (Bender and Laestadius, 2005).

Further, the empirical findings show there are also intervening factors which influence the KIE process, and while they should be not overlooked, these factors cannot be regarded as key drivers of KIE as they refer to a large number of ancillary conditions that influence and modify the KIE process only indirectly, of significance only by having a hindering or promoting effect on it. Such relevant moderating factors include, for instance, aspects of regional proximity, or the possibility and modes of funding of KIE activities. Consequently, innovation policy has to be regarded as an important moderating factor as it can effectively stimulate KIE processes. However, currently it plays only a limited role as a directly decisive factor.

The output of the KIE processes typically takes the form of architectural and modular innovations (Henderson and Clark, 1990). The incremental innovation activities that prevail in mature industries do not overcome established paths and routines, and overall, radical innovation activities are seldom. Quite obviously architectural and modular innovations allow enterprises to gain a considerable competitive edge over ever-increasing global competition. This is because these abilities clear the way for innovation strategies which abandon step-by-step development paths in favor of rapid product changes. These types of innovation not only allow flexible customer-oriented strategies but also open up new market segments and stimulate new customer demands.

To sum up, the main areas for policies to promote KIE in LMT sectors are in the interdependencies between the globally available technologies and knowledge and company-specific capabilities. Both have to be regarded as key drivers of processes for KIE in LMT sectors. In the dynamics between them lies the opportunity to overcome the strong path-dependency of the sectoral LMT system.

10.3   EMPIRICAL FINDINGS: LIMITED SUPPORT FROM PUBLIC MEASURES AND POLICY

As the case-study findings show,[1] KIE activities in LMT sectors usually occur without major targeted industry-specific support of innovation policy measures at the national and European level. This result confirms a general finding of innovation research: that firms in LMT industries are widely neglected by public authorities and innovation policy programs (Jacobson and Heanue, 2005; Hirsch-Kreinsen, 2008). To date, sectors with lower R&D intensity have been regarded as less important for long-term economic growth, and manufacturing in particular has had low priority, both for the EU and national governments. Increasing investment in R&D has been a key policy priority since the Lisbon Strategy set the EU target for R&D spending at 3 per cent of GDP (Hansen and Winther, 2011: 325). Meanwhile, some LMT industries, such as the food or textile sector, have been considered in horizontal and sectoral policy initiatives on industrial policy (COM, 2007).

As the case-study results show, in 16 of 27 cases programs were used but none were industry-specific for LMT industries. Instead the firms called on nonspecific industry programs supporting either innovation, technological or founding activities, or regional growth programs. Thereby the character of these support measures can be termed only 'additional' rather than crucial for the KIE process.

10.3.1   LMT-Specific Support Absent

Regardless of the sample's broad variance among firms as to locations and industries (metal, textile and food), all case-study firms have in common that they are in an LMT industry with no available industry-specific support for knowledge-intensive innovation activities. Only the new LMT firms benefited from policy measures which were generally aimed at founding activities. This holds true for two-thirds of the 15 new firms. All five spin-offs among them received state-funded support and hardly differ from spin-offs in high-tech industries. Compared to this only half of the 12 established companies benefited from policy measures. That means that half of the firms did not participate in any state-funded innovation projects. Nor did they even apply for any government-supported programs, whether regional, national or European. The new firms surveyed by the AEGIS Survey (Caloghirou et al., 2011) indicate more strongly the limited use of public support for new firm creation as well as for the introduction of innovations in LMT industries. In the AEGIS survey sample of the LMT aggregation, 91 per cent indicated their own financial resources for funding the new firm creation, 8 per cent the government as a source of funding and 5 per cent EU funds (ibid.: 50). For 78 per cent of the firms in this sample the innovation introduced was not the result of participation in a publicly supported or subsidized activity, compared to 4 per cent in which the innovation was to a great extent the result of such programs (ibid.: 94).

The reasons for the limited use of policy programs are manifold. A minority of the company representatives interviewed highlighted the generally unfriendly and indifferent attitude to entrepreneurial activity on the part of the public sector, or claimed that they had seen no opportunity for participating in governmental support. This view, however, may be greatly colored by their own limited perception of the public sector and by an aversion to external influences on their company's internal affairs. At least one company representative openly admitted to his fear of the company's losing its independence if it participated in a publicly funded program (CFGE1). Such reluctance to engage in formal programs with external partners is hardly surprising as this attitude is also typical for representatives of SMEs, especially in traditional industries. Furthermore, many of the firms that consciously relinquished external support stressed their financial independence and that they did not want to rely on slow external decisions.

This view is also fuelled by a public-sector situation often considered to be 'lacking awareness' of innovation and economic policy and the needs of non-research-intensive industries. As research on LMT industries has shown (Jacobson and Heanue, 2005; Hirsch-Kreinsen, 2008), government support measures are often proposed in a sector-nonspecific way, or aim to support research in high-tech industries whilst ignoring the specific needs of LMT industries. At best such measures only indirectly promote the innovation ability of LMT companies insofar as they are generally concerned with the improvement of the technological and economic conditions of industrial production.

The majority of interviewees explained their lack of interest in innovation programs by the disproportionately great efforts necessary to apply for governmental support. They speak unanimously of 'too much paperwork and ... bureaucracy' (CFDK2). Especially in the case of KIE at established firms, management normally does not have time to complete applications for subsidies. Furthermore, such projects often go too slowly for companies which normally have to decide quickly about investments and restructuring – they may have to wait too long for final decisions on their applications.

Finally, interviewees admitted that they were often sceptical of state-funded programs. Some justified their reluctance towards policy measures with negative experiences. It seems that program representatives at the regional level often lack the knowledge of the topics relevant to companies' applications, their specific needs and the customers and markets of LMT industries. There may have been 'unpleasant experiences' with consultants from public organizations (CMDK1). In three cases the founders received standardized consulting in financing with risk and venture capital. All the founders rejected this form of financing in favor of long-term financing, for example by an inactive partner.

Further critical remarks highlight the lack of policy programs and measures targeted towards the specific needs of KIE activities in LMT sectors, stressing that support activities and local governmental bodies very often lack knowledge of the typical situations of companies. As a consequence one company owner called for 'more regionally oriented support' which 'could be beneficial for companies' (CMDK2), while a clear majority of interviewees dislike transnational support projects at the European level.

Therefore many LMT firms see only very limited opportunities for participating in the dominant horizontal types of support programs (CFP1; CTGE2), and their negative opinions are directed towards all types and levels of public support. European-funded projects, however, come in for particular criticism. One German company manager underscored the time-consuming application required for an EU project and the fact that 'the decision takes very long as does the arrival of the money'. In addition there is also a lack of transparency among the vast number of EU programs available (CMGE1). Such criticisms of EU innovation policy are similar to those lodged by SME representatives: for smaller companies local funding sources are often the more attractive option since negotiation is often possible with local authorities, whereas the requirements for European funding are non-negotiable.[2]

10.3.2   Only Selective Support from Multiple Policy Levels

The empirical findings show that the case-study companies participated in governmental programs for innovation support only very selectively. Noteworthy here is the difference between founders with limited resources who need seed capital, and established firms setting up KIE as corporate entrepreneurship. For half of the established firms there was no question of support from founding programs. Rather, these firms tried to finance their innovation activities from internal resources or used their private networks for innovation funding. Only when these firms cooperated with research institutes did they benefit from the institutes' knowledge of policy measures and then applied for public funding.

Start-ups often turned to state-funded consultancy firms. An example is a Danish KIE company (CFDK2) that was supported by an export start package offered by the Danish Export Council. This program provides a certain number of hours of consulting with the company regarding export, and the Export Council pays 50 per cent of the fee. The consultancy advises on market analysis, marketing, partner searches, and competition analysis. This KIE firm was planning to export its new product, energy-dense ice cream. The owner of this firm was very satisfied with the program, feeling he got more than he paid for. All the knowledge from the consultancy turned out to be valuable. The empirical findings show that sooner or later export activities become essential for the survival of KIE firms because they all exploit niche markets, and domestic niche markets become rapidly insufficient for production at full capacity. But export and marketing activities abroad still represent a challenge for these small and medium-sized firms. In another example, the German Export Council offers a cross-industrial program that supports innovative start-ups at international trade fairs.

Furthermore, KIE founders often apply for financial support in the founding phase of their new companies. Six of the 27 companies studied received start-up financing from nationwide state-funded programs. Not surprisingly, all these KIE companies were either academic spin-offs or start-ups with a strong technological focus. This, in turn, directly enables companies to overcome the inherent restrictions of their sector and so to open up new business perspectives. This can be described as 'technology push', examples of which are two Portuguese spin-offs (CTP1; CFP1). One of these is a textile firm which combined electronic and new fiber technologies with traditional textile and clothing concepts to develop 'smart textiles'. The other spin-off developed freshly cut 'convenience fruit' adapted to the Portuguese consumer's preferences by using a leading-edge packaging technology. Both firms applied successfully for financial support from a national program (NeoTec), which aimed at promoting new enterprises with high potential growth. The program supported 'technology-based companies with growth potential created particularly by students of higher education and researchers'. NeoTec was divided into three phases: product (process or service) concept; business plan development; and business plan implementation, with a maximum duration allowed of three years. Both firms used the program's support to establish their companies. And, in the words of one founder: 'The money was very well spent', both by the firm and the government. Another example of start-up funding is a German academic spin-off that developed a solar dryer for fruit and a pitting machine for cherries and other stone fruits (CMGE2). The new firm was started with founding capital provided by a national program called EXIST-Seed. It supports the formal establishment of new firms in the early phases of their operations. The founders' business plan had to pass a review, which examined the economic prospects for their venture. They confirmed that getting the grant was vital to their new firm.

These examples show that the technological slant of this type of KIE in LMT sectors is relatively consistent with the predominately high-tech orientation of government programs and that such programs can be useful for founders without major problems. Only one founder reported a refusal of support from an early-stage funding program; the reason was that his metal processing company did not belong to a high-tech sector (CMGE3). However, this experience is found only in a minority of innovative LMT firms. They try to overcome the specific sectoral restrictions by adopting innovation strategies focused on technological opportunities and, at least partly, radical innovation.

These KIE cases underscore, on the one hand, the significance of start-up financing not only for companies belonging to high-tech but also for those in LMT industries. This is because start-ups can be regarded as the driving force behind the dynamic development of mature industries, as this links them to newly emerging technological opportunities. This not only helps stabilize these industries in developed economies but also fosters competition with established firms and the emergence of new industries based on new knowledge and technologies.[3] On the other hand, these characteristics are not at all typical of innovative LMT firms in general. As shown, KIE can emerge in the form of corporate entrepreneurship at existing firms just as well. These face similar risks as start-ups do in betting on new niche markets. Therefore incentives to innovate for established firms in LMT industries deserve more attention from policy-makers.

10.4   POLICY RECOMMENDATIONS

Any discussion of policy measures promoting KIE in LMT sectors should start by considering well-known policies that foster entrepreneurship. These include policies which promote conditions favorable to founding new firms, financial support and venture capital, and offer support in the later stages of firm growth to consolidate the position of companies that have been successful (Malerba and Vonortas, 2010: 299). These general policies have to be specified and targeted to the specific needs not only of KIE activities in general but also to the particular situation and requirements of KIE in LMT sectors. As the examples of selective support presented illustrate, not only nonspecific funding programs have been used for KIE in LMT sectors, but also national innovation measures and regional growth programs beyond the sectoral innovation system have been used. In this regard, two different types of policy recommendations can be discerned:

- general recommendations of a broader nature, that is, not only relevant for KIE in the LMT sector but also for the promotion of entrepreneurial activities and innovation in LMT in general;

- recommendations aimed specifically at the needs of KIE in LMT sectors.

The following recommendations on policy are therefore not only drawn from the findings of research on KIE in LMT sectors but also from the findings of LMT research in general.

10.4.1 General Policy Recommendations

Statements by interviewees critical of the restrictions of government programs and their unattractiveness for KIE in LMT sectors highlight the need for some general policy recommendations. However, the need for such recommendations does not arise from problems specific to KIE in LMT sectors. General issues like remedying the complexity and ineffectiveness of supporting programs, as well as deficiencies in the early-stage financing have been already addressed by the Commission of the European Communities (COM, 2009). Rather, recommendations should underscore the general necessity to improve conditions for innovative LMT companies so that they may participate in state-funded projects. These recommendations therefore address the need to promote innovative LMT firms, as several research projects in recent years have stressed (e.g. Jacobson and Heanue, 2005; Arundel et al., 2008). The following issues may be highlighted:

1) *The policy community should increase its awareness and understanding of innovation processes in LMT industries.*
   The case studies of KIE in LMT sectors and recent research into LMT industries underscore that this aspect should be a basic precondition to promoting entrepreneurial and innovative activities in traditional industrial branches. A key target for future policy should be to support activities and measures which raise awareness about LMT industries and their specific needs and conditions. A fundamental precondition to this is the development of a new and broad understanding of innovation that no longer equates innovative ability with R&D activities. The theoretical basis of that position is the so-called linear model of innovation – the assumption that research and development activities are the starting point for any kind of innovation, and that scientifically generated knowledge gives impetus to the development of new technologies. The statistical basis of this argument is the well-known indicator measuring the ratio of the R&D expenditure to the turnover of a company or a business sector (OECD, 2005).

As innovation research convincingly shows, this perspective has long been insufficient to deal with the complex phenomenon of innovation. At best, it holds only for a minority of innovations (e.g. Fagerberg, 2005). However, in wide areas policy is still focusing on this model and its statistical basis for its simplistic perspective which can be convincingly employed in the public debate. Only recently is the debate within the European Commission and the Organisation for Economic Co-operation and Development (OECD) about new R&D indicators slowly moving in the right direction and should therefore be intensified (OECD, 2010). Generally the practice of innovation policy should be reoriented towards a broader understanding of industrial innovativeness. Finally, the industry-specific and regional actors' attention needs to be drawn to KIE and the possibility of using existing cross-sectoral or nonspecific policy measures.

At the same time it is also true that many firms themselves have only a limited awareness of innovation policies towards LMT industries. Also, policy measures are perceived very differently by different firms. Policy measures that some firms regard as helpful are, as a rule, of a general nature, such as national policies providing tax incentives, subsidies for various activities, or EU policies such as the various 'framework programs'. On the whole though, one can say that there are still great shortcomings in innovation policy when it comes to the specific problems of LMT companies. The mechanisms of and preconditions for entrepreneurial processes in LMT industries remain neglected by most policy-makers.

2) *Policies need to be inclusive.*

This discussion refers to the issue whether Europe should focus exclusively on high-technology or science-based industries in attempting to solve growth and employment problems, or whether it should look to the growth prospects within the industries on which the European economy is actually based: LMT industries in manufacturing and services. For Bender (2006: 70), an important result of LMT research is that the policy issue is not a choice between these apparent alternatives.

As general innovation and entrepreneurial research show, much of output and employment in modern economies is accounted for by both manufacturing and services in LMT. KIE activities in LMT industries reveal that such branches are significant users of the output from the high-tech sector. In a modern economy the levels of performance of high-tech and non-high-tech industries are heavily interdependent, and policy should view the economy as a whole. As a result the promotion of the 90 per cent of the economy that is not high-tech also promotes the welfare of the high-tech sector (Robertson and Patel, 2005). As a corollary, policies need to encourage both the generation of knowledge and its diffusion, and that both operations are carried out rapidly enough to maintain competitive advantage.

3) *Policy measures should focus on the needs of innovative LMT firms and those of entrepreneurial activities in LMT.*

   The bureaucracy surrounding applications for public funding should be reduced, particularly for newly founded and small firms with limited resources and capabilities. Decision-making processes should be accelerated and the transparency of decision criteria improved. A central prerequisite for better public programs is to improve the competence and qualifications of program managers who often lack experience and general knowledge not only of the specifics of LMT but also about the founding of new companies in these industries. Program experts and managers should also be geographically and culturally, that is, in their economic and technological orientation, closer to the LMT sector. As reported above, company representatives often complain that program experts are too inflexible in their thinking and so lack the necessary understanding of KIE activities in LMT sectors.

   If access (especially to European programs) can be made easier, policies of an arguably horizontal nature may help the upgrading of LMT firms, for example, measures promoting the efficient use of energy and water.[4] Another general topic relevant to KIE activities in LMT sectors might be measures promoting the export business of SMEs. As recent research findings show, such measures might be an issue for European SMEs that are looking for niche-player status in global markets (Jacobson and Garibaldo, 2011). A policy measure also worth considering could be to help firms in the clothing, furniture and food industries (for whom consumer tastes are of paramount importance) to access information about trends in key foreign markets. Such a policy could act as a catalyst for LMT firms to learn new technological activities and diffuse new routines. These learning processes would in turn lead to the upgrading of firms' knowledge base (Santamaria et al., 2009).

4) *Start-up funding programs should be more explicitly targeted on KIE processes in LMT.*

   There are many different start-up funding programs available from the EU as well as from national and regional levels. Nominally many of these programs are open to any technology field or innovation activity initiated by start-up firms. An example is the EU program 'Competitiveness and Innovation framework Programme' (CIP, 2007) which, with a budget of over €1bn, currently runs several funding schemes. The target is to facilitate access to loans and equity finance for SMEs for which market gaps have been identified. It is said that up to 400 000 SMEs have benefited from this program. Basically it is open to all forms of innovation in enterprises, but specifically to those which focus on eco-innovation. De facto, this and similar programs do not cater to non-research intensive firms and industries. Critics say that EU innovation policy is too focused on scientific research and is not interested in entrepreneurship and the needs of SMEs (EurActive, 2010).

Companies in mature industries are not actually the main target group for these programs. This is the main reason for the strong perception among LMT firms that the programs are intended instead for high-tech companies. Therefore policy should more explicitly promote programs not only directed at all kinds of innovative start-ups but specifically to highly innovative start-ups in LMT industries. Policy should pursue a strategy to increase the number of successful innovative start-ups instead of its current selective focus on only highly innovative foundations in high-tech industries. To cite Fritsch (2011), a change in policy strategy from the current 'pick the winner policy' towards a 'make more winners' policy would be highly recommendable.

These policy measures should be supplemented by additional policies focused on stimulating activities of innovative LMT firms. Appropriate measures here could be, for example, tax incentives for non-R&D-based innovation activities, financial support for payroll costs accrued by personnel involved in innovation tasks, or for the establishment of specific R&D and design departments (Rammer et al., 2010).

10.4.2 Specific Policy Recommendations

Empirical findings on the key drivers of successful types of KIE in LMT sectors (see Section 2; see also Caloghirou et al. in Chapter 2 in this volume) point to the following possible policy measures to foster KIE activities in LMT:

1) *Given the importance of the specific capabilities of entrepreneurs and LMT firms for successful KIE processes, it is important that policy devise measures and support activities which aim at improving these capabilities.*

   The problem of policy is to support the enhancement of the capabilities of LMT firms and entrepreneurs so that they may access knowledge resources and new technologies in a critical and selective way. Policy should therefore focus on developing firms' capabilities in cross-company cooperation and the corresponding channels of communication, gateways and personnel responsibilities.

In particular, LMT firms and entrepreneurs should have the ability to absorb and integrate knowledge and technologies developed by external players. As outlined above (Section 2), LMT research defines these abilities as transformative capabilities, meaning that the firm is able to identify valuable knowledge in its environment, assimilate it to its existing knowledge stocks and exploit it for successful innovation (Bender and Laestadius, 2005). Transformative capabilities refer to the enduring ability to transform generally available knowledge into firm-specific knowledge. This ability can be regarded as a core competence of LMT industries. Mendonça (2009) stresses this point in a particular way: LMT firms 'demand some degree of endogenous capabilities in order to understand, procure and interact with the partner-suppliers to facilitate the production of renewed traditional goods'.[5]

In practice, policy measures aimed at improving these capabilities should be directed at promoting the different dimensions of, and particularly the preconditions for, developing the capabilities of LMT companies, and organizational conditions and management skills are especially required for a more efficient use of existing knowledge for further development.

Another crucial aspect may be the upgrading and promotion of in-house capacities for R&D-related activities of innovative LMT firms. LMT research has shown this to be the main prerequisite for absorbing external knowledge efficiently (Menrad, 2004; Grimpe and Sofka, 2009). Upgrading may lead to a growing R&D intensity in LMT firms. Another issue for KIE processes and innovative LMT firms is that they should be helped to implement and utilize systematically advanced management methods and organizational concepts. As LMT research has demonstrated, using such methods and concepts routinely improves management's ability greatly to absorb and integrate new knowledge (Bender and Laestadius, 2005).

2) *Policy should devise measures and support activities which aim at improving the skills and knowledge base of LMT firms.*

   A further essential step is to improve firms' capabilities to upgrade the skills of staff or to increase their numbers of professionals, academics and skilled workers. Efforts should be intensified to help firms recruit more skilled personnel, both for management and the shop floor. LMT research has found that management should undergo a process of professionalization by recruiting academics and technical experts and so improve the level of firms' capabilities. Likewise, targeted measures could be taken to train shop floor personnel in order to strengthen continuous improvement activities. This could make an important contribution to upgrading firms' innovativeness (Rammer et al., 2010). These tasks can be realized through support programs at the EU, national and regional levels, though measures aimed at upgrading knowledge and skills may be better developed by local authorities who are closer to the actual LMT firms, as they understand local firms' specific needs better than supranational policy-makers. Such measures could also be developed in a more timely and targeted manner.

In this context the limited resources for recruiting highly educated personnel and R&D staff at LMT firms is often rightly indicated as a constraint. In one of the case-study firms this problem was solved by 'renting' scientists for R&D activities. They were 'offered' by a cooperation partner specializing in innovation processes at SMEs. The advantage of this flexible organization is that the firm need not establish an R&D department or recruit staff. In case of failure, or at completion of the development project, the firm can end the arrangement. Altogether LMT industries need to become more attractive to highly skilled people – particularly also from horizontal or high-tech fields. Firms in LMT industries must compete intensely with the high-tech sector for highly skilled workers.

3) *Given the importance of opportunities to access available technologies and knowledge for processes of KIE in LMT sectors, ways of access should be significantly improved for LMT-SMEs with their limited resources.*

To reach this goal, new innovation networks need to be launched as the key to facilitating collaboration and knowledge transfer. The establishment of externally oriented knowledge and competence networks should be a high priority for policy. Networks should be facilitated in at least two dimensions: first, collaboration should be promoted with actors from the global supply side of new knowledge and technologies, that is, firms from other industries, such as suppliers and producers of new technologies, and non-firm organizations, such as scientific institutions and consultants. At the same time, long-term participants (incumbent firms, industry associations) and established network relations from collaborations, such as potential customers or suppliers, need to be involved and aligned with these new networks. The actors mediating this process and providing opportunities through new cross-industry contacts are crucial to such activities. As LMT research has shown, collaboration activities with scientific organizations leads to an increase in knowledge for LMT firms (Rammer et al., 2010).

Second, possibilities for closer interaction with customers should also be improved, as the impetus to innovate often results from direct customer requests. This has been highlighted in LMT research showing that innovation performance can be strengthened by incorporating customer interaction into funding and incentive schemes for LMT industries (Grimpe and Sofka, 2009).

Policy should therefore promote the creation of networks and upgrade established network arrangements in at least two ways. First, the networking capability of the individual KIE firm and entrepreneur should be thoroughly encouraged, for example, by providing starting capital and passing on the capacities and experiences of network management (see below). Second, networks should be promoted in their entirety. Policy measures need especially to focus on the development of interorganizational cooperation with the corresponding channels of communication, gateways and personnel responsibilities. The empirical findings on KIE in LMT sectors show that the regional proximity of various players is only important for some entrepreneurial activities. In many cases cultural factors (i.e. language, managerial culture) and/or organizational proximity (e.g. harmonization of the level of technology, homogenization of procedures, or a similar approach to quality control) are more important than spatial proximity. Policy should therefore also focus on handling these aspects as they are often responsible for blocking successful cooperation activities.

4) *Policy should especially promote interrelationships between LMT and high-tech.*
    As a consequence policies need to encourage both the generation of knowledge and its diffusion between low-tech and high-tech, as well as promote stronger interrelationships between the sectors. As the findings on KIE in LMT sectors show, opportunities based on globally available technologies and knowledge beyond sectoral and local boundaries are of major significance for successful KIE activities in LMT sectors (see Hirsch-Kreinsen in Chapter 3 in this volume). Therefore the ways of access to these opportunities and actors from high-tech sectors should be promoted by targeted policy measures.

    Crucial obstacles to this new networking process that have to be taken into consideration are strong divergences between the actors and firms from different industries, for example, differing skills and capabilities, deficits in interdisciplinary understanding between entrepreneurs and LMT firms and high-tech or scientific organizations, or differing perceptions of time management and efficiency (especially in collaboration with scientific organizations). Network projects seen to be dealing successfully with these issues should be promoted and their solutions and experiences shared. Additionally, policy measures could include more bridging institutions between LMT industries, science and high-tech firms, as well as continuous consulting in the area of network management and the exchange of experiences with other networks. For instance, trade fairs – but also scientific and specialized congresses – are important external information sources for firms (Eurostat, Community Innovation Survey 2002–04). Therefore opportunities for gathering new knowledge need to be better used in the context of KIE activities.

10.5   CONCLUSIONS

The available empirical findings highlight impressive cases of KIE in new firms, but also at established firms that have successfully transformed knowledge into exceptional innovations. KIE processes in LMT can be characterized by a specific situation that differs from those discussed in the KIE debate in general, which mainly focuses on high-tech. Consequently policy-makers should consider the specific requirements of the LMT sector and address appropriate measures to them. Policy must overcome here the main obstacle to KIE – the strong path-dependency of LMT industries – by devising entrepreneurial programs. The Commission of the European Community has correctly noticed that entrepreneurs are the main driver of innovation. This holds particularly true also for KIE in LMT industries. For this reason policy should reward forerunners conducting research and innovation activities developing new products and processes – also in LMT industries.

A further step in the right direction has been the effort towards a coherent research and innovation system in Europe (COM, 2009). The multiple policy measures assessed in the KIE sample point to the need for better-coordinated activities on the part of political institutions from the European down to the regional level. Existing and newly introduced initiatives favoring SMEs, such as the 'Think small first' principle, can be considered helpful (COM, 2010). Fifteen of the 27 analysed case-study firms (see Hirsch-Kreinsen in Chapter 3 in this volume) conducted activities in eco-efficient processing (such as a new energy-efficient sintering technology) or developed sustainable consumer products. Though necessary stricter regulations in the future will present a considerable challenge to the mostly energy-intensive LMT industries, at the same time this will offer an opportunity for entrepreneurs active in KIE to contribute to sustainable structural change in these industries.

In general, further efforts should be put into more user-friendly policy measures favoring entrepreneurship and innovation that are closer to practice in SMEs, and can thereby also attract established firms and entrepreneurs in LMT industries – instead of policies favoring large-scale demonstration projects in only a few key enabling technologies. Hence despite obstacles, there are considerable opportunities for encouraging KIE activities in LMT sectors that could improve the weak competitive position of many LMT firms. This is confirmed not only by the empirical findings presented in this volume, but also by further studies. Finally, the following issues should be stressed again:

- Long-term empirical studies show that knowledge diversification tends to prevail over a mere deepening of the existing technological paths. They also draw attention to the surprising stability of LMT industries in many OECD countries (Kaloudis et al., 2005). From this it may be concluded that the usual findings tend to 'underestimate the true breadth and depth of entrepreneurial change in mature businesses' (Mendonça, 2009: 479; also Freddi, 2009).

- Recent case-study research emphasizes the innovating ability of the LMT sector and its companies (Bender and Laestadius, 2005; Hirsch-Kreinsen, 2013). Accordingly, LMT companies very often not only pursue incremental innovation strategies, but also try to exit the well-worn paths of knowledge and technology in favor of innovation activities, such as architectural or modular innovation strategies (Hirsch-Kreinsen, 2008). In part, such companies explicitly pursue strategies aimed at achieving a leading position in niche markets beyond the field of standardized, mature products, and then try to upgrade their position as supplier within industrial value chains (Bender, 2006; also Schwinge in Chapter 8 in this volume). They may also attempt to create new market segments.

- Research reveals the impressive success of so-called 'gazelles', that is, fast-growing companies, often from LMT industries, that induce sectoral growth, creating new jobs and markets. Such companies can be found both in Western countries and, in particular, countries of Central and Eastern Europe (see Yudanov in Chapter 6 in this volume).

Because of the persistence and stability of LMT industries, innovative entrepreneurial activities and deviation from established practices and technological paths can hold the promise for them of sustainable competitive advantage and high profitability. For this to happen, policy needs to overcome its restrictive stance towards the needs of mature industries and understand that it can considerably improve the prospects of these industries.

NOTES

1. For a detailed description of the methodological basis and the abbreviations of the cases, see Hirsch-Kreinsen in this volume (Chapter 3).
2. See www.euractiv.com/innovation-enterprise/entrepreneurs-forgotten-eu-innovation-policy-news-495833 (accessed 29 January 2012).
3. A good example of this is the emergence of the sector of 'mechatronics' based on the combination of traditional mechanical engineering and new IT technologies. Daniela Freddi conceptualizes this process as 'technology fusion' of old and new technologies (2008; 2009).
4. We thank Rick Woodward from University of Edinburgh Business School for this note to the relevance of horizontal programs for LMT firms.
5. This concept can be linked to the open innovation approach that assumes that firms can and should use external ideas as well as internal ideas, and internal and external paths to markets, as the firms look to advance their technology level and innovation. The boundaries between a firm and its environment have become more permeable; innovations can easily transfer inwardly and outwardly (Chesbrough, 2003). This means that LMT firms should be put in a position to implement the basics of this approach.

REFERENCES

Arundel, A., C. Bordoy and M. Kanerva (2008), 'Neglected Innovators: How Do Innovative Firms that Do Not Perform R&D Innovate? Results of an Analysis of the Innobarometer 2007 Survey No. 215', INNO-Metrics Working Paper, available at http://arno.unimaas.nl/show.cgi?fid=15406 (accessed 15 February 2013).

Bender, G. (2006), 'Peculiarities and Relevance of Non-Research-Intensive Industries in the Knowledge-Based Economy', final report of the project PILOT, Policy and Innovation in Low-Tech, available at http://citeseerx.ist.psu.edu/viewdoc/download?rep=rep1&type=pdf&doi=10.1.1.134.743 (accessed 23 May 2013).

Bender, Gerd and Staffan Laestadius (2005), 'Non-Science Based Innovativeness: On Capabilities Relevant to Generate Profitable Novelty', in Gerd Bender, David Jacobson and Paul L. Robertson (eds), *Non-Research-Intensive Industries in the Knowledge Economy*, published in *Perspectives on Economic Political and Social Integration*, **XI** (1–2), special issue, 123–70.

Caloghirou, Y., A. Protogerou and A. Tsakanikas (2011), 'Final Report Summarizing Survey Methods and Results', Deliverable 7.1.5 AEGIS project, available at www.aegis-fp7.eu/index.php?option=com_docman&task=cat_view&gid=97&Itemid=12 (accessed 10 June 2013).

Chesbrough, Henry W. (2003), *Open Innovation: The New Imperative for Creating and Profiting from Technology*, Boston, MA, USA: Harvard Business School Press.

CIP (2007), 'Competitiveness and Innovation Framework Programme of the

European Commission', available at http://ec.europa.eu/enterprise/policies/finance/cip-financial-instruments/index_en.htm (accessed 27 January 2012).

Commission of the European Communities (COM) (2007), 'Communication from the Commission to the European Parliament, the Council, the European Economic and Social Committee and the Committee of the Regions: Mid-Term Review of Industrial Policy – A Contribution to the EU's Growth and Jobs Strategy', available at http://eur-lex.europa.eu/LexUriServ/LexUriServ.do?uri=COM:2007:0374:FIN:en:PDF (accessed 6 November 2009).

COM (2009), 'Communication from the Commission to the European Parliament, the Council, the European Economic and Social Committee and the Committee of the Regions: Reviewing Community Innovation Policy in a Changing World', available at http://ec.europa.eu/enterprise/policies/innovation/files/com%282009%29442final_en.pdf (accessed 25 September 2009).

COM (2010), 'Communication from the Commission to the European Parliament, the Council, the European Economic and Social Committee and the Committee of the Regions: An Integrated Industrial Policy for the Globalisation Era – Putting Competitiveness and Sustainability at Centre Stage', available at http://ec.europa.eu/enterprise/policies/industrial-competitiveness/industrial-policy/files/communication_on_industrial_policy_en.pdf (accessed 16 February 2012).

EurActiv (2010), 'Entrepreneurs "Forgotten" in EU Innovation Policy', available at www.euractiv.com/innovation-enterprise/entrepreneurs-forgotten-eu-innovation-policy-news-495833 (accessed 29 January 2012).

Deutschmann, Christoph (2008), *Kapitalistische Dynamik: Eine gesellschaftstheoretische Perspektive*, Wiesbaden, Germany: VS-Verlag.

Eurostat, Community Innovation Survey (CIS) 2002–04, available at http://epp.eurostat.ec.europa.eu/portal/page/portal/science_technology_innovation/data/database (accessed 20 December 2013).

Fagerberg, Jan (2005), 'Innovation: A Guide to the Literature', in Jan Fagerberg, David C. Mowery and Richard R. Nelson (eds), *The Oxford Handbook of Innovation*, Oxford, UK: Oxford University Press, pp. 1–27.

Freddi, Daniela (2008), 'Technology Fusion and Organizational Structures in Low- and Medium-Tech Companies', in Hartmut Hirsch-Kreinsen and David Jacobson (eds), *Innovation in Low-Tech Firms and Industries*, Cheltenham, UK and Northampton, MA, USA: Edward Elgar, pp. 140–59.

Freddi, D. (2009), 'The Integration of Old and New Technological Paradigms in LMT Sectors: The Case of Mechatronics', *Research Policy*, **38** (3), 548–58.

Fritsch, Michael (2011), 'Start-ups in Innovative Industries: Causes and Effects', in David B. Audretsch, Oliver Falck, Stephan Heblich and Adam Lederer (eds), *Handbook of Research on Innovation and Entrepreneurship*, Cheltenham, UK and Northampton, MA, USA: Edward Elgar, pp. 365–80.

Grimpe, C. and W. Sofka (2009), 'Search Patterns and Absorptive Capacity: Low- and High-Technology Sectors in European Countries', *Research Policy*, **38** (3), 495–506.

Hansen, T. and L. Winther (2011), 'Innovation, Regional Development and Relations between High- and Low-Tech Industries', *European Urban and Regional Studies*, **18** (3), 321–39.

Henderson, R.M. and K.B. Clark (1990), 'Architectural Innovation: The Reconfiguration of Existing Product Technologies and the Failure of Established Firms', *Administrative Science Quarterly*, **35** (1), 9–30.

Hirsch-Kreinsen, H. (2008), '"Low-Tech" Innovation', *Industry and Innovation*, **15** (1), 19–43.

Hirsch-Kreinsen, H. (2013), '"Low-Tech" Research Revisited', paper presented at the 35th DRUID Conference, Barcelona, 17–19 June 2013.

Jacobson, David and Kevin Heanue (2005), 'Policy Conclusions and Recommendations', in Gerd Bender, David Jacobson and Paul L. Robertson (eds), *Non-Research-Intensive Industries in the Knowledge Economy*, published in *Perspectives on Economic Political and Social Integration*, **XI** (1–2), special issue, 359–416.

Jacobson, David and Francesco Garibaldo (2011), 'The Role of Company Networks in Low-Tech Industries', in Paul L. Robertson and David Jacobson (eds), *Knowledge Transfer and Technology Diffusion*, Cheltenham, UK and Northampton, MA, USA: Edward Elgar, pp. 90–106.

Kaloudis, Aris, Tore Sandven and Keith Smith (2005), 'Structural Change, Growth and Innovation: The Roles of Medium and Low Tech Industries, 1980–2000', in Gerd Bender, David Jacobsen and Paul L. Robertson (eds), *Non-Research-Intensive Industries in the Knowledge Economy*, published in *Perspectives on Economic, Political and Social Integration*, **XI** (1–2), special issue, 49–74.

Malerba, Franco and Nicholas Vonortas (2010), 'Knowledge-Intensive Entrepreneurship in Europe: Some Policy Conclusions', in Franco Malerba (ed.), *Knowledge-Intensive Entrepreneurship and Innovation Systems: Evidence from Europe*, London, UK and New York, USA: Routledge, pp. 299–311.

Mendonça, S. (2009), 'Brave Old World: Accounting for "High-Tech" Knowledge in "Low-Tech" Industries', *Research Policy*, **38** (3), 470–82.

Menrad, K. (2004), 'Innovations in the Food Industry in Germany', *Research Policy*, **33** (10), 845–78.

OECD (2005), *Oslo-Manual, Proposed Guidelines for Collecting and Interpreting Technological Innovation Data*, 3rd edn, Paris, France: OECD.

OECD (2010), *SMEs, Entrepreneurship and Innovation*, Paris, France: OECD.

Rammer, C., C. Köhler, M. Murmann, A. Pesau, F. Schwiebacher, S. Kinkel, E. Kirner, T. Schubert and Oliver Som (2010), 'Innovationen ohne Forschung und Entwicklung, Studien zum deutschen Innovationssystem', working paper, available at www.e-fi.de/fileadmin/Studien/StuDIS_2011/StuDIS_15_2011.pdf (accessed 23 March 2013).

Robertson, Paul L. and Primal R. Patel (2005), 'New Wine in Old Bottles: Technological Diffusion in Developed Economies', in Gerd Bender, David Jacobsen and Paul L. Robertson (eds), *Non-Research-Intensive Industries in the Knowledge Economy*, published in *Perspectives on Economic, Political and Social Integration*, **XI** (1–2), special issue, 271–304.

Santamaria, L., M. Nieto and A. Barge-Gil (2009), 'Beyond Formal R&D: Taking Advantage of Other Sources of Innovation in Low- and Medium-Technology Industries', *Research Policy*, **38** (3), 507–17.

Index